WAGE INEQUALITY
IN LATIN AMERICA

WAGE INEQUALITY IN LATIN AMERICA

Understanding the Past to Prepare for the Future

Julián Messina and Joana Silva

 WORLD BANK GROUP

Latin American Development Forum Series

This series was created in 2003 to promote debate, disseminate information and analysis, and convey the excitement and complexity of the most topical issues in economic and social development in Latin America and the Caribbean. It is sponsored by the Inter-American Development Bank, the United Nations Economic Commission for Latin America and the Caribbean, and the World Bank, and represents the highest quality in each institution's research and activity output. Titles in the series have been selected for their relevance to the academic community, policy makers, researchers, and interested readers, and have been subjected to rigorous anonymous peer review prior to publication.

Advisory Committee Members

Alicia Bárcena Ibarra, Executive Secretary, Economic Commission for Latin America and the Caribbean, United Nations

Inés Bustillo, Director, Washington Office, Economic Commission for Latin America and the Caribbean, United Nations

Daniel Lederman, Deputy Chief Economist, Latin America and the Caribbean Region, World Bank

Santiago Levy, Vice President for Sectors and Knowledge, Inter-American Development Bank

Roberto Rigobon, Professor of Applied Economics, Sloan School of Management, Massachusetts Institute of Technology

José Juan Ruiz, Chief Economist and Manager of the Research Department, Inter-American Development Bank

Ernesto Talvi, Director, Brookings Global-CERES Economic and Social Policy in Latin America Initiative

Carlos Végh, Chief Economist, Latin America and the Caribbean Region, World Bank

Andrés Velasco, CIEPLAN (Corporación de Estudios para Latinoamérica), Chile

Titles in the Latin American Development Forum Series

Stop the Violence in Latin America: A Look at Prevention from Cradle to Adulthood (2017) by Laura Chioda

Innovative Experiences in Access to Finance: Market-Friendly Roles for the Visible Hand? (2017) by Augusto de la Torre, Juan Carlos Gozzi, and Sergio L. Schmukler

Beyond Commodities: The Growth Challenge of Latin America and the Caribbean (2016) by Jorge Thompson Araujo, Ekaterina Vostroknutova, Markus Brueckner, Mateo Clavijo, and Konstantin M. Wacker

Left Behind: Chronic Poverty in Latin America and the Caribbean (2016) by Renos Vakis, Jamele Rigolini, and Leonardo Lucchetti

Cashing In on Education: Women, Childcare, and Prosperity in Latin America and the Caribbean (2016) by Mercedes Mateo Díaz and Lourdes Rodriguez-Chamussy

Work and Family: Latin American and Caribbean Women in Search of a New Balance (2016) by Laura Chioda

Great Teachers: How to Raise Student Learning in Latin America and the Caribbean (2014) by Barbara Bruns and Javier Luque

Entrepreneurship in Latin America: A Step Up the Social Ladder? (2013) by Eduardo Lora and Francesca Castellani, editors

Emerging Issues in Financial Development: Lessons from Latin America (2013) by Tatiana Didier and Sergio L. Schmukler, editors

New Century, Old Disparities: Gaps in Ethnic and Gender Earnings in Latin America and the Caribbean (2012) by Hugo Ñopo

Does What You Export Matter? In Search of Empirical Guidance for Industrial Policies (2012) by Daniel Lederman and William F. Maloney

Investor Protection and Corporate Governance: Firm-Level Evidence across Latin America (2007) by Alberto Chong and Florencio López-de-Silanes, editors

Natural Resources: Neither Curse nor Destiny (2007) by Daniel Lederman and William F. Maloney, editors

The State of State Reform in Latin America (2006) by Eduardo Lora, editor

Emerging Capital Markets and Globalization: The Latin American Experience (2006) by Augusto de la Torre and Sergio L. Schmukler

Beyond Survival: Protecting Households from Health Shocks in Latin America (2006) by Cristian C. Baeza and Truman G. Packard

Beyond Reforms: Structural Dynamics and Macroeconomic Vulnerability (2005) by José Antonio Ocampo, editor

Privatization in Latin America: Myths and Reality (2005) by Alberto Chong and Florencio López-de-Silanes, editors

Keeping the Promise of Social Security in Latin America (2004) by Indermit S. Gill, Truman G. Packard, and Juan Yermo

Lessons from NAFTA for Latin America and the Caribbean (2004) by Daniel Lederman, William F. Maloney, and Luis Servén

The Limits of Stabilization: Infrastructure, Public Deficits, and Growth in Latin America (2003) by William Easterly and Luis Servén, editors

Globalization and Development: A Latin American and Caribbean Perspective (2003) by José Antonio Ocampo and Juan Martin, editors

Is Geography Destiny? Lessons from Latin America (2003) by John Luke Gallup, Alejandro Gaviria, and Eduardo Lora

Contents

Chapter 3: The Role of Labor Supply in Wage Inequality Trends   95

Chapter 4: The Role of Labor Demand Conditions in Wage Inequality Trends   117

Boxes

Figures

Tables

Acknowledgments

This book was written by Julián Messina, a lead economist for the Inter-American Development Bank, and Joana Silva, a senior economist for the World Bank. However, it would have been impossible without the collaboration of a generous team of colleagues and collaborators. Special thanks are due to Augusto de la Torre, chief economist for Latin America and the Caribbean, World Bank; Nora Lustig, professor of economics, Tulane University; Luis F. López-Calva, lead economist, World Bank; and Daniel Lederman, deputy regional chief economist for Latin America and the Caribbean, World Bank. They provided valuable comments and suggestions at different stages during production of this book. We also gratefully acknowledge several colleagues who provided comments on particular chapters of the book, including Alain Ize, senior consultant, World Bank (chapter 3); Carlos Rodríguez-Castelán, senior economist, World Bank (chapter 2); and Sergei Soares, economist, Institute for Applied Economic Research (chapter 5).

Substantive inputs were provided by Ciro Avitabile, Maria Marta Ferreyra, Samuel Pienknagura, Rafael Prado Proença, Martin Sasson, Miguel Székely, and Daniel Valderrama. We are very grateful for their feedback. Alejandra Martinez Cubillos and Juan Pablo Uribe provided outstanding research assistance.

The book greatly benefited from the comments and suggestions of our peer reviewers at the World Bank Concept Note and Decision Meetings, including David Autor, professor of economics, Massachusetts Institute of Technology; Samuel Freije-Rodriguez, lead economist, World Bank; Roberta Gatti, chief economist, Human Development, World Bank; Mary Hallward-Driemeier, senior economic adviser, World Bank; William Maloney, chief economist, Equitable Growth, Finance, and Institutions, World Bank; and Naércio Menezes-Filho, professor of economics, Institute of Education and Research and University of São Paulo.

The book was also discussed in a dedicated session at the Fourth World Bank-Banco de España Research Conference, "Labor Markets: Growth, Productivity and Inequality," held June 16–17, 2016. We are very grateful for insightful comments and suggestions from reviewers at that session, including David Card, professor of economics, University of California, Berkeley; Angel Estrada, economist, Bank of Spain; Adriana Kugler, professor at the McCourt School of Public Policy, Georgetown University; and Santiago Levy, vice president, Inter-American Development Bank.

We also thank the participants in the authors' workshops organized in Washington, DC. In particular, we are extremely grateful to João Pedro Azevedo and Josefina Posadas. This report builds on a series of background papers (further described in annex 1A in chapter 1). The team is grateful to all authors of these papers. Last, but not least, this report would not have been possible without the unfailing administrative support of Ruth Delgado and Jacqueline Larrabure.

About the Authors

Julián Messina is lead research economist in the research department of the Inter-American Development Bank (IDB). Before joining the IDB, he worked at the World Bank and the European Central Bank, and he taught at the Universities of Barcelona GSE, Frankfurt, Georgetown, Girona, and Mainz. He has coauthored two World Bank Latin American flagship reports and is coeditor of the IDB flagship report *Learning Better: Public Policy for Skills Development*. His research focuses on labor market dynamics, skills, wage determination, and inequality. His work has been published in leading academic journals, including the *American Economic Journal: Macroeconomics, Journal of Economic Perspectives, Economic Journal, Journal of the European Economic Association,* and *Labour Economics* and is often featured in popular blogs and media outlets. He has extensive experience advising governments in Latin America, Europe, and Asia. Julián obtained his PhD in economics from the European University Institute in 2002.

Joana Silva is a senior economist in the Office of the Chief Economist for Latin America and the Caribbean of the World Bank. She has expertise in labor economics, international trade, poverty and inequality, firm productivity, and policy evaluation. Her research has been published in leading academic journals, including the *American Economic Review, Journal of International Economics, Economics Letters, Review of International Economics,* and *Review of World Economics*. She has authored four books, including a World Bank flagship report. She is currently leading the research program on labor market adjustment in Latin America, as well as a number of impact evaluations and research on globalization and its impacts on growth and inequality. She has extensive experience advising governments in Latin America and the Caribbean, Europe, and the Middle East and North Africa. Before joining the World Bank, Joana worked for the Globalization and Economic Policy Research Center and taught at the University of Nottingham. She holds a PhD in economics from the University of Nottingham.

Abbreviations

CCT	conditional cash transfer
CEDLAS	Universidad Nacional de la Plata (Argentina)
EU	European Union
GATT	General Agreement on Tariffs and Trade
GDP	gross domestic product
G-7	Group of Seven
ICT	information and communication technology
LABLAC	Labor Database for Latin America and the Caribbean
LAC	Latin America and the Caribbean
NAFTA	North American Free Trade Agreement
OECD	Organisation for Economic Co-operation and Development
OLS	ordinary least squares
PPP	purchasing power parity
RAIS	Annual Social Information Report (Brazil)
SBTC	skill-biased technological change
SEDLAC	Socio-Economic Database for Latin America and the Caribbean
STEP	Skills Toward Employment and Productivity surveys
WTO	World Trade Organization

1
Introduction

Rationale

Latin America achieved something truly remarkable during the first decade of the 21st century: it sustained vigorous economic growth with declining inequality. Other regions in the world grew strongly during this period, but this growth was not shared equitably—in fact, inequality increased in most countries outside Latin America (Milanovic 2016). In a period characterized by rising global inequality, Latin America demonstrated that an inclusive growth path is possible. This was an encouraging development not only for Latin America, but perhaps also for the rest of the world.

Lower commodity prices and slower growth in China, however, have reduced Latin America's growth prospects. Since the beginning of the slowdown in 2011, the reduction in inequality has stalled in many countries (Cord et al. 2014; Rodríguez-Castelán et al. 2016). Thus, several countries in the region have faced a difficult and protracted transition to a new equilibrium, a "new normal." Unlike the systemic crises of the 1980s and 1990s, the economic pain of the second decade of the 21st century is not driven by a sudden stop in capital inflows, a banking system failure, or a sovereign debt crisis. The slowdown arrived at the end of a growth episode driven by growth of domestic demand beyond that of output.

In this low-growth scenario, it is important to ask whether the social gains of the 2000s can be sustained. Will there be lower growth across all segments of the population in Latin America, or will the slowdown disproportionately hurt those who have less? In other words, will the economic slowdown put the brakes on the reduction of inequality in Latin America?

To answer these forward-looking questions—and to know what to expect—it is essential to understand the causes of the observed changes in inequality in past decades. The downward trend in inequality in Latin America in the 2000s was

1

nothing short of a historic breakthrough for a region that, ever since the 19th-century writings of explorer Alexander von Humboldt, has been seen as the "land of inequalities" (Engerman and Sokoloff 1997; Williamson 2015). What was different about the 2000s relative to previous decades, and what might change in the decades to come?

This book focuses on the determinants of changes in wage inequality, which is the main driver of the region's changes in income inequality (Cord et al. 2014; López-Calva and Lustig 2010).[1] Undeniably, other factors, such as the emergence of conditional cash transfer (CCT) programs, the expansion of pension coverage, and changes in household demographics, also played roles in the reduction of inequality in the 2000s. However, their contributions were small compared with that of falling wage inequality (Cord et al. 2014), and studying their effects on income and wage inequality goes beyond the scope of this book, which instead focuses on labor market dynamics.[2] In Latin America, labor earnings represent the lion's share of most households' total income, and thus they are the biggest determinant of overall trends in income inequality. Moreover, although inequality in households' assets is important for distributional equity and economic efficiency, it is a more static factor: the large majority of Latin Americans rely on labor earnings as their main source of income, trading skills for income through labor markets.

Understanding the drivers of wage inequality is economically and socially consequential for several reasons. Inequality plays a mediating role in the relationship between economic growth and poverty reduction, partially explaining countries' relative long-term performance in reducing poverty (Allwine, Rigolini, and López-Calva 2013; Bourguignon 2002; Ravallion 2015). Inequality also matters because it tends to be associated with social mobility (Chetty and Hendren 2015). In other words, when the distance between steps in the income ladder increases, the ladder becomes more difficult to climb. Persistent inequality thus helps to explain why poverty persists over time and reduces the aspirations of groups at the bottom of the income distribution (Genicot and Ray 2014). As such, it becomes difficult to dissociate income inequality as an outcome from inequality of opportunity—whereby circumstances such as where you are born and who your parents are can define an individual's lifelong earnings profile. Finally, inequality is also a source of social unrest, and excessive inequality is often perceived as a source of political turmoil. A dynamic labor market that provides opportunities to put individual skills into practice and rewards the effort exerted to acquire those skills is essential for social cohesion (World Bank 2014).

Road Map of the Book

This book sheds light on the drivers of recent trends in wage inequality in Latin America. It summarizes the findings of a large research study that included (1) the production of nine background papers in partnership with researchers at several universities and international institutions (see the list of papers in annex 1A);

(2) complementary original research on the region that combines different data sources (administrative data and household, labor force, and census data); and (3) a review of the existing literature. In addition to summarizing the findings of the background papers, the book also puts them in the context of the broader labor literature and presents original research.

The book is structured as follows:

Chapter 2, "Wage Inequality Changes since 1990: Key Trends and Stylized Facts," describes the main earnings-inequality trends, distinguishing the evolution of inequality between labor market groups (for example, industry, firm, education, experience, and occupation) and within each of those groups. It documents changes in the relative supply of labor since the mid-1990s and measures the contribution of the education and experience premiums, as well as the male-female, urban-rural, and formal-informal earnings gaps, to the levels and changes of earnings inequality in Latin America.

Chapter 3, "The Role of Labor Supply in Wage Inequality Trends," discusses and quantifies the role of the changing quantity, quality, and composition of the labor skill supply in the observed evolution of the skill premium and, through this channel, wage inequality.

Chapter 4, "The Role of Labor Demand Conditions in Wage Inequality Trends," argues that the role of changes in aggregate demand might have been downplayed in the literature on developed countries (where business cycles are less pronounced), but appears to be of great importance in Latin America. The chapter also offers new evidence that in South America in the 2000s exchange rate appreciation from the commodity boom led to falling interfirm wage differences among similar workers of the same sector and therefore reduced wage inequality. In addition, this chapter highlights the reasons why skill-biased technological change, job polarization, and the traditional trade channels do not explain the decline in wage inequality in Latin America.

Chapter 5, "Exploring the Role of Minimum Wages and Unions in Recent Inequality Trends," assesses the role of minimum wage policy and decreasing unionization in the wage inequality trend.

Chapter 6, "Conclusions and Policy Reflections," presents the book's conclusions and puts forth policy recommendations.

Annex 1A. Background Papers for This Book

The nine background papers listed in this annex were produced during the preparation of this book.

Title: **"Understanding the Dynamics of Labor Income Inequality in Latin America"** **(World Bank Policy Research Working Paper 7795)**
    Authors: Carlos Rodríguez-Castelán (World Bank), Luis F. López-Calva (World Bank), Nora Lustig (Tulane University), and Daniel Valderrama (World Bank)

Abstract: This paper shows that the decline in the Gini coefficient for labor income inequality, which dropped from 47.3 in 2002 to 41.0 in 2013, was supported by a substantial expansion in real hourly earnings at the bottom of the wage distribution. The paper finds that, although the relative supply of skills grew steadily throughout the period, this factor alone is only weakly associated with the observed decline in the earnings gap between skilled and less-skilled workers. This paper concludes that the decline in labor inequality in Latin America was strongly associated with a constant but slow decline in the education premium since the mid-1990s, coupled with a steady decline in the experience premium observed since the early 2000s.

Title: **"Skill Premium, Labor Supply and Changes in the Structure of Wages in Latin America" (Inter-American Development Bank Working Paper 786)**

Authors: Manuel Fernández (University of Oxford) and Julián Messina (Inter-American Development Bank)

Abstract: Earnings inequality declined rapidly in Argentina, Brazil, and Chile during the 2000s. A reduction in the experience premium is a fundamental driver of declines in upper-tail (90/50) inequality, while a decline in the education premium is the primary determinant of the evolution of lower-tail (50/10) inequality. Relative labor supply is important for explaining changes in skill premiums. Relative demand trends favored high-skilled workers during the 1990s, shifting in favor of low-skilled workers during the 2000s. Changes in the minimum wage, and more important, commodity-led terms-of-trade improvements, are key factors behind these relative skill demand trends.

Title: **"Ageing Poorly? Accounting for the Decline in Earnings Inequality in Brazil, 1995-2012" (World Bank Policy Research Working Paper 8018)**

Authors: Francisco H. G. Ferreira (World Bank), Sergio P. Firpo (São Paulo School of Economics at Getulio Vargas Foundation), and Julián Messina (Inter-American Development Bank)

Abstract: This paper investigates the determinants of the decline in wage inequality in Brazil during 1995–2012. It uses a rigorous statistical decomposition technique (a recentered influence function regression) to assess the relative magnitudes of each one of four groups of candidate explanatory factors, namely human capital, labor market institutions, demographic composition of the labor force, and spatial segmentation. The analysis suggests that substantial reductions in the gender, race, and spatial wage gaps—conditional on human capital and institutional variables—explain the lion's share of the decline in earnings inequality. It also points out that, although rising minimum wages contributed to the decline during 2004–12, they had no such effect during 1995–2002.

Title: **"Declining Wages for College-Educated Workers in Mexico: Are Younger or Older Cohorts Hurt the Most?" (World Bank Policy Research Working Paper 7546)**

Authors: Raymundo M. Campos-Vázquez (El Colegio de Mexico), Luis F. López-Calva (World Bank), and Nora Lustig (Tulane University)

Abstract: Wage inequality has declined in Mexico since 2000. Using data from Mexican labor surveys for the period between 2000 and 2014, this paper investigates whether the decline was driven by wages declining more sharply for younger or older workers. It finds that wages of older workers declined and that the older the cohort, the more pronounced the decline. This would seem to support the hypothesis that older workers' skills have become obsolete.

Title: **"Education Expansion and Decline in Tertiary Premium in Brazil: 1995–2013" (Tulane Economics Working Paper 1525)**
Author: Yang Wang (Tulane University)
Abstract: According to Brazil National Household Survey 1995–2013 data, the decline in the relative wage of tertiary-educated workers coincides with an education expansion that shifted the relative supply and might also change the quality composition of the tertiary group. This paper tries to decompose the change in the tertiary premium in Brazil during the 1995–2013 period into the "price effect" (which refers to the change in educational premium caused by the shifts in supply and demand) and the "composition effect" (which refers to whether there was any significant decline in the average quality of tertiary-educated workers among recent cohorts and how the changes in cohort quality impacted the relative wage of the tertiary group).

Title: **"The Expansion of Higher Education in Colombia: Bad Students or Bad Programs?" (Inter-American Development Bank Discussion Paper 452)**
Authors: Adriana Camacho (Los Andes University), Julián Messina (Inter-American Development Bank), and Juan Pablo Uribe (Brown University)
Abstract: During the 2000s, Colombia witnessed a rapid expansion in the demand for postsecondary education. This rising demand triggered an explosion of new programs and institutions. This paper uses rich administrative data matching detailed socioeconomic characteristics of the young graduates, school admissions, wages in the early stages of their careers, and standardized test scores (pre- and post-tertiary education) to assess the heterogeneity in the value-added generated by these new programs.

Title: **"Tracking Wage Inequality Trends with Prices and Different Trade Models: Evidence from Mexico" (World Bank Policy Research Working Paper 7471)**
Authors: Timothy Halliday (University of Hawaii), Daniel Lederman (World Bank), and Raymond Robertson (Macalester College)
Abstract: Mexican wage inequality rose following Mexico's accession to the General Agreement on Tariffs and Trade/World Trade Organization in 1986. Since the mid-1990s, however, wage inequality has been falling. Since most trade models suggest that output prices can affect factor prices, this paper explores the relationship between output prices and wage inequality. The rise of inequality can

be explained by the evolution of the relative price of skill-intensive goods relative to unskilled-intensive goods, but these prices flattened by 1999 and thus cannot explain the subsequent decline in wage inequality. An alternative trade model with firm heterogeneity driven by variations in the relative price of tradable goods relative to nontradable goods can explain the decline in wage inequality. The paper compares this model's predictions with Mexican inequality statistics using data on output prices, census data, and quarterly household survey data. In spite of the model's simplicity, the model's predictions match Mexican variables reasonably well during the years when wage inequality fell.

Title: **"Job Polarization in Latin America" (Inter-American Development Bank, unpublished)**

Authors: Julián Messina (Inter-American Development Bank), Giovanni Pica (University of Milan), and Ana María Oviedo (World Bank)

Abstract: The objective of the paper is to document whether job and wage polarization occurred in Latin American countries over recent decades. The authors exploit the Skills Toward Employment and Productivity (STEP) Surveys conducted in Bolivia, Colombia, and El Salvador to measure the routine/abstract/manual content of jobs in Latin America. A first comparison with the United States shows that the task intensity of Latin American occupations is remarkably different, exhibiting a higher manual content. The paper merges the information on the task intensity of Latin American occupations with individual-level data from Chile and Mexico. This allows the authors to show that job polarization seems to have taken place in both countries in 2000, with employment changes happening mostly at the bottom and top ends of the abstract and routine task distributions.

Title: **"Labor Supply Elasticities: Evidence for Latin America" (World Bank Policy Research Working Paper, forthcoming)**

Authors: Olivier Bargain (Aix-Marseille University) and Joana Silva (World Bank)

Abstract: The authors put forth the first comprehensive characterization of wage and income elasticities of labor supply and transition across sectors for Latin America, using a comparative framework for four large countries in the region. Precisely, the paper uses microdata for Argentina, Brazil, Chile, and Mexico to estimate wage and income elasticities of participation and worked hours. To attenuate concerns regarding the endogeneity of wage rates, the authors pool repeated cross-sections over the 2000–14 period and construct pseudo-panels for grouped estimations. Results show that participation elasticities are in a range of values that is similar to what is found in richer countries and especially in southern Europe, where female participation was still relatively low in the 2000s. Another feature shared with these countries is that the low-skilled workers seem to be less responsive to wage changes than the high-skilled workers, at least in the largest labor force reservoir of married women. This fact, combined with strong domestic demand in South America, could concur to explain the faster progression of low-skill wages and the decline in overall wage inequality observed in the recent period. The paper also estimates the responsiveness to wage changes of formal versus informal employment. Formal employment seems procyclical to the variation in average wages, yet a wage increase mainly triggers a decline in informal employment for men and a decline in non-employment for women.

Notes

1. The terms "labor earnings inequality" and "wage inequality" entail different concepts. This book focuses on labor earnings inequality, which includes inequality in earnings from work of wage employees and self-employed full-time workers. We use the term "wage inequality" because this may be a more familiar concept, although our results always refer to labor earnings inequality.

2. Factors such as CCTs had important effects on poverty reduction and human capital formation (Fiszbein and Schady 2009). They are also likely to have had general equilibrium effects because of their positive effects on health and on skill levels for given years of schooling (Behrman and Parker 2010; Glewwe and Olinto 2004; Maluccio and Flores 2005; Schultz 2004), and, through these routes, on wage inequality. However, because of their relatively small size, CCTs are unlikely to have had large effects on labor market decisions and thus to have been the source of large shifts in wage inequality (Alzúa, Cruces, and Ripani 2013; Banerjee et al. 2016; Parker and Skoufias 2000). Noncontributory pension systems are likely to have larger effects on labor market decisions and are an area of active research (Frölich et al. 2013; World Bank 2012). For a detailed description of pension coverage expansion, see Levy and Schady (2013) and World Bank (2014).

References

Allwine, M., J. Rigolini, and L. F. López-Calva. 2013. "The Unfairness of (Poverty) Targets." Policy Research Working Paper 6361, World Bank, Washington, DC.

Alzúa, M. L., G. Cruces, and L. Ripani. 2013. "Welfare Programs and Labor Supply in Developing Countries: Experimental Evidence from Latin America." *Journal of Population Economics* 26 (4): 1255–84.

Banerjee, A., R. Hanna, G. Kreindler, and B. Olken. 2016. "Debunking the Stereotype of the Lazy Welfare Recipient: Evidence from Cash Transfer Programs Worldwide." Harvard Kennedy School (HKS) Faculty Research Working Paper No. 76, John F. Kennedy School of Government, Harvard University, Cambridge, MA.

Bargain, O., and J. Silva. Forthcoming. "Labor Supply Elasticities: Evidence for Latin America." Policy Research Working Paper, World Bank, Washington, DC. Available at: https://sites.google.com/site/joanasilvaweb/.

Behrman, J. R., and S. W. Parker. 2010. "The Impacts of Conditional Cash Transfer Programs on Education." In *Conditional Cash Transfers in Latin America*, edited by M. Adato and J. Hoddinott. Baltimore: Johns Hopkins University Press for the International Food Policy Research Institute.

Bourguignon, F. 2002. "Growth and Inequality: Issues and Policy Implications." CESifo, Munich, January.

Camacho, A., J. Messina, and J. P. Uribe. 2016. "The Expansion of Higher Education in Colombia: Bad Students or Bad Programs?" IDB Discussion Paper 452, Inter-American Development Bank, Washington, DC.

Campos-Vázquez, R. M., L. F. López-Calva, and N. Lustig. 2016. "Declining Wages for College-Educated Workers in Mexico: Are Younger or Older Cohorts Hurt the Most?" Policy Research Working Paper 7546, World Bank, Washington, DC.

Chetty, R., and N. Hendren. 2015. "The Impacts of Neighborhoods on Intergenerational Mobility: Childhood Exposure Effects and County-Level Estimates." Study for the Equality of Opportunity Project, Harvard University and National Bureau of Economic Research, Cambridge, MA.

Cord, L. J., O. B. Cabanillas, L. Lucchetti, C. Rodríguez-Castelán, L. D. Sousa, and D. Valderrama. 2014. "Inequality Stagnation in Latin America in the Aftermath of the Global Financial Crisis." Policy Research Working Paper 7146, World Bank, Washington, DC.

Engerman, S. L., and K. L. Sokoloff. 1997. "Factor Endowments, Institutions, and Differential Paths of Growth among New World Economies: A View from Economic Historians of the United States." In *How Latin America Fell Behind: Essays on the Economic Histories of Brazil and Mexico, 1800–1914*, edited by S. Haber. Stanford, CA: Stanford University Press.

Fernández, M., and J. Messina. 2017. "Skill Premium, Labor Supply and Changes in the Structure of Wages in Latin America." IDB Working Paper 786, Inter-American Development Bank, Washington, DC.

Ferreira, F. H. G., S. P. Firpo, and J. Messina. 2017. "Ageing Poorly? Accounting for the Decline in Earnings Inequality in Brazil, 1995–2012." Policy Research Working Paper 8018, World Bank, Washington, DC.

Fiszbein, A., and N. Schady. 2009. *Conditional Cash Transfers: Reducing Present and Future Poverty*. Washington, DC: World Bank.

Frölich, M., D. Kaplan, C. Pagés, J. Rigolini, and D. Robalino, eds. 2013. *Social Insurance, Informality, and Labour Markets: How to Protect Workers while Creating Good Jobs*. Oxford, UK: Oxford University Press.

Genicot, G., and D. Ray. 2014. "Aspirations and Inequality." NBER Working Paper 19976, National Bureau of Economic Research, Cambridge, MA.

Glewwe, P., and P. Olinto. 2004. "Evaluating the Impact of Conditional Cash Transfers on Schooling: An Experimental Analysis of Honduras's PRAF Program." Final report for the U.S. Agency for International Development. International Food Policy Research Institute, Washington, DC.

Halliday, T., D. Lederman, and R. Robertson. 2015. "Tracking Wage Inequality Trends with Prices and Different Trade Models: Evidence from Mexico." Policy Research Working Paper 7471, World Bank, Washington, DC.

Levy, S., and N. Schady. 2013. "Latin America's Social Policy Challenge: Education, Social Insurance, Redistribution." *Journal of Economic Perspectives* 27 (2): 193–218.

López-Calva, L. F., and N. Lustig, eds. 2010. *Declining Inequality in Latin America: A Decade of Progress?* Washington, DC: Brookings Institution Press; New York: United Nations Development Programme.

Maluccio, J., and R. Flores. 2005. "Impact Evaluation of a Conditional Cash Transfer Program: The Nicaraguan Red de Protección Social." Report 141, International Food Policy Research Institute, Washington, DC.

Messina, J., G. Pica, and A. M. Oviedo. 2016. "Job Polarization in Latin America." Inter-American Development Bank, Washington, DC. Unpublished. Available at: http://www.jsmessina.com.

Milanovic, B. 2016. *Global Inequality: A New Approach for the Age of Globalization*. Cambridge, MA: Harvard University Press.

Parker, S. W., and E. Skoufias. 2000. "The Impact of PROGRESA on Work, Leisure, and Time Allocation." Final report submitted to the Programa de Educación, Salud y Alimentación

(PROGRESA), Government of Mexico, by the International Food Policy Research Institute, Washington, DC.

Ravallion, M. 2015. *The Economics of Poverty: History, Measurement, and Policy.* Oxford, UK: Oxford University Press.

Rodríguez-Castelán, C., L. F. López-Calva, N. Lustig, and D. Valderrama. 2016. "Understanding the Dynamics of Labor Income Inequality in Latin America." Policy Research Working Paper 7795, World Bank, Washington, DC.

Schultz, P. 2004. "School Subsidies for the Poor: Evaluating the Mexican Progresa Poverty Program." *Journal of Development Economics* 74 (1): 199–250.

Wang, Y. 2015. "Education Expansion and Decline in Tertiary Premium in Brazil: 1995–2013." Tulane Economics Working Paper 1525, Tulane University, New Orleans.

Williamson, J. G. 2015. "Latin American Inequality: Colonial Origins, Commodity Booms, or a Missed 20th Century Leveling?" NBER Working Paper 20915, National Bureau of Economic Research, Cambridge, MA.

World Bank. 2012. *World Development Report 2013: Jobs.* Washington, DC: World Bank.

———. 2014. "Social Gains in the Balance: A Fiscal Policy Challenge for Latin America and the Caribbean." LAC Poverty and Labor Brief (February), World Bank, Washington, DC.

2
Wage Inequality Changes since 1990: Key Trends and Stylized Facts

Introduction

While the 1990s was a period of moderate increases in wage inequality in Latin America, the 2000s was characterized by a decline in wage inequality in the region—an important historical breakthrough. This happened as most developed countries faced a persistent rise in earnings inequality (Autor 2014).

This chapter describes the main wage inequality trends in the region since the 1990s and documents key stylized facts that accompanied this evolution. It uses standardized household survey and labor force survey data for all countries in the region that have a time series covering this period. It presents different types of summary measures and disentangles the evolution of wage inequality at the top and bottom of the wage distribution. This is important, given that inequality can fall either because (1) wages at the top are falling, (2) wages at the bottom are rising, (3) both are falling but the top is falling faster, or (4) both are rising but the bottom is rising faster. Each explanation has different implications for the drivers of inequality trends, and ultimately policy implications.

Through the use of decomposition techniques, this chapter also differentiates between observed wage inequality and residual wage inequality and thoroughly documents secular trends in observable worker skills. It considers the roles of the skill (education) premium and of changes in gender, urban-rural, and formal-informal wage gaps in the level and evolution of earnings inequality in the region. In addition to characterizing the changes in economic payoffs to key characteristics and relative wages across groups of workers with different observable characteristics (between-group wage differentials), the chapter quantifies the contribution of within-group (residual) wage differentials. It also characterizes the key trends in skill supply and demand with which any valid explanation of the region's wage inequality evolution (discussed in chapters 3, 4, and 5) must be consistent.

Trends in Overall Inequality

Persistence of High Inequality in the Region

High (income or consumption) household inequality is a persistent economic fact in Latin America, where for decades it has been nearly the highest in the world (Alvaredo and Gasparini 2015; Lakner and Milanovic 2013; Williamson 2015). In fact, Latin America, along with Sub-Saharan Africa, is the region with the greatest inequality in the world (figure 2.1).[1] The most recent measurements of income inequality reveal that, among the world's 20 most-unequal countries, 8 are in Latin America, with the rest in Sub-Saharan Africa.[2]

FIGURE 2.1: **Wage and Total Income Inequality in Latin America, 1995–2015**

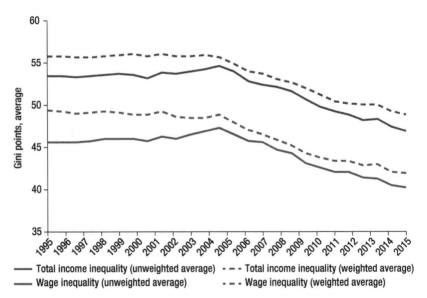

— Total income inequality (unweighted average)   - - - Total income inequality (weighted average)
— Wage inequality (unweighted average)   - - - Wage inequality (weighted average)

Source: Rodríguez-Castelán et al. (2016), based on the Socio-Economic Database for Latin America and the Caribbean (SEDLAC), Universidad Nacional de la Plata (CEDLAS) and World Bank (http://sedlac.econo.unlp.edu.ar/eng/).
Note: The regional aggregate is the average of the Gini points from 17 countries. The Gini coefficient measures the equality of income distribution, ranging from zero (perfect equality) to 100 (maximal inequality). Dashed lines show Gini points averaged across Latin American countries using population size as weights, while solid lines show unweighted averages. If a specific country did not have information available for a particular year, a simple interpolation was applied. Colombia data for the 1990s were complemented with wage inequality data from the International Labour Organization and total income inequality data from the Mission for the Design of a Strategy for Reducing Poverty and Inequality.

Significant Reduction in Inequality in the 2000s

A growing body of literature suggests that, after a long period of growing or stagnant inequality, the trajectory of household income inequality in Latin America shows a visible kink around 2002—rising from the 1990s until about 2002, when it started to decline (López-Calva and Lustig 2010). This trend of decreasing inequality was particularly steep during the commodity-driven boom period of 2003–11, before flattening out during the post-2011 slowdown.

The region's average Gini coefficient for household income per capita increased from 53.4 to 54.7 (1.3 points) between 1990 and 2002, but fell by 5.9 points to 48.8 between 2002 and 2011 (figure 2.1).[3] The trajectory during the 2000s contrasts with that of Latin America in previous periods and with the trajectories of other regions during the same period (Alvaredo and Gasparini 2015; Cord et al. 2014; Cornia 2014; De Ferranti et al. 2004; De la Torre, Messina, and Pienknagura 2012; De la Torre et al. 2014; Gasparini and Lustig 2011; Rodríguez-Castelán et al. 2016; Székely and Hilgert 1999; Székely and Mendoza 2015; World Bank 2011).

Putting numbers in a recent historical perspective, Latin America from the 1970s through the 1990s was nearly 10 Gini points more unequal than Asia, 17.5 points more unequal than the 30 countries in the Organisation for Economic Co-operation and Development (OECD), and 20.4 points more unequal than Eastern Europe (De Ferranti et al. 2004). During the 2000s, however, the data clearly indicate an inequality convergence: while inequality was *decreasing* in Latin America, it was *increasing* in the world's more-equal countries (Alvaredo and Gasparini 2015). By the end of the decade, Latin America was only 3.4 points more unequal than East Asia and the Pacific, 7.7 points more unequal than South Asia, and 11.9 points more unequal than Eastern Europe and Central Asia (figure 2.2).[4]

The decline in income inequality was not driven by a single country or group of countries; it was shared across 16 of the 17 countries in which we can consistently measure household income inequality in Latin America. The only exception was Costa Rica, where inequality increased by 1.7 Gini points.[5] In spite of the common trends, the reductions are heterogeneous in their magnitude, ranging from reductions of 1.4 annual Gini points in Nicaragua (2005–09) to 0.09 annual Gini points in Colombia (2003–12) (Cord et al. 2014).

Furthermore, the decline in income inequality is robust to the choice of index: the reductions are actually larger when measured by the Theil (T) index[6] and very similar when measured by the 90–10 percentile ratio,[7] at 11.4 percent and 9.4 percent, respectively.[8] However, during the post-2011 slowdown, income inequality trends have flattened (as shown in figure 2.1), raising concerns about the sustainability of the welcomed trends in a low-growth scenario (Cord et al. 2014).

FIGURE 2.2: Household Income Inequality in Latin America Compared with Other Regions, 2013

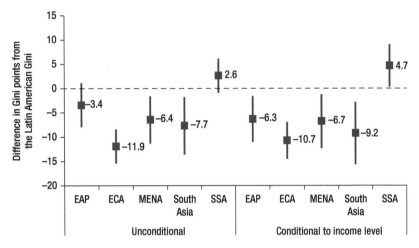

Source: Rodríguez-Castelán et al. (2016) based on June 2015 PovcalNet data, World Bank (http://iresearch.worldbank.org /PovcalNet/).

Note: EAP = East Asia and the Pacific; ECA = Eastern Europe and Central Asia; MENA = Middle East and North Africa; SSA = Sub-Saharan Africa. Numbers shown represent the value of the coefficient of a regional dummy variable of a linear regression model that has as a dependent variable the latest available Gini coefficient (which measures the equality of income distribution, ranging from zero [perfect equality] to 100 [maximal inequality]). "Unconditional" results are those not conditioned to income level. For the results that are "conditional to income level," we include as an independent variable the log of per capita GDP. These calculations use data from the most recent year available for each of the 147 countries included in this analysis. Approximately 95 percent of the most recent data points are from 2000–08, and the rest are from 1990s data. To compare income Gini coefficients with consumption Gini coefficients, following Alvaredo and Gasparini (2015), the analysis multiplies all Gini coefficients of household per capita income by a factor of 0.86. This transformation corresponds with a Latin America–specific average of consumption-income Gini ratios, calculated using data from seven Latin American countries that have frequent information on consumption and income. All the reported differences between Latin America and other regions are statistically significant except for the region's differences relative to Sub-Saharan Africa and East Asia and the Pacific.

Trends in Wage Inequality

Synchrony of Income and Wage Inequality Trends

The same sharp declining trend in income inequality in the 2000s after a decade of stagnation is observed for wage inequality, as shown in figure 2.1. Specifically, the average Gini index for labor income rose from 45.6 in 1990 to 47.3 in 2002, but fell from 47.3 in 2002 to 42.0 in 2011. In fact, in Latin America there is a close relationship between household income inequality and individual earnings inequality, as discussed further in box 2.1 (Cord et al. 2014; De la Torre et al. 2014; De la Torre, Beylis, and Ize 2015; Rodríguez-Castelán et al. 2016; World Bank 2015b).[9] This relationship is not surprising, since labor income accounts, on average, for 73 percent of the total household income captured in Latin American household surveys in 2012.

The correlation or comovement over time of income and earnings inequality is evident in changes in earnings and total inequality during the 1990s and 2000s, as shown in figure 2.1. Annex 2A presents the evolution of earnings and income inequality in each Latin American country for which time series data are available (figure 2A.1). The common patterns between the two series are remarkable. For example, earnings and income inequality in Argentina increased sharply up to 2002 and declined rapidly thereafter. When earnings inequality in Brazil was declining slowly, income inequality was almost stagnant. After 2002, when earnings inequality declined rapidly, the inequality of household income followed at a similar pace.

The Latin American wage inequality trends in the 2000s differ from those in other regions. In fact, while wage inequality declined significantly in Latin America in the 2000s, it increased in most countries outside Latin America. In 2013, wage inequality in Latin America was about 6 Gini points *below* the value in 2002, while in non-Latin American countries it was about 1.3 Gini points *above* the value in 2002 (figure 2.3).[10]

The recent economic slowdown in Latin America is already affecting wage inequality. Between 2012 and 2015, the average Gini index for labor income fell from 41.4 to 40.2, a much smaller annual reduction than the one observed between 2003 and 2011.

Wage Inequality Relative to 2002: Latin American Countries Compared with Countries Outside the Region, 1993–2013

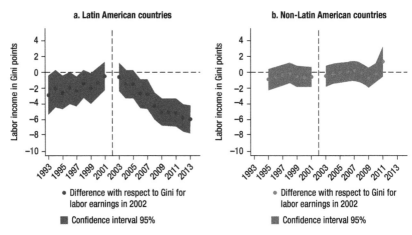

a. Latin American countries   b. Non-Latin American countries

● Difference with respect to Gini for labor earnings in 2002

■ Confidence interval 95%

● Difference with respect to Gini for labor earnings in 2002

■ Confidence interval 95%

Sources: For Latin American countries, based on Rodríguez-Castelán et al. (2016), based on the Socio-Economic Database for Latin America and the Caribbean (SEDLAC), Universidad Nacional de la Plata (CEDLAS) and the World Bank (http://sedlac.econo.unlp.edu.ar/eng/). For non-Latin American countries, based on the International Labour Organization's *Global Wage Report*. *Note:* The underlying data represent the hourly wage Gini among paid workers 15–65 years of age for each country and year, multiplied by 100. The Gini coefficient measures the equality of income distribution, ranging from zero (perfect equality) to 100 (maximal inequality). The values of the 1st and 100th percentiles of the earnings distribution were trimmed by each gender education cell. The figure uses only the information (noninterpolated) available for each country. It shows the average difference between the labor income Ginis in any year with respect to the value in 2002. Each average value and its standard errors are estimated as part of a simple panel data specification with country fixed effects. The *Global Wage Report* data are not strictly comparable with SEDLAC data. In some countries, different types of surveys were used, and the sample and trimming criteria are different.

Earnings Inequality Declines as the Main Contributors to Household Income Inequality Decline

In addition to higher labor earnings per worker, other factors contributed to changes in household per capita income (Cord et al. 2014; De la Torre, Messina, and Pienknagura 2012; Gasparini and Cruces 2013; López-Calva and Lustig 2010; World Bank 2011):[11]

- Better job opportunities and increasing female labor force participation, translating into more people employed in the household

- Improved transfer policies for the poor with the introduction of conditional cash transfer programs and reinvigorated redistribution through noncontributory pension systems, translating into higher nonlabor income

- Decline in fertility rates, particularly among low-income households.

Applying a decomposition method based on counterfactual simulations proposed by Barros et al. (2010) for distinguishing the main contributors to inequality changes in Latin America in the 1990s and 2000s, Rodríguez-Castelán et al. (2016) find that all of these forces had some explanatory power. However, the reduction of earnings inequality stands out as the main contributor to declining household income inequality in most countries in the 2000s. The exceptions were Colombia and Peru, where the main contributor to declining inequality was the increased average number of people employed in the household; Guatemala and Mexico, where the contribution of nonlabor income (such as pensions and other social transfers) was larger than that of labor income; and Brazil, where the contribution of labor and nonlabor income were similar, with pension income alone contributing to 18 percent of the total reduction in income inequality (figure 2.4). In the region as a whole, labor earnings account for two-thirds of the overall reduction in income inequality (Rodríguez-Castelán et al. 2016).

Notwithstanding the crucial role of labor income—the main asset of the poor—in reducing household income inequality, the contribution of nonlabor income cannot

FIGURE 2.4: Decomposition of Average Annual Changes in Household Income Inequality, Selected Latin American Countries, 1990–2003 and 2003–11

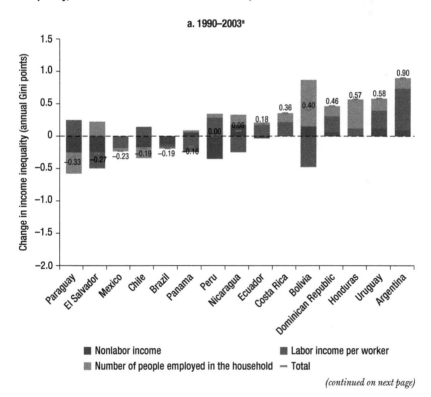

(continued on next page)

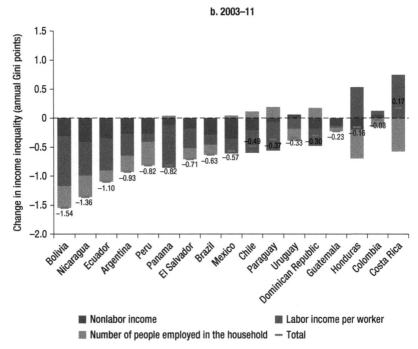

b. 2003–11

Source: Rodríguez-Castelán et al. (2016), based on the Socio-Economic Database for Latin America and the Caribbean (SEDLAC), Universidad Nacional de la Plata (CEDLAS) and the World Bank (http://sedlac.econo.unlp.edu.ar/eng/).

Note: The Gini coefficients—which measure the equality of income distribution from zero (perfect equality) to 100 (maximal inequality)—have been multiplied by 100 to create an index. The figures illustrate changes in Gini points, ranked from the country with the largest decline in the Gini to the country with the largest increase in the Gini over 1990–2003 (panel a) and 2003–11 (panel b). For each country in each period, the figures show the contribution of three factors to changes in the Gini: household nonlabor income (such as remittances, rents, and capital income); labor income per working adult in the household; and the number of working adults in the household. The bars represent the total change in the Gini. The numbers correspond to the Shapley nonparametric decomposition of inequality changes following a method proposed by Paes de Barros, Foguel, and Ulyssea (2007). The period for each country may be different, and, to ensure comparability across periods, we have selected pairs of comparable years.

a. The 1990–2003 data do not include Colombia and Guatemala because early 1990s data were not available for these countries.

be disregarded as minor. Perhaps what is more remarkable is that nonlabor income has had a much more consistent role in reducing inequality during the 2000s than in the 1990s. In 14 of the 17 countries analyzed, nonlabor income had an important redistribution component during the most recent period. Only in Uruguay and Colombia did nonlabor income exacerbate inequality. The contribution of nonlabor income is all the more remarkable during times when the capital income share in gross domestic product (GDP) was on the rise (Karabarbounis and Neiman 2014). Because capital tends to be more concentrated than labor, increases in the capital share are usually associated with increases in inequality (Piketty 2014). The limited evidence available for Latin America suggests that the region shared these global trends, as the labor share declined mildly in Mexico and Brazil (ILO 2010/11). This suggests that other forces (possibly transfers and taxes) became more progressive during the last few years.

Changes in Wage Structure

The structure of wages changed markedly in Latin America during the past two decades. Remuneration for observable skill-related characteristics, particularly education and experience, moved hand-in-hand with the inequality dynamics. In particular, the returns to education and experience declined during the 2000s, when earnings inequality was also in decline. Other gaps—including differences between urban and rural earnings and the differences in pay between men and women and between the majority of the population and ethnic minorities—declined as well. Behind all of these closing gaps was a sharp increase of the wages at the bottom of the wage distribution. Let us review each of the factors, starting with the latter.

• *Sizable expansion of real wages at the bottom of the wage distribution*

Although the (unweighted) average earnings in Latin America increased for the bottom, middle, and top of the labor income distribution over the past decade—following no change during the 1990s—the largest increase in wages occurred for those workers at the bottom of the earnings distribution.

In particular, between 2002 and 2013, labor earnings of workers at the 10th percentile of the distribution (the highest-paid workers in the bottom decile of the earnings distribution) rose by more than 50 percent in real terms. This increase was significantly greater than the 15 percent wage growth for workers at the 90th percentile of the distribution (the lowest-paid workers in the top decile of the earnings distribution). It was also higher than the 32 percent wage growth for the workers at the 50th percentile of the distribution (those at the earnings midpoint in the labor earnings distribution) (figure 2.5). For information on the evolution of earnings inequality at the top and bottom of the income distribution in each country see annex table 2A.1.

This evolution is in sharp contrast with the evolution of the upper and lower tails of the earnings distribution in high-income economies. Alvaredo et al. (2013) present evidence that the main force behind the recent increase in wage inequality in several high-income economies was a dynamic increase at the upper tail (90th percentile and above) of real wages and a stagnant trend in real wages at the lower tail (wages below the median) of the wage distribution. This was particularly true for the United States.

• *Changes in the education premium*

The earnings premium for a college education versus primary school was 67 percent in the 1980s (Manacorda, Sánchez-Páramo, and Schady 2010),[12] increased

Index of Labor Earnings in Latin America: 10th Percentile vs. 50th and 90th Percentiles of the Income Distribution, 1990–2013

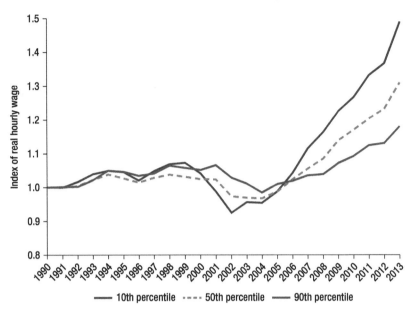

Source: Rodríguez-Castelán et al. (2016), based on the Socio-Economic Database for Latin America and the Caribbean (SEDLAC), Universidad Nacional de la Plata (CEDLAS) and the World Bank (http://sedlac.econo.unlp.edu.ar/eng/).

Note: Index base: 1990 = 1. The regional aggregate is an unweighted average of the index of hourly earnings in 17 countries. If no country data are available for a year in the middle of two points in the series, the missing data are estimated using a simple linear interpolation. To address missing data at the beginning or the end of the series, the first or the last figure available was replaced, respectively. Estimations are based on samples of female and male workers (self-employed, salaried, and employer) who work full-time (at least 35 hours per week) and are ages 15–65. Labor income in 2005 purchasing power parity (PPP) terms trimmed the 1st and 99th percentiles by gender and education level in each country-year subgroup. If a specific country did not have information available for a particular year, a simple interpolation was applied.

moderately in the 1990s (by around 10 percent), and has decreased sharply since 2003 (by around 25 percent), following a trend similar to that of earnings inequality. In contrast, there has been a steady but very slow decline of the college versus high school premium since the mid-1990s. Rodríguez-Castelán et al. (2016), who use a standard Mincerian framework, find that, since 2003, the average (unweighted) gap between college-educated workers and workers with primary schooling or less declined from about 330 percent to 240 percent (figure 2.6, panel a). As discussed in annex 2B, these results are robust to alternative methodologies to compute returns to schooling and are consistent with larger earnings increases for unskilled workers than for high-skilled workers in the 2000s (in other words, they represent an increase in the primary school premium relative to other educational levels). Accounting for differences in the propensity to participate in the labor market across different skill groups does not change the main conclusions.

- *Changes in the experience premium*

Work experience premiums remained relatively stable in the 1990s but fell in the 2000s, a trajectory similar to that of wage inequality (figure 2.6, panel b). That is, the gap between those with more years of experience and those with less experience remained relatively constant during the 1990s, and then fell in the early 2000s. This evident fall in labor earnings for the most-experienced workers relative to less-experienced workers implies that skills gained through years in the labor market might be losing value since the past decade and may represent lower wages for older cohorts. For example, the experience premium for the groups with the largest difference in years of experience (those with 21–30 years of potential experience relative to those with 0–5 years of potential experience) dropped from 56 percent in 1993 to 50 percent in 2004, but since then, has declined significantly faster to 33 percent in 2013.

FIGURE 2.6: **Returns to Education, Experience, and Relative Gender and Urban-Rural Wage Gap Trends, Latin America, 1993–2013**

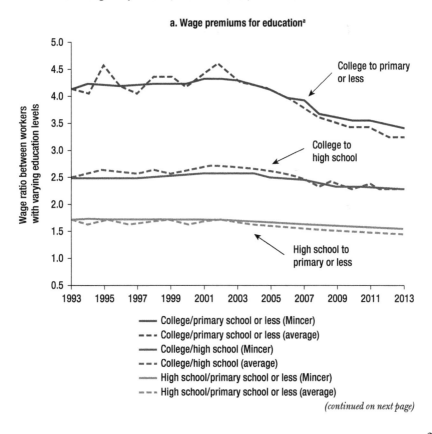

a. Wage premiums for education[a]

College/primary school or less (Mincer)
College/primary school or less (average)
College/high school (Mincer)
College/high school (average)
High school/primary school or less (Mincer)
High school/primary school or less (average)

(continued on next page)

Returns to Education, Experience, and Relative Gender and Urban-Rural Wage Gap Trends, Latin America, 1993–2013 *(continued)*

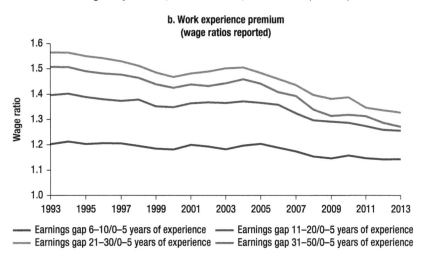

b. Work experience premium
(wage ratios reported)

— Earnings gap 6–10/0–5 years of experience — Earnings gap 11–20/0–5 years of experience
— Earnings gap 21–30/0–5 years of experience — Earnings gap 31–50/0–5 years of experience

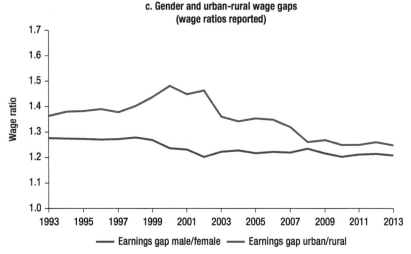

c. Gender and urban-rural wage gaps
(wage ratios reported)

— Earnings gap male/female — Earnings gap urban/rural

Source: Adapted from Rodríguez-Castelán et al. (2016) using the Socio-Economic Database for Latin America and the Caribbean (SEDLAC), Universidad Nacional de la Plata (CEDLAS) and the World Bank (http://sedlac.econo.unlp.edu.ar/eng/).
Note: Sample restricted to the working-age population (ages 15–65). Calculations use only full-time workers and exclude outliers (1st and 99th percentile values) of the wage distribution, and use ordinary least squares models including dummies for four key observable characteristics that are part of a traditional Mincerian equation: education, tenure, gender, and urban/rural dummy. The panels report ratios expressing the number of times a specific category (such as wages of college-educated workers) varies from the base category (wages of workers with primary education or less) of each characteristic (in this case, education).
a. The ratios of college to primary education and of high school to primary education were computed using an exponential function of the coefficients. Coefficients are the average difference *between* the returns to a specific category (such as college-educated workers) and the base category (workers with primary education or less), controlling for the rest of the observable characteristics. The ratio of college to high school education is the ratio of the exponential of the coefficient of college and the exponential of the coefficient of high school.

In comparison, the experience premium for the group with 6–10 years of potential experience relative to the group with 0–5 years of potential experience had a less dramatic decline over the past two decades. The timing of changes in the experience premiums also coincides with the evolution of earnings inequality. That is, the gap of returns to experience remained relatively constant during the 1990s, but then narrowed in the early 2000s.

- *Changes in the gender, race, and urban-rural wage gaps*

During the 2000s, most labor market gaps narrowed in the region (gender, race, and spatial wage gaps). There were changes in the gender composition of the labor force (with an increase in female labor force participation) and in the corresponding wage gap of male workers compared to female workers. However, in a divergence from overall wage inequality trends, the gender gap remained relatively stable over 1993–99 (figure 2.6, panel c). In contrast, the urban-rural gap increased from 36 percent in 1993 to 46 percent in 2002, followed by a significant decline from 46 percent in 2002 to 25 percent in 2013 (figure 2.6, panel c). This decline may have been triggered by the commodity boom, which boosted the supply of agricultural goods and other commodities.

A country-by-country analysis of the urban-rural labor earnings gap shows that changes in wage compression were rather small in the period between 1990 and 2003. Only Colombia, El Salvador, and Paraguay showed a negative annual growth rate of the urban-rural gap larger than 5 percent. However, during the second period (between 2003 and 2010) half of the 17 Latin American countries studied experienced larger declines in the urban-rural wage gap. As expected, this substantial compression in the urban-rural earnings distribution was particularly strong in countries that were more favored by the commodity boom of the 2000s. Wage growth was high in countries with favorable terms-of-trade shocks driven by the commodity boom, but it was particularly higher for unskilled and low-skilled workers in tradable sectors, which include primary activities, mining, and manufacturing (World Bank 2015a).[13] Interestingly, the countries that benefited from the commodity boom (fundamentally South American countries), plus Costa Rica, El Salvador, Nicaragua, and Panama, are the ones that showed the largest decline in the urban-rural wage gap after 2003 (Rodríguez-Castelán et al. 2016).

Other gaps also narrowed during the 2000s. The race earnings gap between whites and nonwhites declined in most countries of the region (Ñopo, Daza, and Ramos 2012), and differences in pay between formal and informal employees declined in Brazil (Ferreira, Firpo, and Messina 2017) and possibly other countries.

Two Groups of Countries, Two Different Wage Trends

Although the reduction of wage inequality in Latin America was a regionwide phenomenon, two regional subgroups exhibited important differences in terms of the timing and magnitude of the reduction in the 21st century. In the 1990s, wage inequality increased slightly in most of the region's countries (the exceptions being Brazil,

El Salvador, and Nicaragua, where inequality started to fall slowly in the mid-to-late 1990s, although 2003 was when this decline became sharp). In the 2000s, wage inequality fell broadly across Latin America with only one exception: Costa Rica. The biggest difference across countries occurred in the magnitude of the reduction in wage inequality in the 2000s across two geographically distinct country subgroups: South America and Central America plus Mexico. Although wage inequality fell throughout the region in the 2000s, it fell more strongly in South America than in Central America and Mexico (figure 2.7).

This difference reflected wage patterns by educational level that diverged between these two groups of countries. In South America, earnings at the top and bottom deciles increased faster than the regional average, and the gap between the two deciles closed as earnings at the bottom grew faster than at the top. In contrast, in Central America and Mexico, earnings in the upper decile were stagnant to declining, while earnings at the bottom increased, albeit at a significantly lower rate than in the region as a whole (figure 2.8, panel a). In other words, the decline in earnings inequality in

FIGURE 2.7: **Wage Inequality Trends in Latin America Compared with Other Regions and by Country Subgroup**

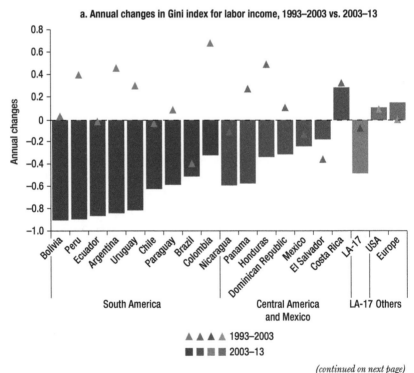

a. Annual changes in Gini index for labor income, 1993–2003 vs. 2003–13

▲ ▲ ▲ ▲ 1993–2003
■ ■ ■ ■ 2003–13

(continued on next page)

b. Wage and income inequality dynamics, South America vs. Central America and Mexico, 1990–2012

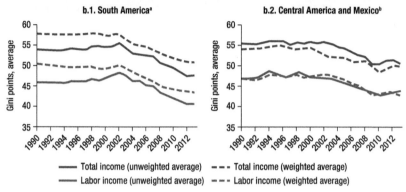

b.1. South America[a]

b.2. Central America and Mexico[b]

——— Total income (unweighted average)   – – – Total income (weighted average)
——— Labor income (unweighted average)   – – – Labor income (weighted average)

Source: Rodríguez-Castelán et al. (2016), based on the Socio-Economic Database for Latin America and the Caribbean (SEDLAC), Universidad Nacional de la Plata (CEDLAS) and the World Bank (http://sedlac.econo.unlp.edu.ar/eng/).
Note: LA in panel a = Latin America. The Gini index measures the equality of income distribution, ranging from zero (perfect equality) to 100 (maximal inequality).
a. The regional aggregate for South America is the average of Argentina, Bolivia, Brazil, Chile, Colombia, Ecuador, Paraguay, Peru, and Uruguay.
b. The regional aggregate for Central America and Mexico is the average for Guatemala, Honduras, Mexico, Nicaragua, and Panama.

FIGURE 2.8: **Labor Earnings Dynamics in Selected Latin American Countries**

a. Evolution of real hourly wage index, selected percentiles, 1990–2012[a]

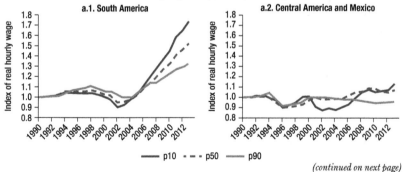

a.1. South America

a.2. Central America and Mexico

——— p10   – – – p50   ——— p90

(continued on next page)

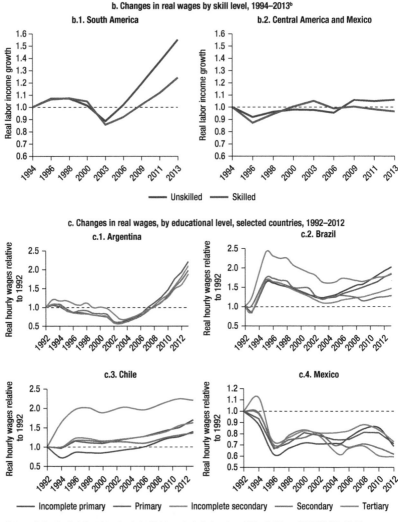

b. Changes in real wages by skill level, 1994–2013[b]

b.1. South America

b.2. Central America and Mexico

Unskilled ——— Skilled

c. Changes in real wages, by educational level, selected countries, 1992–2012

c.1. Argentina

c.2. Brazil

c.3. Chile

c.4. Mexico

——— Incomplete primary ——— Primary ——— Incomplete secondary ——— Secondary ——— Tertiary

Sources: Authors' calculations based on Labor Database for Latin America and the Caribbean (LABLAC) (http://lablac.econo
.unlp.edu.ar/eng/index.php); Socio-Economic Database for Latin America and the Caribbean (SEDLAC), Universidad Nacional de
la Plata (CEDLAS) and the World Bank (http://sedlac.econo.unlp.edu.ar/eng/).

Note: Wages are deflated using national deflators. If no country data are available for a year in the middle of two points in the
series, the missing figure was estimated using a simple linear interpolation. South American countries include Argentina, Brazil,
Chile, Ecuador, and Uruguay. Central American and Mexico countries include Costa Rica, Honduras, Mexico, and Panama.
a. p10 refers to the bottom 10 percent of the income distribution, p50 to the 50th percentile, and p90 to the 90th percentile (the
top 10 percent of the income distribution). Graphs show the ratio between the real hourly wage of each year and the real hourly
wage in the earliest year by skilled and unskilled workers.
b. "Unskilled" refers to completed primary education or less. "Skilled" refers to completed tertiary education or more. Graphs
show the ratio between the real wage of each year and the real wage reported in the earliest year for each educational level.

Central America and Mexico was driven by a reduction of earnings at the top and modest growth at the bottom, while in South America the decline was driven by much more vigorous growth at the bottom in a context of overall earnings growth.

Similarly, the two subregions differed in terms of changes in the education premium. In South American countries, real earnings of both college-educated workers and those with a primary school education or less increased, but earnings of unskilled workers grew faster than those of skilled workers, matching the overall regional pattern. In contrast, in Central America and Mexico, real earnings of college-educated workers declined, while those of workers with a primary education or less modestly increased (figure 2.8, panel b). In Mexico, for example, average hourly earnings of workers who had completed either college or high school declined during the 2000s; meanwhile, the wages of the rest of the workers rose until the 2008 global financial crisis and subsequently declined, albeit more slowly than the wages of college-educated workers, as shown in figure 2.8, panel c (Campos-Vázquez, López-Calva, and Lustig 2016).

Contribution of Skills and Education to the Changes in Overall Wage Inequality

Much of the discussion on changes in wage inequality focuses on returns to skills and education—that is, the pay differential among skilled and unskilled workers. Because education is the most important predictor of labor earnings that can be consistently measured over time, changes in returns to schooling have important implications for the evolution of income inequality.[14]

Figure 2.9 depicts the evolution of the labor income Gini, household income per capita Gini, and tertiary versus primary education premium. As can be seen, inequality has had the same trend as the education premium—increasing in the 1990s and decreasing throughout the 2000s. The correlation between the changes in the premium and the average growth rate of the Gini index across countries is stronger for the 2003–10 period. The parallel trends between the reductions in the schooling premium and wage inequality are shared across the vast majority of Latin American countries. The correlation between changes in earnings inequality and changes in the skill premium is 0.63 and highly significant.

Returns to skills, and in particular, returns to education, are central to changes in wage inequality in Latin America for the three main reasons discussed below.[15]

First, the education premium accounts for a large share (around 27 percent) of wage inequality (measured by the log-wage variance) in Latin America at any point in time during the 1997–2013 period.[16] Combined, education and experience account for an even larger share (around 32 percent). Adding other observable worker characteristics (such as whether the worker lives in an urban or rural area) increases the explained share to about 40 percent of overall earnings inequality. The other 60 percent is accounted for by within-group (residual) wage inequality (that is, wage

Income and Wage Inequality Trends Relative to the Education Premium in Latin America, 1993–2013

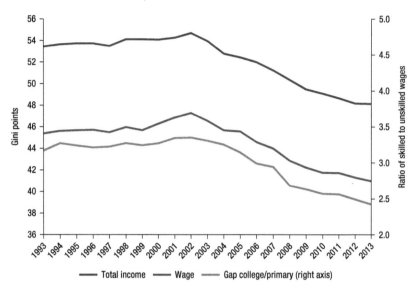

Total income — Wage — Gap college/primary (right axis)

Source: Calculations based on data from the Socio-Economic Database for Latin America and the Caribbean (SEDLAC), Universidad Nacional de la Plata (CEDLAS) and World Bank (http://sedlac.econo.unlp.edu.ar/eng).
Note: These regional aggregates are unweighted averages of the Gini coefficients of 17 countries. If no country data are available for a year in the middle of the series, the missing point is interpolated. Our regional estimates of returns to schooling correspond to the unweighted average for the 17 countries in the SEDLAC. Labor earnings consider both wage employees and self-employed full-time workers ages 15–65. All education categories (college, high school, and primary education) follow country-specific classifications for university degrees, secondary education, and primary education defined in each household survey. The college-educated labor force comprises persons who have completed a university degree or higher. "High school education" includes completed secondary education and incomplete college education. "Primary education" includes no formal education, incomplete primary, complete primary, and incomplete secondary education. The values of the 1st and 100th percentiles of the earnings distribution were trimmed by each gender-education pair. "Skilled" refers to an education level of completed tertiary education or more. "Unskilled" refers to an education level of completed primary education or less.

inequality among observationally equivalent workers).[17] The contribution of observable worker attributes to the log-wage variance drops after 2001, indicating that within-group inequality has increased its contribution to the levels of overall wage inequality in Latin America since the early 2000s (see table 2.1 in the next section).[18]

Second, among observable worker attributes (that is, concentrating on the contribution of the between-group component in the variance of wages), education is the characteristic with the largest average contribution (70 percent) (table 2.1).

Third, inequality reduction is not only well traced by changes in the wage premium of observable worker characteristics, but is also followed closely by changes in residual inequality. Hence, within-group (residual), between-group, and observed inequality follow similar paths in Latin America (figure 2.10). Looking in further detail at Argentina, Brazil, Chile, and Mexico, it can be seen that residual inequality co-moves

Within-Group, Between-Group, and Total Wage Inequality, Selected Latin American Countries

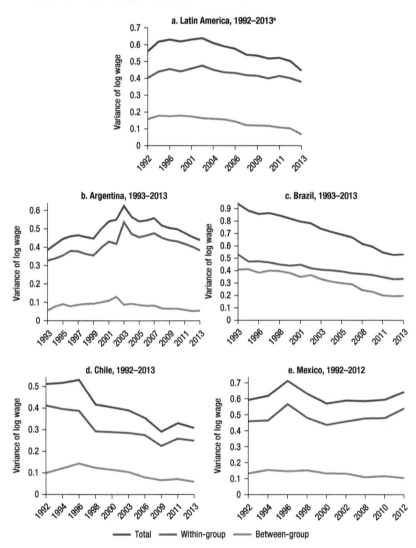

Source: Calculations based on data from the Socio-Economic Database for Latin America and the Caribbean (SEDLAC), Universidad Nacional de la Plata (CEDLAS) and the World Bank (http://sedlac.econo.unlp.edu.ar/eng).
Note: Estimations are based on a sample of female and male workers (self-employed, salaried, and employer) who are full-time workers (at least 35 hours per week) and ages 15–65. Interpolation for missing data is done using a simple arithmetic average. Labor income in 2005 purchasing power parity trimmed the 1st and 99th percentile by gender and education level in each country-year subgroup. Log wage is regressed on a full set of dummies for years of experience (0–39 years) and years of education (0–16 years). Residual (within-group) inequality is measured using the residuals of the regression.
a. Data for Latin America are estimated by a simple average of each individual component in a decomposition done separately for each country. Countries covered are Argentina, Brazil, Chile, Mexico, Panama, Paraguay, and Uruguay.

with observed inequality even more closely than the between-group component. This suggests that returns to unobservable skills correlate positively with those of education and experience—predicting that, in the region, within- and between-group inequality move together (Acemoglu 2002).

Contribution of Pay Differentials among Workers with Similar Skills to Overall Wage Inequality

Changes in pay differentials across workers with similar skills also explain changes in wage inequality. In what follows, we characterize their contribution to the overall change in wage inequality in Latin America and further decompose the within-group component of falling pay differentials. We distinguish the evolution of inequality between labor market groups (for example, industry, firm, education, experience, and occupation) and within each of those groups.

Changes in Within-Group versus Between-Group Components

Table 2.1 and table 2A.2 (in annex 2A) present the results of the decomposition of *overall level* of wage inequality in Latin America into within-group and between-group components. The worker groups considered in the estimations in table 2.1 are similar in terms of their observable demographic characteristics, including education, years of experience, gender, and location. Table 2A.2 replicates the analysis in table 2.1 but considers an additional dimension in which worker groups are similar: the sector of employment. This dimension is added by including a comprehensive set of dummy variables for the employment sector of each worker (that is, industry-fixed effects). Table 2A.2 presents results using a different number of categories for sector of employment (5 large sectors versus 17 detailed sectors). Results indicate that the participation of the within-group variance in the total wage variance is more than 50 percent in all cases, and this result is robust to the size and definition of the industries.[19]

Figure 2.11 presents the results of the decomposition of the *changes over time* in wage inequality into within- and between-group components, following the methodology proposed by Lemieux (2006). The method allows for comparison of the variance component changes over time, assuming that the distribution of a set of observable characteristics did not change. Figure 2.11 shows that during 2001–13, the contribution of changes in the between-group component to changes in the variance of wages was 48 percent.[20] The remaining 52 percent was associated with the contribution of changes in the within-group (observable worker characteristics) component to changes in the variance. Over 1997–2001, the change in the between-group variance accounts for 34 percent of the change in the overall variance of wages, and the rest is explained by differences within skill groups.[21]

In summary, while the change in pay differentials among workers with similar skills and education (between-group inequality) accounts for a large share of the

TABLE 2.1: Decomposition of Overall Wage Inequality (Log-Wage Variance) in Latin America, 1997–2013

Component	Level of contribution to wage inequality				
	1997	2001	2005	2009	2013
Overall	0.80	0.87	0.75	0.69	0.66
Residual (within-group)	0.46	0.52	0.46	0.45	0.43
Between-group	0.34	0.35	0.29	0.24	0.23
Share of overall from between-group (%)	43	40	39	34	35
Education	0.27	0.26	0.24	0.18	0.16
Experience	0.05	0.05	0.04	0.03	0.02
Urban	0.02	0.02	0.01	0.01	0.01
Country	0.03	0.05	0.02	0.02	0.03
Covariance	−0.04	−0.02	−0.03	0.00	0.01
Share of between-group from education (%)	79	73	82	77	70

Source: Calculations based on data from the Socio-Economic Database for Latin America and the Caribbean (SEDLAC), Universidad Nacional de la Plata (CEDLAS) and the World Bank (http://sedlac.econo.unlp.edu.ar/eng/).
Note: Sample of full-time male workers (salaried, self-employed, employers) from the household surveys in each country. Log labor income in main occupation regressed on dummies for the country (14 countries), years of experience (0–39), years of education (0–16), and region (urban dummy). Countries are Argentina, Bolivia, Brazil, Chile, Costa Rica, Dominican Republic, Ecuador, El Salvador, Honduras, Mexico, Panama, Paraguay, Peru, and Uruguay.

change in overall inequality, more than half of overall wage inequality occurs among workers with similar education, labor market experience, gender, location, and working in the same sector (within-group inequality).

Within-Group Wage Inequality

While the previous sections focused on changes in wage dispersion across workers abstracting from the firm (within each industry) and occupation dimension, this section uses detailed administrative matched employer-employee data for Brazil to document the important role of changes within industry-occupation pay differentials. In addition, it documents the key role of interfirm pay differences (within the same sector) among workers employed by various types of employers—and the changes in those pay differences.

Table 2.2 reports the results of a decomposition of wage inequality within sector-occupations into within-group and between-group components, using detailed administrative matched employer-employee data covering all formal employment from Brazil's Annual Social Information Report (RAIS).[22] The analysis finds that most overall wage inequality in Brazil takes place within sector-occupations.

Decomposition of Changes in Wage Inequality into Within-Group and Between-Group Components, Latin America, 1997–2001 vs. 2001–13

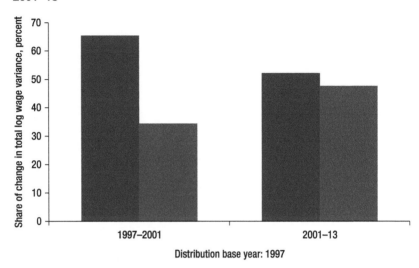

Distribution base year: 1997

■ Change in variance of wages within-group   ■ Change in variance of wages between-group

Source: Authors' calculations based on data from the Socio-Economic Database for Latin America and the Caribbean (SEDLAC), Universidad Nacional de la Plata (CEDLAS) and the World Bank (http://sedlac.econo.unlp.edu.ar/eng/).
Note: Sample of full-time male workers (salaried, self-employed, employers) from the household surveys in each country. Log labor income in main occupation regressed on dummies for country (13 countries), years of experience (0–39), years of education (0–16), sector of employment (17 sectors), and region (urban dummy). Countries are Argentina, Bolivia, Brazil, Costa Rica, Dominican Republic, Ecuador, El Salvador, Honduras, Mexico, Panama, Paraguay, Peru, and Uruguay. This decomposition and the calculations follow Lemieux (2006). The method allows for comparison of the variance component changes over time, assuming that the distribution of a set of observable characteristics did not change. Estimates were done by selecting a base year (1997) and finding counterfactual weights for all the years to be compared against the base year by estimating a logit model of the probability of being in a given year based on observables. Estimations of the decomposition variances and covariances are done using the new weights.

This within-component accounted for 54 percent and 53 percent of overall wage inequality among sector-detailed occupations in 2003 and 2012, respectively. In all specifications, inequality that occurs *within* sector-occupations contributes more to overall wage inequality than inequality that occurs *between* sector-occupations. In most cases, the contribution of inequality within sector-occupation to overall wage inequality increased in the 2000s (relative to the 1990s). Moreover, the result that most of the wage dispersion occurs *within* sector-occupations is robust to the size and definition of sectors (see table 2.2).

However, pay differentials for workers who are employed in the same sector and occupation could occur because of pay differences either between firms

TABLE 2.2: Decomposition of Wage Inequality within Sector-Occupations into Within-Group and Between-Group Components in Brazil, 1994, 2003, and 2012

	Contribution		
	1994	2003	2012
Components	(1)	(2)	(3)
I. Occupation			
Overall inequality	n.a.	0.551	0.384
Between-group	n.a.	0.054	0.038
Within-group	n.a.	0.497	0.346
Percent within in overall	*82*	*90*	*90*
II. Sector (17 sectors)			
Overall inequality	n.a.	0.555	0.390
Between-group	n.a.	0.108	0.064
Within-group	n.a.	0.447	0.326
Percent within in overall	*83*	*81*	*84*
III. Sector-occupation			
Overall inequality	n.a.	0.552	0.385
Between-group	n.a.	0.153	0.096
Within-group	n.a.	0.399	0.289
Percent within in overall	*68*	*72*	*75*
IV. Detailed occupation			
Overall inequality	n.a.	0.556	0.391
Between-group	n.a.	0.217	0.159
Within-group	n.a.	0.339	0.232
Percent within in overall	*61*	*61*	*59*
V. Sector-detailed occupation			
Overall	n.a.	0.556	0.391
Between-group	n.a.	0.255	0.183
Within-group	n.a.	0.302	0.208
Percent within in overall	*56*	*54*	*53*

(continued on next page)

TABLE 2.2: **Decomposition of Wage Inequality within Sector-Occupations into Within-Group and Between-Group Components in Brazil, 1994, 2003, and 2012** *(continued)*

	Contribution		
	1994	2003	2012
Components	(1)	(2)	(3)
VI. Detailed sector-occupation			
Overall	n.a.	0.499	0.344
Between-group	n.a.	0.317	0.226
Within-group	n.a.	0.183	0.118
Percent within in overall	*n.a.*	*63*	*66*

Sources: Estimates for 1994 (column 1) from Helpman, Itskhoki, and Redding (2010); authors' estimates for 2003 and 2012 (columns 2 and 3) from Brazil's Annual Social Information Report (RAIS) data.
Note: n.a. = not available. For 2003 and 2012, we regress log wage by sector-occupation groups per year including firm fixed effects, and normalize to zero each fixed effect for each sector-occupation-year. Then we estimate the variance on log wages for the residual and the firm fixed effects between all sector-occupations (60 groups). "Contribution" shows the participation of the variance between- and within-group in the total wage variance.

TABLE 2.3: **Decomposition of Wage Inequality within Sector-Occupations in Brazil, 1986–95 vs. 2003–12**
(percent)

	Unconditional firm wage component			
	Level		Change	
	1994	2003	1986–95	2003–12
Interfirm wage inequality	55	56	115	70
Intrafirm wage inequality	45	46	−15	30

Source: 1986–95 values are from Helpman, Itskhoki, and Redding (2010); calculations based on 2003–12 data are from Brazil's Annual Social Information Report (RAIS).
Note: For 2003 and 2012, we regress log wage by sector-occupation groups per year including firm fixed effects and normalize to zero each fixed effect for each sector-occupation-year. Then we estimate the variance on log wages for the residual and the firm fixed effects between all sector-occupations (60 groups). "Level" shows the participation on the overall wage inequality of the interfirm (line 4) and intrafirm (line 5) wage inequality. The entry in both lines under the "Change" column for 2003–12 are estimated by normalizing 2003 and estimating the share of each change over the total change.

(with more-productive firms paying more to attract better workers) or within firms (with firms' pay policies allowing for large pay gaps among workers employed in the same occupation but in different departments or areas). Table 2.3 decomposes wage inequality among workers of the same sector-occupation into the contributions of interfirm and intrafirm wage dispersion (following Abowd, Kramarz, and

Margolis 1999; Abowd et al. 2001; Davis and Haltiwanger 1991; Helpman, Itskhoki, and Redding 2010; and Katz and Murphy 1992).

For each sector-occupation-year cell, we decompose wage inequality across workers in that cell into interfirm and intrafirm components by regressing log worker wages on firm fixed effects and observable worker characteristics for each sector-occupation-year separately; therefore, the resulting firm-occupation-year fixed effect varies over time and across occupations. The results show that most initial wage inequality within sector-occupations and its decline in Brazil occurred inter firms of the same sector (relative to intra firms), which points toward frameworks that explicitly consider interfirm heterogeneity as the relevant framework for understanding wage inequality across workers with similar observed characteristics, which will be the focus of chapter 4.

Labor Supply Trends: Rising Numbers of More-Educated Workers

Labor supply developments are a primary suspect to explain changes in the wage premiums for education and experience. In a competitive labor market, if relative labor demand across education groups remains constant, an increase (or decline) in the relative supply of a particular worker type (for example, college-educated workers) translates into a decline (or increase) in the education premium. The same logic would apply to workers with different experience levels.

At least since the 1990s, the region has experienced a rapid increase in the supply of more-educated workers. In all Latin American countries, educational attainment increased and the population aged, raising the skill levels of the workforce. The average years of schooling of individuals ages 18 and older increased from 5.8 in 1990 to 8.26 in 2010 (Barro and Lee 2013). The proportion of the labor force that had at least completed high school rose from 21 to 36 percent during the same period. The unweighted average share of the working-age population that completed secondary education in the 15 countries for which data are available rose from 14 percent in 1990 to 20 percent in 2013. This rise is all the more remarkable if we consider the weighted (by population) average, which rose from 11 to 23 percent in the same period (Barro and Lee 2013).[23]

The expansion of tertiary education was equally important to the expansion of secondary education, and therefore the ratio of workers with tertiary to secondary education increased only slightly in the 2000s (figure 2.12, panel a). Led by Argentina, Chile, Honduras, and Panama, the weighted average share of workers who had completed college more than doubled, rising from 6 percent in 1990 to 14 percent in 2010 (or from 7 to 14 percent if we consider the unweighted average) (Rodríguez-Castelán et al. 2016). The share of people between 15 and 24 years old attending higher education institutions also doubled during that period, from 10 to 20 percent. In Brazil and El Salvador, the ranks of working-age individuals who had completed secondary and tertiary education more than doubled as well. In a third group of countries (Bolivia, Colombia, Costa Rica, the Dominican Republic, Paraguay, and Peru), the improvements in educational attainment were significant but more modest.

These broad patterns of large shifts in workforce education in Latin America hide substantial country-specific differences in the educational attainment of the labor force during the 1990s and 2000s. Some countries (Colombia, Costa Rica, and Paraguay) achieved gains in years of schooling only during the 2000s, after a decade of stagnation or, in the case of Paraguay, after a severe deterioration of educational attainment. Others (Brazil and Ecuador) rapidly expanded secondary education in the 1990s, followed by a more intense expansion of tertiary education in the 2000s. But in contrast to the reductions in inequality, which were mostly concentrated during the 2000s, several Latin American countries (notably El Salvador and Uruguay) expanded education more rapidly in the 1990s than in the 2000s.[24]

Although education has expanded, there is no evidence of a regime shift since the 1990s, which stands in contrast to the case of wage inequality (figure 2.12). Specifically, there is no evidence of a strong acceleration in the supply of highly educated workers in the 2000s. In fact, the expansion of the supply of highly educated labor appears to be a secular, long-term phenomenon. Figure 2.12, panel b, presents the mean years of schooling at age 30 by birth cohort for Argentina, Brazil, Chile, and Mexico (the four Latin American countries where comparable data since the 1980s were available).

FIGURE 2.12: **Education Expansion in Latin America, by Education Level**

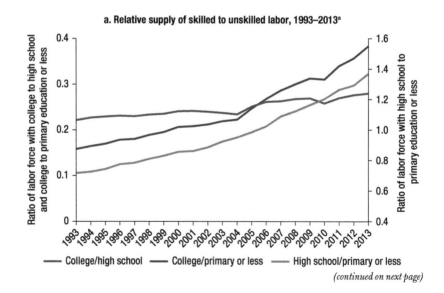

a. Relative supply of skilled to unskilled labor, 1993–2013[a]

— College/high school   — College/primary or less   — High school/primary or less

(continued on next page)

FIGURE 2.12: **Education Expansion in Latin America, by Education Level**
(continued)

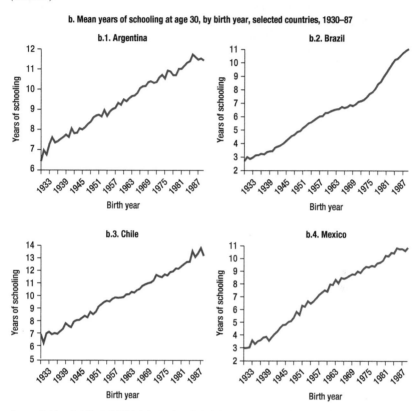

b. Mean years of schooling at age 30, by birth year, selected countries, 1930–87

Sources: Rodríguez-Castelán et al. (2016); Labor Database for Latin America and the Caribbean (LABLAC) (http://lablac.econo
.unlp.edu.ar/eng/index.php); and the Socio-Economic Database for Latin America and the Caribbean (SEDLAC), Universidad
Nacional de la Plata (CEDLAS) and the World Bank (http://sedlac.econo.unlp.edu.ar/eng/).
Note: Relative supply constructed from unweighted averages of the share of different education groups participating in the
labor force (includes employed and unemployed populations). All education categories (college, high school, and primary)
follow country-specific classifications for university degrees, upper-secondary education, and primary education. The college-
educated labor force comprises workers who completed a university degree or higher. "High school education" includes
completed secondary education and incomplete college education. "Primary education" includes no formal education,
incomplete primary, complete primary, and incomplete secondary education. If no country data are available for a year in the
middle of two points in the series, the missing figure was estimated using a simple linear interpolation. To address missing data
at the beginning or the end of the series, the first or the last figure available, respectively, was replaced.
a. "Skilled" refers to completed tertiary education or more. "Unskilled" refers to completed primary education or less.

There is no clear shift in any of the cohorts, suggesting that no regime shift has
occurred since the 1990s, in sharp contrast with trends of decreased inequality and
returns to schooling. The divergent patterns between education expansion and returns
to education suggest that the changes in labor supply alone are unlikely to explain the
observed changes in the wage inequality.

Within-country relative supply reflects the same trends as the supply depicted at the regional level. During the first decade of the 2000s, all of the 17 countries for which data were available experienced sustained growth in the relative supply of both college-educated and high-school-educated workers relative to the primary-school-educated labor force. Moreover, the relative supply of the college-educated to primary-educated labor force grew faster than the high-school-educated to primary-school-educated labor force.

Figure 2.13 presents the average annual growth of the relative labor supply by education level—that is, the growth of the ratio of the secondary- and tertiary-educated labor force to the primary-educated labor force. This figure includes 17 Latin American countries and the Russian Federation, South Africa, Sri Lanka, Turkey, and the United States.

An interesting pattern is that those countries with the largest decline in labor income inequality appear to be those with the highest growth rate of the relative supply in the college to primary labor force (Bolivia, Nicaragua, and Russia). This finding provides some evidence in favor of relative labor supply trends as one of the plausible mechanisms that may be behind the trend reversal in labor income inequality. Also, it is interesting to observe that in the United States—the only country for which we observe a decline in the relative supply of both the college to primary labor force and the high school to primary labor force—labor income inequality has been increasing.

Moreover, although an increase in the stock of human capital is expected to increase pay levels, its effect on wage inequality is more mixed for several reasons:

- As Ferreira, Firpo, and Messina (2017) point out, education expansion can increase inequality because a greater mass of the distribution of workers has educational levels corresponding to the steepest segments of the earnings-education profile—an example of what is known as the "paradox of progress" (Battistón, García-Domench, and Gasparini 2014; Bourguignon, Ferreira, and Lustig 2005).

- Moreover, in a rapidly expanding educational system, younger cohorts are likely to be more educated than older cohorts, putting downward pressure on the education premium of workers with little experience in the labor market. These trends may be exacerbated if the rapidly increasing demand for education exerts such pressure on the educational system that a degradation of educational diplomas results (Campos-Vázquez, López-Calva, and Lustig 2016).

- Older, more educated workers usually have more dispersed earnings. As a consequence, changes in the distribution of education and experience of the labor force may give rise to higher or lower inequality in a mechanical way, simply by changing the employment share of groups that have more or less dispersed earnings (Lemieux 2006).

FIGURE 2.13: **Skill Growth in 17 Latin American Countries Relative to the Russian Federation, South Africa, Sri Lanka, Turkey, and the United States, 2003–10**

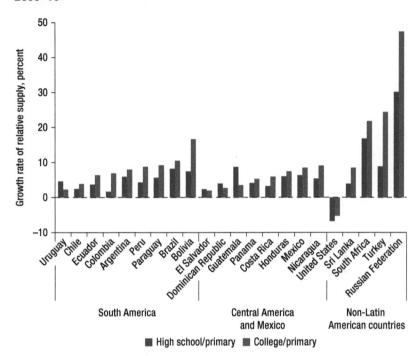

Sources: Rodríguez-Castelán et al. (2016), based on the Socio-Economic Database for Latin America and the Caribbean (SEDLAC), Universidad Nacional de la Plata (CEDLAS) and the World Bank for the 17 Latin American countries; the Longitudinal Monitoring Survey (RLMS) for the Russian Federation; the Post Apartheid Labour Market Series (PALMS) for South Africa; the International Income Distribution Database (I2D2; World Bank) for Sri Lanka; the Household Income and Expenditure Survey (HIES) for Turkey; and the U.S. Census for the United States.
Note: The relative supply is constructed from the share of different education groups participating in the labor force (including the employed and unemployed populations). All education categories (college, high school, and primary) follow country-specific classifications for university degrees, upper-secondary education, and primary education defined in each household survey. The college-educated labor force comprises those who completed a university degree or higher. "High school education" includes completed secondary education and incomplete college education. "Primary education" includes no formal education, incomplete primary, complete primary, and incomplete secondary education. Countries are sorted from smallest to largest growth in college/primary in each group of countries.

Macroeconomic Conditions and Labor Demand Shifts

The 1990s and 2000s were periods of large aggregate demand fluctuations. Aggregate domestic demand fell between the late 1990s and 2002 and increased between 2002 and 2010.[25] After a decade of disappointing growth, the region's economy expanded rapidly in the 2000s in the wake of rising commodity prices and high growth globally, particularly in China and the Group of Seven (G-7) major advanced economies.[26]

During the same period, the terms of trade improved across South America, whereas they fell (or remained flat) in Central America and Mexico. It is precisely the South American countries that recorded improvements in the terms of trade that also recorded the larger expansions in aggregate demand, while those countries with less-favorable terms of trade had only a small expansion of aggregate domestic demand in the same period (De la Torre, Beylis, and Ize 2015).

Similarly, in South America the nominal exchange rate depreciated significantly in the second half of the 1990s and appreciated significantly in the 2000s. Hence, the prices of tradable goods fell relative to nontradable goods in the second half of the 1990s and rose during the 2000s boom period. In contrast, in Central America and Mexico the relative price of tradable goods was much more stable (with the exception of the Mexican peso crisis of 1994–95—also called the "Tequila crisis"). It rose starting in the mid-1990s, but this trend changed in the 2000s when prices of tradable goods relative to nontradable goods either leveled off or rose slightly. The joint effects of nominal exchange rate adjustments and relative prices can be observed in the movements in the real exchange rate (figure 2.14).

FIGURE 2.14: **Real Effective Exchange Rate in Latin America, by Subregion, 1990–2015**

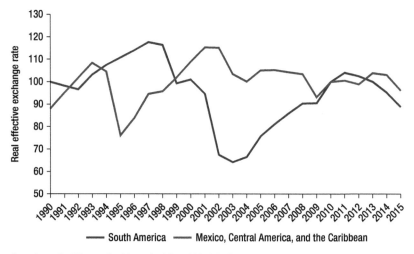

Source: International Monetary Fund, International Financial Statistics Database.
Note: Index base: 2010 = 100. The series shows weighted averages. South America includes Argentina, Bolivia, Brazil, Chile, Colombia, Ecuador, Guyana, Paraguay, Peru, Suriname, and Uruguay. Mexico, Central America, and the Caribbean include Antigua and Barbuda, Barbados, Belize, Costa Rica, Dominica, the Dominican Republic, El Salvador, Grenada, Guatemala, Haiti, Honduras, Jamaica, Mexico, Nicaragua, Panama, St. Kitts and Nevis, St. Lucia, St. Vincent and the Grenadines, and Trinidad and Tobago.

Because the prices of tradable versus nontradable goods presumably affect the demand for labor across sectors, these trends are important to understanding how the demand for goods and services affects labor demand, whose role in wage inequality will be discussed later.

What is the relationship between changes in aggregate demand and inequality? Chapter 4 will discuss this issue in detail, but there is suggestive evidence that demand shifts may help explain differences across countries in the intensity and timing of changes in inequality. Between 1995 and 2014, reductions in domestic demand were accompanied by increases in the wage Gini for the region, while expansions were accompanied by reductions in wage inequality (figure 2.15, panel a). In a specification controlling for supply-side effects and time and country dummies, De la Torre and Ize (2016) find that declines of wage inequality in the 2000s were more pronounced in South America than in Central America and Mexico. They also highlight that these declines had different characteristics in each of these subgroups, with demand making a stronger contribution to changes in inequality in South America (where terms of trade were more favorable) than in Central America and Mexico (where spending [demand] effects from terms-of-trade shocks were smaller). Differences in aggregate demand between South America and Central America and Mexico are shown in figure 2.15, panel b.

FIGURE 2.15: **Wage Inequality and Domestic Demand Trends in Latin America**

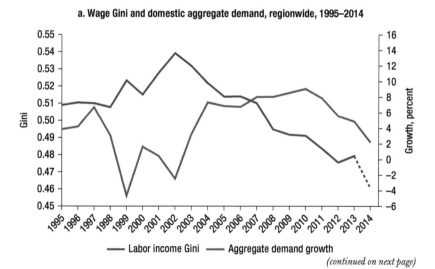

a. Wage Gini and domestic aggregate demand, regionwide, 1995–2014

—— Labor income Gini —— Aggregate demand growth

(continued on next page)

b. Domestic aggregate demand: South America vs.
Central America and Mexico, 1994–2014[a]

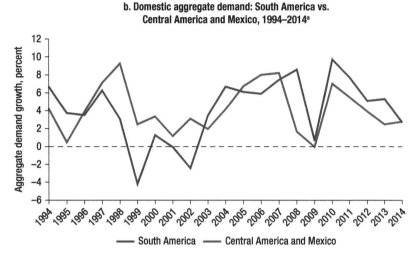

— South America — Central America and Mexico

Sources: Calculations based on data from the Labor Database for Latin America and the Caribbean (LABLAC) (http://lablac .econo.unlp.edu.ar/eng/index.php); the Socio-Economic Database for Latin America and the Caribbean (SEDLAC), Universidad Nacional de la Plata (CEDLAS) and the World Bank (http://sedlac.econo.unlp.edu.ar/eng/); and the World Bank's World Development Indicators Database (http://data.worldbank.org/data-catalog/world-development-indicators).
a. The figure plots the average across countries of the labor income Gini and the growth of domestic demand. Countries included are Argentina, Bolivia, Brazil, Chile, Colombia, Costa Rica, the Dominican Republic, Ecuador, Mexico, Panama, Paraguay, Peru, and Uruguay.

The Labor Market of Skilled and Unskilled Workers and Differences across Tradable and Nontradable Sectors

Skilled workers have a higher employment rate than unskilled workers in most Latin American countries. Similarly, college graduates tend to have a higher employment rate than unskilled individuals (figure 2.16). These stylized facts are common across both South America and Central America and Mexico. However, there are important differences in the evolution of the employment and unemployment rates across groups and geographical areas.

In South America, the employment rate of all groups dipped slightly in the years just before and after 2000 (figure 2.16, panel a). During the same period, the unemployment rates of college-educated and less-educated workers converged, driven by the sharp reduction of unemployment among the least educated (those with less than a secondary degree completed). In Central America and Mexico, on the other hand,

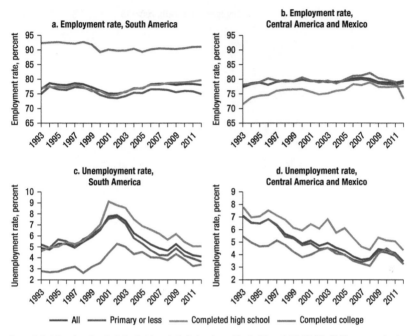

FIGURE 2.16: **Employment and Unemployment Rates, by Education and Regional Subgroup, Latin America, 1993–2012**

Source: Calculations based on the Labor Database for Latin America and the Caribbean (LABLAC) (http://lablac.econo.unlp.edu.ar/eng/index.php).

Note: Based on the male population. The unemployment rate estimate is based on the ratio of unemployed to working-age population (aged 15–65 years). "Primary or less" refers to individuals with incomplete secondary school or less. "Completed high school" includes incomplete tertiary students. "Completed college" includes only those who have completed tertiary education. South American countries include Argentina, Bolivia, Brazil, Chile, Colombia, Ecuador, Peru, and Uruguay. Central American countries listed with Mexico include Costa Rica, the Dominican Republic, El Salvador, Guatemala, Honduras, Mexico, Nicaragua, and Panama. For missing observations we used imputations of simple constant growth rates.

it was the employment rate among those who had completed high school that increased quite rapidly (figure 2.16, panel b). In spite of slow economic growth, the unemployment rate declined during the period for all groups as well.

To discuss the role of domestic aggregate demand, it is important to understand differences in skill intensity across sectors. Changes in aggregate domestic demand and terms of trade will have different implications for the skill premium depending on which sectors they favor and the skill content of those different sectors. During 2002–13, employment in South America grew faster in the nontradable sector than in the tradable sector (figure 2.17, panel a). In South America, the nontradable sector is more skill-intensive on average than the tradable sector, and this difference became slightly more pronounced throughout the 2000s (figure 2.17, panel b). The gap

FIGURE 2.17: Employment and Skill-Use Growth, by Sector Type, in South America

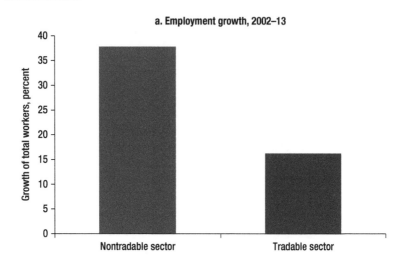

a. Employment growth, 2002–13

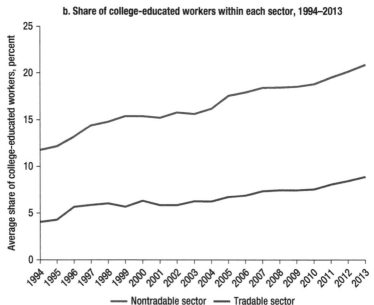

b. Share of college-educated workers within each sector, 1994–2013

Source: Calculations based on Socio-Economic Database for Latin America and the Caribbean (SEDLAC), Universidad Nacional de la Plata (CEDLAS) and the World Bank (http://sedlac.econo.unlp.edu.ar/eng/).
Note: The tradable sector includes agriculture and mining (primary sector), manufacturing, restaurants and hotels, and financial services; the nontradable sector includes all other services. The panel b figure plots the average across countries of the share of workers within each sector who have completed tertiary (college) education in the following countries: Argentina, Brazil, Chile, Colombia, Ecuador, Mexico, Peru, and Uruguay.

between the tradable and nontradable sectors in the share of workers with tertiary education was more than 10 percentage points by 2010. These results are robust regardless of whether service sectors such as restaurants and hotels and financial services are considered to be tradable sectors (as in figure 2.17) or nontradable sectors (as in annex 2C, figure 2C.1).

In fact, the largest segment of the nontradable sector includes mostly high-paying services such as education, electricity, health, real estate, and transportation. However, the sector also includes large shares of employment in construction and wholesale and retail industries, all of which are intensive in unskilled work. Thus, the importance of aggregate demand and terms-of-trade shocks for the skill premium will largely depend on which subindustries within the tradable and nontradable sectors were more affected, as discussed in chapter 4.

Informality and Wage Inequality

The level of formal or informal employment is not a policy variable but rather an outcome associated not only with labor market policies but also with fiscal and social policies, as well as with the functioning of other markets (such as the market for credit). However, formalization does play a mediating role in the relationship between labor market institutions (for example, the minimum wage and employment protection policies) and inequality levels, and it can be influenced by policies such as stricter enforcement of labor regulations and social security laws. In countries with high informality, an increase in the minimum wage may have smaller effects on wage inequality than it would in countries with relatively low informality.[27] At the same time, increased enforcement of regulations may result in higher formality to the extent that wages adjust. On the other hand, if the minimum wage is highly binding, increases in labor law enforcement might backfire, resulting in higher levels of informality.

Informality may dampen or enhance inequality. To the extent that identical workers are paid different wages if they work in formal versus informal sectors, the effects of informality on inequality would be positive. This effect is probably magnified because informal workers tend to be low-skilled, and hence low-earning workers. However, informality can also reduce inequality through the introduction of allocative distortions that compress the skill premium. Levy and López-Calva (2016) show that the persistence of distortions that misallocate resources toward less-productive firms—a distortion reflected in the size-distribution of firms—limits the dispersion of wages across educational groups because smaller, informal firms are substantially less intensive in educated workers than are more-productive firms. This effect becomes even more important when the supply of higher-educated workers is increasing.

More broadly, the contribution of changes in informality to inequality depends on three aspects: (1) the evolution of the wage premium (or penalty) of formal employment relative to informal employment; (2) the changing distribution of this wage premium (or penalty) across skill groups; and (3) changes in formality across skill groups. Ferreira, Firpo, and Messina (2017) find that the reduction of the formal-informal wage gap from 1995 to 2012 in Brazil contributed to a reduction of 1.7 Gini points of the total inequality reduction of 9 Gini points. Amarante, Arim, and Yapor (2016) also report a significant impact in Uruguay. Are these findings generalizable across the region? This section examines the three forces just outlined and assesses the contributions of changes in formal employment to changes in inequality during the past decade.

Changes in the Wage Premium for Formal versus Informal Employment

During the Mexican peso crisis of 1994–95 (the "Tequila crisis") and the Brazilian crisis of 1999, informality increased in those countries while unemployment rose. In contrast, during the boom years of 2002–13, informality decreased significantly (figure 2.18). To a greater or lesser extent, the rate of informality declined during the 2000s in the vast majority of the countries in the region, regardless of how informality is measured.

It is not immediately obvious that increased formalization leads to a reduction in inequality. A first aspect that mediates this relationship is whether there is a wage penalty for informal employment (or, in other words, a premium for formal employment). If equivalent workers (that is, with the same human capital) are paid differently in the formal and informal sectors, reductions in informality will mechanically reduce wage inequality by eliminating within-group differences in wages. We label this the "within-group effect."

Figure 2.19 shows that the wage distribution for informal workers is located to the left relative to the wage distribution for formal workers. Note that this shift does not necessarily reflect a wage penalty for informal employment, because more-skilled workers are likely to concentrate in the formal sector. To assess whether a wage penalty exists, we need to compare workers in the two sectors of the same skill level, a feature that will be examined below.

Changes in the Formal Wage Premium for Skilled versus Unskilled Workers

Informality can also affect inequality across skill groups. This may be the case if the wage premium of formal workers (or wage penalty of informal workers) is different across skill groups. For example, if the wage penalty of informal employment is higher among unskilled workers than among skilled workers, reductions in informality will reduce the wage differences across these groups, thus reducing inequality. The opposite would be true if the wage penalty of high-earning workers were larger than the wage penalty of low-earning workers.

Informal Employment Trends, Selected Latin American Countries, 1995, 2002, and 2013

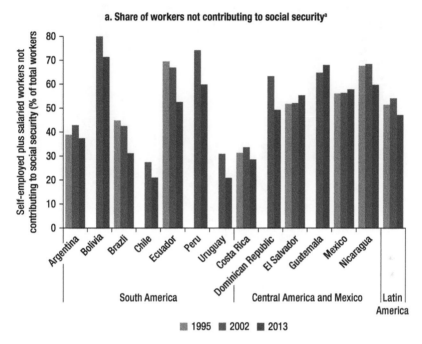

a. Share of workers not contributing to social security[a]

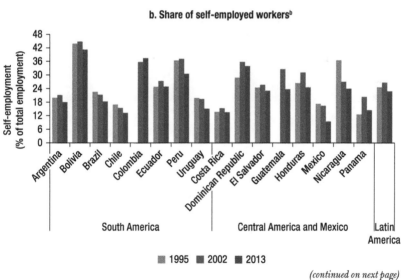

b. Share of self-employed workers[b]

(continued on next page)

Informal Employment Trends, Selected Latin American Countries, 1995, 2002, and 2013 *(continued)*

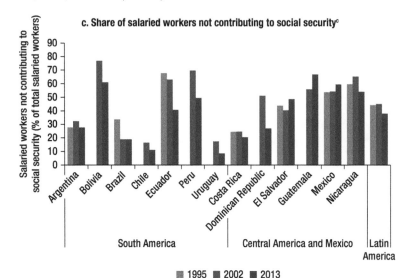

c. Share of salaried workers not contributing to social security[c]

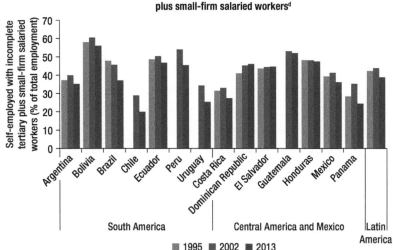

d. Share of self-employed workers with incomplete tertiary plus small-firm salaried workers[d]

Source: Authors' calculations based on data from the Socio-Economic Database for Latin America and the Caribbean (SEDLAC), Universidad Nacional de la Plata (CEDLAS) and the World Bank (http://sedlac.econo.unlp.edu.ar/eng/). For more details on changes in informality see table 2E.1 in annex 2E.

Note: The definition of informality in this figure corresponds to SEDLAC's definition of informality using a "productivity" perspective.

a. "Workers not contributing to social security" includes all self-employed plus salaried workers not contributing to social security. Estimation includes only full-time salaried and self-employed workers who are ages 15–65.

b. Estimation considers only full-time, self-employed workers who are ages 15–65.

c. Estimation considers full-time salaried workers who are ages 15–65.

d. Estimation considers self-employed workers and full-time, salaried workers of small firms.

To assess the potential role of informality on within- and between-group inequalities, we divide workers into skill groups defined by age and education levels. We consider 408 age-education groups (consisting of 51 age groups and 8 education groups for each country) and plot 2002 data contrasting the average wage of each skill cell in the formal and informal sectors. Figure 2.20 shows differences in wages between the formal and informal sectors across groups for Argentina, Bolivia, Brazil, Chile, Mexico, Peru, and Uruguay. If wages for each group were the same for the two sectors, we would observe the points aligned with a 45-degree line.[28] The figure clearly indicates the existence of a formalization premium in the vast majority of cells—that is, the data points lie above the 45-degree line. Thus, reductions in informality that occur across the board would push inequality downward, just by reducing the formal-informal wage gap. In other words, formalization is likely to have reduced within-group inequality.

FIGURE 2.19: **Distribution of Wages for Formal and Informal Male Workers, Selected Latin American Countries, 2002**

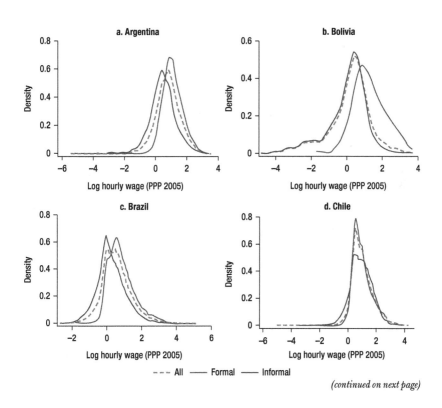

(continued on next page)

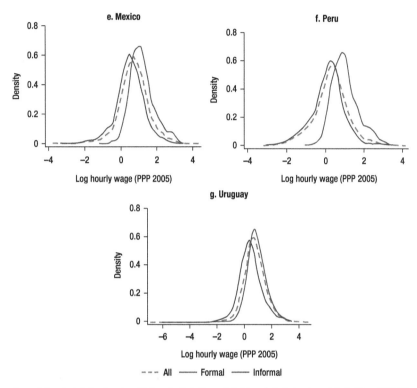

Source: Authors' calculations based on data from the Socio-Economic Database for Latin America and the Caribbean (SEDLAC), Universidad Nacional de la Plata (CEDLAS) and the World Bank (http://sedlac.econo.unlp.edu.ar/eng/).
Note: Estimation for full-time males who are employed formally or informally (including self-employed) (ages 15–65). The 1st and 99th percentiles of each year's wage distribution by education level and year group are excluded. All hourly wages are reported in purchasing power parity (PPP) 2005 terms. "Formal" workers are all employees who contribute to social security. "Informal" workers include the self-employed and employees who do not contribute to social security.

Figure 2.20 also shows that, perhaps with the exception of Brazil and Chile, the informality penalty is larger among low-earning workers. Thus, informality is also widening wage differentials across skill groups, which implies that reductions in informality may reduce inequality via lower between-group inequality.[29]

Changes in Formality across Skill Groups: Who Is Becoming Formal Matters

The third force that mediates the relationship between changes in informality and inequality relates to *who* is becoming formal. Considering that there is a formality premium, if the workers becoming formal are in the upper part of the wage distribution, formalization could exacerbate inequality. Conversely, if they are in the bottom of the wage distribution, formalization would lead to a more equal wage distribution.

The panels in figure 2.21 show the changes in formalization by percentile in Argentina, Brazil, and Bolivia (high-formality, medium-to-high-formality, and low-formality countries, respectively).[30] In all three countries, the changes from the mid-1990s to the early 2000s coincided with increased inequality, with workers below the median wage becoming more informal, and workers above the median wage increasing their formalization. In contrast, from 2002 onward, the formalization process appeared to be strongly equalizing in all three countries, particularly Brazil.

The importance of informality to wage inequality in 2002 and 2012 is assessed in table 2.4, which closely follows the analysis of Card, Lemieux, and Riddell (2003) on the effect of unions on wage inequality. The first row shows that informality declined in all countries. The informality rate declined by more than 10 percentage points in Brazil, Peru, and Uruguay; by 7–8 percentage points in Argentina, Bolivia, and Chile;

FIGURE 2.20: **Relative Wages of Formal Male Workers and Informal Male Workers, Selected Latin American Countries, 2002**

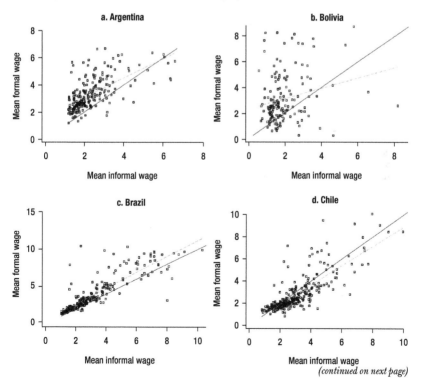

(continued on next page)

FIGURE 2.20: **Relative Wages of Formal Male Workers and Informal Male Workers, Selected Latin American Countries, 2002** *(continued)*

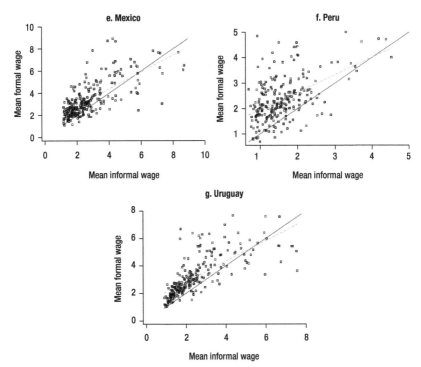

Source: Authors' calculations based on data from the Socio-Economic Database for Latin America and the Caribbean (SEDLAC), Universidad Nacional de la Plata (CEDLAS) and the World Bank (http://sedlac.econo.unlp.edu.ar/eng/).
Note: Estimation for full-time male workers, employed or self-employed, who are ages 15–65. The 408 groups consist of 51 age groups and 8 education groups for each country. The 1st and 99th percentiles of each year's wage distribution per education level and year group are excluded. All hourly wages are reported in purchasing power parity (PPP) 2005 terms. "Formal" workers are all employees who contribute to social security. "Informal" workers include the self-employed as well as employees who do not contribute to social security.

and by 2 percentage points in Mexico. Thus, changes in formality were large and potentially affected wage inequality significantly.

The next rows show that there is a positive wage premium among formal workers on average in all countries and in both years. Perhaps more interestingly, the premium has declined in all countries. The reductions are significant if we look just at the unadjusted mean differences, ranging from 0.59 log points in Bolivia to 0.002 points in Chile, where the penalty was much lower to start with. Naturally, a large part of the wage premium of formal employment is due to skills, because more-educated and more-experienced workers are more likely to work in this sector. This is visible when we calculate the adjusted wage gap (the gap that remains after a full set of dummies for

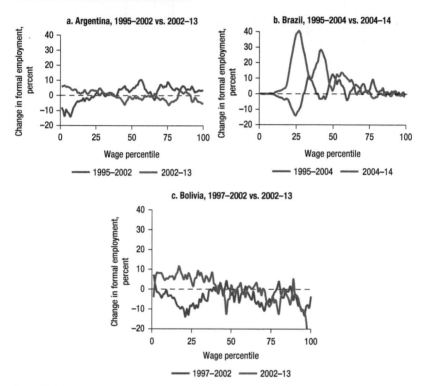

FIGURE 2.21: **Changes in Formal Employment, by Wage Percentile, Selected Latin American Countries**

a. Argentina, 1995–2002 vs. 2002–13

b. Brazil, 1995–2004 vs. 2004–14

c. Bolivia, 1997–2002 vs. 2002–13

Source: Calculations based on data from the Socio-Economic Database for Latin America and the Caribbean (SEDLAC), Universidad Nacional de la Plata (CEDLAS) and the World Bank (http://sedlac.econo.unlp.edu.ar/eng/).
Note: The figures reflect main occupation income data for full-time employers, employees, and self-employed workers ages 15–65. Income was trimmed for the 99th percentile and for those reporting no income. "Informal" workers are defined as those who are self-employed without tertiary education plus workers in small firms.

skill groups are included in the regression). But the main message remains that differences in the adjusted wage gap declined over time in all countries with the exception of Chile and Mexico, where differences increased slightly.

The standard deviation of wages shows that inequality of pay is higher in the informal sector across the board, indicating another channel through which informality increases inequality. The variance gap between formal and informal wages evolved differently across countries but remained fairly stable with the exceptions of Chile and Uruguay, where the gap increased during the past decade, and Argentina, where it declined substantially.

Panel b of table 2.4 presents two simulations of the effects of formalization on inequality in 2002 and 2012. The two-sector model ignores differences in the

TABLE 2.4: Effects of Formality on Wage Structure, Selected Latin American Countries, 2002 and 2012

Variable	Argentina			Bolivia			Brazil		
	2002	2012	Difference	2002	2012	Difference	2002	2012	Difference
a. Formalization and wage gap trends									
Fraction of informal workers	0.490	0.411	**−0.079**	0.868	0.793	**−0.075**	0.499	0.383	**−0.117**
Mean log wages									
Informal workers	5.846	6.289	**0.444**	5.376	6.054	**0.678**	5.539	6.017	**0.479**
Formal workers	6.405	6.819	**0.415**	6.611	6.693	**0.083**	6.069	6.347	**0.278**
Wage gap (unadjusted)	−0.559	−0.530	**0.029**	−1.235	−0.639	**0.595**	−0.530	−0.330	**0.200**
Wage gap (adjusted)	−0.460	−0.450	**0.010**	−0.646	−0.392	**0.254**	−0.279	−0.153	**0.126**
Standard deviation of log wages									
Informal workers	0.802	0.630	**−0.172**	1.154	0.863	**−0.291**	0.820	0.720	**−0.101**
Formal workers	0.577	0.466	**−0.110**	0.830	0.520	**−0.310**	0.723	0.617	**−0.106**
Standard deviation gap	0.225	0.163	**−0.062**	0.324	0.343	**0.019**	0.097	0.102	**0.005**

(continued on next page)

TABLE 2.4: **Effects of Formality on Wage Structure, Selected Latin American Countries, 2002 and 2012** *(continued)*

Variable	Argentina			Bolivia			Brazil		
	2002	2012	Difference	2002	2012	Difference	2002	2012	Difference
b. Variance decomposition in within-sector and between-sector									
Overall variance	0.563	0.359	**−0.203**	1.421	0.713	**−0.708**	0.668	0.459	**−0.209**
Two-sector model									
Within-sector effect	0.152	0.074	**−0.078**	0.558	0.376	**−0.182**	0.075	0.052	**−0.023**
Between-sector effect	0.078	0.068	**−0.010**	0.175	0.067	**−0.108**	0.070	0.026	**−0.045**
Total effect	0.230	0.141	**−0.088**	0.733	0.443	**−0.290**	0.145	0.078	**−0.067**
Model with skill groups									
Within-sector effect	0.160	0.094	**−0.066**	0.307	0.357	**0.050**	0.091	0.063	**−0.029**
Between-sector effect	0.066	0.047	**−0.020**	0.077	0.046	**−0.031**	0.018	0.014	**−0.003**
Dispersion across groups	0.138	0.042	**−0.096**	0.179	0.140	**−0.039**	0.102	0.053	**−0.049**
Total effect	0.364	0.183	**−0.182**	0.564	0.543	**−0.021**	0.212	0.131	**−0.081**
Sample size	*19,413*	*35,670*		*3,305*	*11,330*		*145,267*	*71,625*	
Number of skill groups	*35*	*35*		*35*	*35*		*35*	*35*	

(continued on next page)

TABLE 2.4: **Effects of Formality on Wage Structure, Selected Latin American Countries, 2002 and 2012** *(continued)*

Variable	Chile			Mexico			Peru			Uruguay		
	2002	2012	Difference	2002	2012	Difference	2002	2012	Difference	2002	2012	Difference
a. Formalization and wage gap trends												
Fraction of informal workers	0.306	0.236	**−0.070**	0.658	0.637	**−0.021**	0.805	0.637	**−0.168**	0.360	0.243	**−0.117**
Mean log wages												
Informal workers	6.290	6.655	**0.364**	5.823	5.934	**0.111**	5.431	5.812	**0.381**	5.766	6.186	**0.420**
Formal workers	6.324	6.686	**0.363**	6.498	6.506	**0.008**	6.359	6.414	**0.056**	6.200	6.518	**0.318**
Wage gap (unadjusted)	−0.033	−0.032	**0.002**	−0.675	−0.572	**0.103**	−0.927	−0.602	**0.325**	−0.434	−0.332	**0.102**
Wage gap (adjusted)	0.117	0.101	**−0.016**	−0.357	−0.381	**−0.024**	−0.496	−0.374	**0.122**	−0.345	−0.285	**0.060**
Standard deviation of log wages												
Informal workers	0.789	0.816	**0.027**	0.806	0.689	**−0.117**	0.891	0.759	**−0.132**	0.815	0.738	**−0.076**
Formal workers	0.683	0.676	**−0.007**	0.638	0.616	**−0.022**	0.651	0.537	**−0.114**	0.667	0.545	**−0.122**
Standard deviation gap	0.106	0.140	**0.034**	0.168	0.073	**−0.095**	0.240	0.222	**−0.018**	0.147	0.193	**0.046**

(continued on next page)

TABLE 2.4: **Effects of Formality on Wage Structure, Selected Latin American Countries, 2002 and 2012** *(continued)*

Variable	Chile			Mexico			Peru			Uruguay		
	2002	2012	Difference	2002	2012	Difference	2002	2012	Difference	2002	2012	Difference
b. Variance decomposition in within-sector and between-sector												
Overall variance	0.514	0.506	**−0.008**	0.669	0.516	**−0.153**	0.856	0.555	**−0.301**	0.567	0.377	**−0.190**
Two-sector model												
Within-sector effect	0.048	0.049	**0.002**	0.160	0.061	**−0.099**	0.298	0.183	**−0.115**	0.079	0.060	**−0.018**
Between-sector effect	0.000	0.000	**0.000**	0.102	0.076	**−0.027**	0.135	0.084	**−0.051**	0.043	0.020	**−0.023**
Total effect	0.048	0.050	**0.002**	0.262	0.137	**−0.126**	0.433	0.267	**−0.166**	0.122	0.080	**−0.042**
Model with skill groups												
Within-sector effect	0.087	0.095	**0.007**	0.196	0.167	**−0.029**	0.302	0.249	**−0.053**	0.074	0.070	**−0.005**
Between-sector effect	0.006	0.010	**0.004**	0.029	0.034	**0.006**	0.037	0.044	**0.007**	0.027	0.030	**0.004**
Dispersion across groups	0.024	0.018	**−0.007**	0.192	0.093	**−0.099**	0.266	0.128	**−0.139**	0.092	0.056	**−0.036**
Total effect	0.118	0.122	**0.004**	0.417	0.295	**−0.123**	0.606	0.421	**−0.185**	0.193	0.156	**−0.037**
Sample size	*43,096*	*39,656*		*13,068*	*18,798*		*20,008*	*35,606*		*17,001*	*44,674*	
Number of skill groups	*35*	*35*		*35*	*35*		*35*	*35*		*35*	*35*	

Source: Socio-Economic Database for Latin America and the Caribbean (SEDLAC), Universidad Nacional de la Plata (CEDLAS) and the World Bank (http://sedlac.econo.unlp.edu.ar/eng/).

Note: Estimation for full-time male workers, employed or self-employed, who are ages 15–65. The 1st and 99th percentiles of each year's wage distribution per education level and year group are excluded. All hourly wages are reported in purchasing power parity (PPP) 2005 terms. "Formal" workers are all employees who contribute to social security. "Informal" workers include the self-employed as well as employees who do not contribute to social security. The 35 skill groups consist of 7 education levels and 5 age groups (dividing age in groups of 10).

skill composition across the formal and informal sectors. The counterfactual exercises measure the contribution of formality to inequality at each point in time, and hence allow for an assessment of how this contribution has changed over time. The total effect thus is the difference between the observed variance of wages and the one that would prevail if all workers were formal. Further, this overall contribution is decomposed into two effects: a within-sector effect (which amounts to differential evolutions across sectors in the variance of wages) and a between-sector effect (which captures changes in the wage gap between formal and informal workers over time).

The analysis of changes in the contribution of informality to the reduction of inequality of this simple two-sector model suggests a nontrivial role in Bolivia, Brazil, Peru, and Uruguay. Take Brazil, for example. According to the two-sector model, changes in informality contributed to a reduction of inequality of −0.067 points. If we consider that the variance of wages declined by −0.21 points, this amounts to 32 percent of the total reduction. In Peru, this percentage jumps to 50 percent. Both the within- and between-sector effects contributed to the decline in inequality according to this simple model.

The importance of the between-sector effect is obviously overstated in the two-sector model, as it does not take into account that formal workers are more educated and experienced. The "model with skill groups" in panel b of table 2.4 presents simulations accounting for this factor and shows that, in all cases, the between-sector effect is smaller than in the two-sector model, and in general the overall contribution of changes in informality to reducing inequality is smaller. However, there is an additional effect in this decomposition, labeled "dispersion across groups," which is a combination of two forces: (1) the additional variance in wages that results from the fact that the informal wage penalty may differ across workers, and (2) the effect stemming from differences in the wage penalty of formalization across groups.

In sum, the reductions in informality and changes in the wage and variance gaps across formal/informal workers remain important factors in explaining changes in wage inequality in Argentina, Brazil, Mexico, Peru, and Uruguay. These effects are also quantitatively important. The contributions to inequality reduction of changes in informality range from some 3 percent in Bolivia to almost 90 percent in Argentina. This obviously begs the question of what forces were behind the formalization wave of the 2000s. The demand changes discussed in chapter 4 are likely to be important factors.

Cross-Country Heterogeneity in Main Trends, and Correlations between Key Inequality-Related Indicators

In spite of the common trends, the reductions in *income inequality* are heterogeneous in their magnitude. During the period from 2003 to 2013, the income inequality reductions ranged from 1.1 annual Gini points in Argentina (followed by Bolivia, Peru, and Ecuador) to 0.2 in Mexico. Similarly, the changes in *wage inequality* ranged from a reduction of 0.9 annual Gini points in Bolivia and Ecuador to an increase of 0.3 annual Gini points in Costa Rica. In Mexico and El Salvador, wage inequality fell but at a low rate of 0.2 annual Gini points (table 2D.1 in annex 2D).

In these two indicators, the biggest difference was the larger magnitude of the income and wage inequality reductions during the 2000s in the South American countries than in Central America and Mexico. Despite this general trend, the Central American countries of Nicaragua and Panama registered impressive reductions in both income and wage inequality—larger than those of Colombia in South America—but they remain the exceptions in Central America (table 2D.1).

The only country where wage inequality increased, Costa Rica, was also the only country that recorded an increase in returns to schooling in the 2000s (measured as the percentage point change in the wage gap between completed tertiary education and primary or less). This was in line with the increase, in all countries, of the supply of skilled versus unskilled labor (completed tertiary education versus primary education) in the 2003–13 period. In addition, in all countries during the 2000s, the fall in the returns to completed tertiary versus primary education was larger than the returns to tertiary versus completed high school—as was the change in the supply of tertiary-to primary-educated workers (relative to tertiary-educated to high school–educated workers).

In the 1990s, the overall regional pattern was more heterogeneous. The wage gap between workers with completed tertiary education and those with primary education or less fell in several countries (including Argentina, Brazil, Chile, El Salvador, Mexico, and Nicaragua), whereas the wage gap between those with completed tertiary and those with a high school education fell only in Argentina, Nicaragua, and Panama.

A less-close link in the 1990s was between countries with the largest drop in returns to education and those with the largest expansion in their relative skilled-labor supply. For example, Brazil—the country that had the largest decline in returns to education in South America—recorded only a small increase (0.6 annual percentage points) in the ratio of skilled workers (with tertiary education) to unskilled workers (with primary education) compared with that in Argentina or Chile (where the skilled-to-unskilled ratio increased by 3.2 and 3.5 annual percentage points, respectively). Similarly, in the Dominican Republic—where the increase in returns to education was second only to Bolivia—the change in the relative supply of skilled labor was very small (table 2D.1).

The expansion of aggregate domestic demand (and the linked shift in terms of trade) around 2003 was observed in all countries in South America, while in Central America and Mexico aggregate domestic demand remained at similar levels in 1995–2003 and 2003–13. Similarly, all of the South American countries saw an appreciation of the real exchange rate in the 2000s. The only exception was Ecuador, where the nominal exchange rate appreciated but not the real exchange rate, linked with the dollarization of the economy (a characteristic also shared by El Salvador and Panama). In contrast, in the 1990s, most South American countries saw a depreciation of their real exchange rate, with the exceptions of Bolivia and Peru. In Central America and Mexico, the real exchange rate changes were much more similar in the 1990s and 2000s (table 2D.1).

In terms of correlations of these aggregates across Latin American countries, our results suggest a high, statistically significant correlation between changes in the labor Gini and changes in the total income Gini, in line with the parallel evolution of these two indicators. We also observe that the correlation between changes in earnings inequality and changes in the skill premium is 0.6 and highly significant, in line with the importance of the education expansion to the reduction in wage inequality (table 2D.2).

On the demand side, changes in aggregate domestic demand are negatively associated with the changes in returns to skill, and this correlation is statistically significant. Hence, the expansions of education and aggregate domestic demand have confounding effects on the skill premium, as both decrease the skill premium. The next chapters will present evidence detailing the main mechanisms through which each of these forces operate and identifying the direction of their effects on wage inequality in Latin America.

Conclusions

This chapter documented the key empirical patterns of wage inequality in Latin America. In so doing, it identified and elaborated upon the seven stylized facts summarized as follows:

Fact 1: Labor earnings (and household income) inequality in Latin America, after a decade of stagnation or moderate increase, decreased sharply in the first decade of the 2000s in 16 out of 17 countries.

In Latin America there is a close relationship between individual earnings inequality and household income inequality, which move in synchrony over time. This is not surprising, since labor income accounts on average for 73 percent of the total household income captured in Latin American household surveys in 2012. Earnings inequality in Latin America, after a decade of stagnation or moderate increase (from an average Gini index of 45 in 1993 to 47 in 2002), decreased sharply in the 2000s (from a Gini index of 47 in 2002 to 41 in 2013). This decline was observed in all countries in the region except Costa Rica.

Earnings inequality fell more sharply in South America than in Central America and Mexico during the 2000s. In particular, it decreased from an average Gini index of 57 in 2002 to 51 in 2013 in South America, while it decreased from an average Gini index of 52 in 2002 to 49 in 2013 in Central America and Mexico. Furthermore, the overall declining trend in Latin America was observed in only a few countries outside the region (for example, Italy, the Kyrgyz Republic, New Zealand, Poland, and the United Kingdom), and in all of those countries, the movements were of much smaller magnitude, with changes in the average Gini index close to zero.

Fact 2: Earnings were relatively stable in the 1990s (when inequality was stagnant to increasing) and grew faster for unskilled workers than for skilled workers in the 2000s (when inequality decreased). Trends in the first decade of the 2000s were stronger in South America than in Central America and Mexico.

Worker earnings in the top 10 percent and the bottom 10 percent of the earnings distribution moved along similar paths during the 1990s, but the gap between them started to narrow in the early 2000s. The associated decline in earnings inequality was supported by a substantial expansion in real hourly earnings at the bottom of the wage distribution, which was larger than the expansion of wages at the top and in the middle of the distribution. Specifically, since 2002 in Latin America, real earnings at the lower tail rose by more than 50 percent while those in the middle rose by 32 percent and those at the upper tail rose by 15 percent (Rodríguez-Castelán et al. 2016). Hence, the gap narrowed between the upper and lower tails of the real earnings distribution during the 2000s because of a significant expansion of earnings at the bottom. These trends contrasted sharply with those observed in the United States and other high-income economies, characterized by dynamic growth at the upper tail of real wages and moderate growth at the lower tail (Alvaredo et al. 2013; Autor, Katz, and Kearny 2008).

There also had been a moderate increase in the education premium in the 1990s, which contrasted with the declining education premium in the 2000s in 16 of 17 Latin American countries. This trend followed a track similar to that of wage inequality. The wage premium for college education versus high school remained stable in both decades. It was the wage of workers with primary education or less that increased sharply during the 2000s, catching up with high school and college graduates. As of 2014, the earnings ratio of college-educated workers to those with primary education or less was around 2.25, and the earnings ratio of college-educated to high-school-educated workers was 1.5, after controlling for various individual characteristics.[31]

Although this stylized fact was seen throughout the region, this overall picture hides important heterogeneity across subgroups of countries. In South America, earnings in both the top and bottom deciles increased. In contrast, in Central America and Mexico, earnings in the upper decile were stagnant to declining; wages at the bottom increased but at a significantly lower rate than in the region as a whole. Similarly, in most of South America, wages of both skilled and unskilled workers grew in the 2000s (with unskilled wages growing faster). In Central America and Mexico, however, skilled workers' wages declined while those of unskilled workers increased (albeit less than unskilled wages in South America). During the previous decade of the 1990s, both skilled and unskilled wages had declined in South America and were relatively stagnant in Central America and Mexico. It was in the mid-1990s that relative wage trends started markedly diverging between the northern and southern parts of the region.

Fact 3: The skilled labor supply has risen gradually since the late 1980s (when wage inequality was still increasing) and continued increasing through the 2000s.

The share of educated workers in the total labor force has grown steadily since the late 1980s in Latin America. On average, the share of workers with less than primary education declined from 54 to 39 percent between 1990 and 2010 (Rodríguez-Castelán et al. 2016). In contrast, the share of college graduates doubled during the same period (Ferreyra et al. 2016). The increase in the relative supply of college-educated workers was a trend across the region, observed with similar intensity in most Latin American countries.

Fact 4: In both the 1990s and the first decade of the 2000s, individual worker characteristics (such as gender, education, experience, and whether the family lives in an urban or rural area) explain less than 50 percent of the total wage differential across workers. Similarly, changes in these characteristics explain less than half of the changes in the total wage differential across workers. Most of the decline in total wage inequality is explained by falling within-group wage inequality.

Among the individual worker characteristics used in standard Mincerian regressions (gender, education, experience) plus rural-versus-urban-area indicators, education is the single observable characteristic with the largest contribution to wage inequality. In a decomposition of overall wage inequality (log-wage variance) in Latin America, the contribution of workers' education accounts for about 30 percent of the level of inequality. However, all these characteristics explain no more than 50 percent of the observed inequality levels. Similar numbers are obtained when changes in inequality are analyzed. In most countries changes in workers' observable characteristics and the returns to these characteristics explain less than 50 percent of the observed changes in inequality. Falling within-group wage inequality accounted for most of the decline in total wage inequality.

Fact 5: The region's labor market improved during the first decade of the 2000s, with unemployment falling and employment increasing. However, the employment rates of skilled and unskilled workers rose at a similar pace.

The period was one of rapid economic growth. Unemployment declined rapidly and the employment rate increased in most countries. These trends are more marked in South America than in Central America and Mexico. Interestingly, the employment rates of skilled and unskilled workers increased at similar rates. This happened despite the secular upward trend in the skilled labor supply and a higher wage increase for unskilled workers than for skilled workers. Moreover, relative employment of skilled workers increased in both tradable and nontradable sectors.

Fact 6: Terms-of-trade movements differed across countries. During the first decade of the 2000s, these movements favored South America but were relatively stable in Central America and Mexico.

In South America, the exchange rate depreciated significantly in the second half of the 1990s and appreciated significantly in the 2000s. Hence, the prices of tradable goods rose relative to nontradable goods in the second half of the 1990s and fell during the 2000s boom period. In contrast, in Central America and Mexico, the relative price of tradable goods was much more stable (except during the Tequila crisis). It fell after the mid-1990s, but this trend changed in the 2000s, when prices of tradable goods relative to nontradable goods either leveled off or fell slightly.

Fact 7: In Argentina, Brazil, Mexico, and Peru, there was a sizable reduction of informal employment in the 2000s that contributed to reducing wage inequality, since most of those who became formal were low-wage workers.

With some exceptions, the growth of the first decade of the 2000s—and, in some countries, policy change—translated into a sizable reduction of informal employment. Results also indicate that, in the 1990s, only high-wage workers exited from informality, while in the 2000s, most of those who became formal were low-wage workers. Reductions in informality, especially when concentrated among the unskilled, help reduce inequality though two channels: (1) reduction of *within-group* inequality, as workers with equivalent skills are paid less in the informal sector; and (2) reduction of *between-group* inequality, as the wage penalty of being informal is not evenly distributed across skill groups and concentrates among unskilled workers. The decompositions in this book suggest that declining informality has contributed to reductions in inequality during the 2000s in Argentina, Brazil, Mexico, and Peru. In Bolivia, Chile, and Uruguay, the contribution was smaller.

These seven stylized facts show the extent to which wage inequality is multifaceted, and that, despite common trends, there is substantial heterogeneity across countries. In the chapters that follow, this book challenges unicausal explanations that link single causes to single effects. Instead, it discusses the combined role of labor market supply-side and demand-side factors that determine the observed wage inequality changes in each period as well as how institutional factors such as minimum wage policies were at work. It will also discuss the channels through which such factors operated in search of hints about the sustainability of recent trends over the next few years.

Annex 2A. Supplementary Wage and Income Inequality Figures

TABLE 2A.1: **Evolution of Earnings Inequality, Top and Bottom of the Income Distribution, Selected Latin American Countries, 1995–2013**

a. Log(p90/p50)

Year	Argentina	Bolivia	Brazil	Chile	Colombia	Ecuador	El Salvador	Mexico	Panama	Paraguay	Peru	Uruguay
1995	0.85		1.25						1.01	0.92		0.86
1996	0.82		1.25	1.10				1.07				0.86
1997	0.81	1.20	1.21						0.98	0.89	0.91	0.89
1998	0.91	1.23	1.21	1.11		0.98	0.99	1.10	0.96		0.98	0.87
1999	0.92	1.20	1.22			1.00	1.01		0.99	0.89	0.92	
2000	0.92	1.09		1.10		0.98	1.05	0.98	1.02		0.89	0.88
2001	0.97	1.06	1.19		0.89		1.06		0.98	0.95	0.95	0.98
2002	1.02	1.04	1.20	1.10	1.00		1.02	0.98	1.01	0.98	0.97	1.02
2003	1.01	1.12	1.16		0.97	0.94	1.01		1.02	1.00	0.99	0.99
2004	0.92	1.14	1.17		1.00	0.98	0.98		1.02	0.89	0.93	1.02
2005	0.90	1.14	1.12		0.98	0.96	1.04		1.00	0.93	0.94	1.02
2006	0.87	0.96	1.12	1.06		0.90	0.94		0.99	0.91	0.93	1.02
2007	0.83	0.92	0.99			0.96	0.94		0.90	0.85	0.95	1.02
2008	0.83	0.88	1.05		0.96	0.92	0.97	0.88	0.90	0.88	0.91	0.94
2009	0.76	0.93	1.09	1.04	0.94	0.88	0.97		0.90	0.87	0.91	0.94
2010	0.76	0.90		0.96	0.89	0.92	0.92	0.92	0.83	0.83	0.86	0.92
2011	0.79		0.98	1.07	0.93	0.86	0.88		0.85	0.83	0.85	0.88
2012	0.72		1.00		0.93	0.85	0.89	0.96	0.88	0.79	0.83	0.81
2013	0.73		0.97	0.99	0.91	0.82	0.89		0.80	0.87	0.82	0.79

(continued on next page)

TABLE 2A.1: **Evolution of Earnings Inequality, Top and Bottom of the Income Distribution, Selected Latin American Countries, 1995–2013** *(continued)*

b. Log(p50/p10)

Year	Argentina	Bolivia	Brazil	Chile	Colombia	Ecuador	El Salvador	Mexico	Panama	Paraguay	Peru	Uruguay
1995	0.80		0.92						0.91	1.17		0.91
1996	0.81		0.94	0.78			1.88					0.93
1997	0.84	1.42	0.96						0.95	1.23	1.06	0.92
1998	0.90	2.03	0.92	0.71	1.10	2.31		0.95	0.93		1.02	0.91
1999	0.88	1.82	0.89		2.01	1.15			0.87	1.16	0.99	
2000	0.97	1.62		0.69	1.14	1.01		0.94	0.85		1.12	0.87
2001	1.08	1.65	0.87		1.06	1.13			1.10	1.30	1.19	0.94
2002	1.07	1.27	0.82	0.63	1.17	1.20		1.00	1.24	1.26	1.19	0.99
2003	1.33	1.54	0.78		1.10	1.18			1.22	1.18	1.14	0.97
2004	1.25	1.59	0.78	1.07	1.10	0.98			1.17	1.12	1.09	0.97
2005	1.16	1.49	0.72	1.03	1.12	0.88			1.10	1.19	1.10	0.93
2006	1.12	1.42	0.73	0.62	0.94	0.90			1.10	1.14	1.05	0.97
2007	1.05	1.51	0.91		0.99	0.78			1.04	1.13	1.02	1.01
2008	1.03	1.22	0.67	0.98	1.05	0.82		0.89	0.97	1.12	0.98	0.98
2009	1.10	1.46	0.66	0.53	0.97	1.06		0.81	0.93	1.16	0.95	0.93
2010	1.01	1.43		1.01	1.02	0.81		0.90	0.93	1.06	0.95	0.93
2011	0.99		0.60	0.47	0.96	0.99		0.80	0.83	1.17	0.91	0.90
2012	0.95		0.56	1.00	0.96	0.82		0.89	0.81	1.14	0.95	0.89
2013	0.96		0.55	0.52	1.01	0.88		0.82	0.80	1.05	0.96	0.85

Source: World Bank, Office of the Chief Economist for Latin America and the Caribbean, based on the Socio-Economic Database for Latin America and the Caribbean (SEDLAC), Universidad Nacional de la Plata (CEDLAS) and the World Bank (http://sedlac .econo.unlp.edu.ar/eng/).

Note: The sample comprises male and female full-time workers (working at least 35 hours a week) who were either employed or self-employed and ages 15–65. The 1st and 99th percentiles were trimmed in the year-country level. Finally, p90 refers to the top 10 percent of the income distribution, p50 to the 50th percentile, and p10 to the 10th percentile (the bottom 10 percent of the income distribution).

TABLE 2A.2: Decomposition of Wage Inequality into Within-Group and Between-Group Components Using a Different Number of Categories for Sector of Employment, Latin America, 1997–2013

	Level of contribution to wage inequality considering 5 sectors					Level of contribution to wage inequality considering 17 sectors				
	1997	2001	2005	2009	2013	1997	2001	2005	2009	2013
Overall	0.804	0.895	0.751	0.690	0.661	0.804	0.895	0.751	0.690	0.661
Residual (within-group)	0.443	0.515	0.441	0.433	0.409	0.435	0.503	0.430	0.421	0.395
Between-group	0.361	0.379	0.310	0.257	0.252	0.369	0.391	0.321	0.269	0.266
Sector (5 categories)	0.025	0.047	0.024	0.022	0.019					
Sector (17 ISIC categories)						0.037	0.069	0.039	0.037	0.034
Education	0.256	0.183	0.219	0.166	0.152	0.234	0.165	0.198	0.149	0.137
Experience	0.057	0.032	0.045	0.030	0.025	0.056	0.031	0.044	0.029	0.025
Urban	0.002	0.004	0.001	0.000	0.001	0.001	0.002	0.000	0.000	0.000
Country	0.029	0.045	0.022	0.020	0.032	0.029	0.044	0.021	0.020	0.032
Covariance	−0.007	0.069	0.000	0.019	0.023	0.012	0.080	0.019	0.034	0.038

Source: Calculations based on the Socio-Economic Database for Latin America and the Caribbean (SEDLAC), Universidad Nacional de la Plata (CEDLAS) and the World Bank (http://sedlac.econo.unlp.edu.ar/eng/).
Note: ISIC = International Standard Industrial Classification of All Economic Activities.

FIGURE 2A.1: Wage and Total Income Inequality in Latin America, by Country

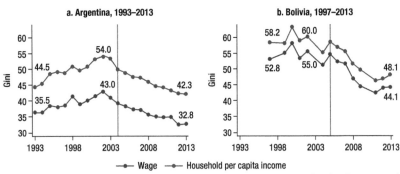

a. Argentina, 1993–2013

b. Bolivia, 1997–2013

— Wage   — Household per capita income

(continued on next page)

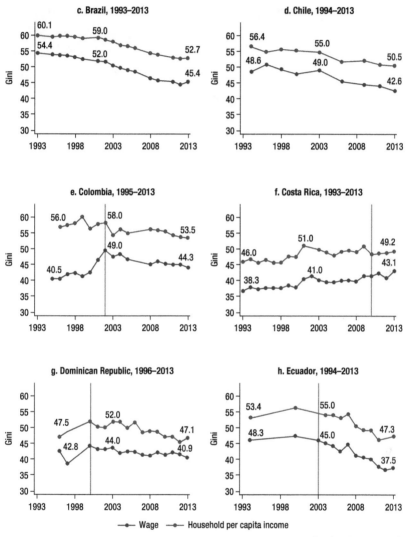

c. Brazil, 1993–2013

d. Chile, 1994–2013

e. Colombia, 1995–2013

f. Costa Rica, 1993–2013

g. Dominican Republic, 1996–2013

h. Ecuador, 1994–2013

Wage   Household per capita income

(continued on next page)

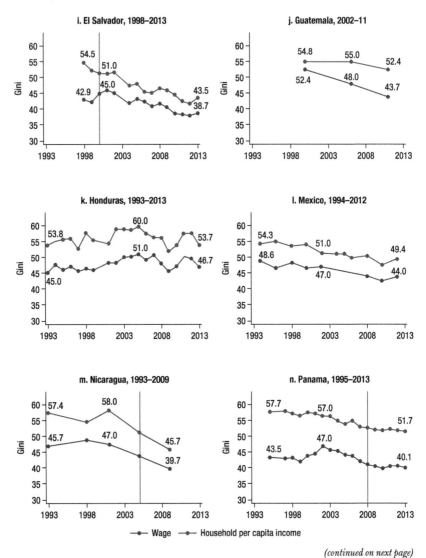

i. El Salvador, 1998–2013

j. Guatemala, 2002–11

k. Honduras, 1993–2013

l. Mexico, 1994–2012

m. Nicaragua, 1993–2009

n. Panama, 1995–2013

Wage — Household per capita income

(continued on next page)

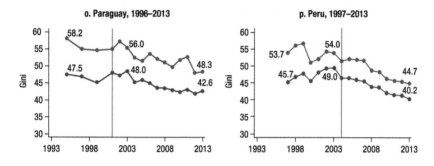

o. Paraguay, 1996–2013

p. Peru, 1997–2013

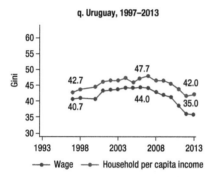

q. Uruguay, 1997–2013

—•— Wage   —•— Household per capita income

Source: Authors' calculations based on data from the Socio-Economic Database for Latin America and the Caribbean (SEDLAC), Universidad Nacional de la Plata (CEDLAS) and the World Bank (http://sedlac.econo.unlp.edu.ar/eng/).
Note: Vertical lines mark the year of a comparability breakpoint, when the country-specific data reflect a methodological change.

Annex 2B. Robustness of Returns to Skill to Different Estimation Methodologies

In this discussion, we assume that skills are proxied by a worker's educational attainment, and we estimate skill premiums by Mincerian equations for the hourly wage on educational attainment, controlling for the most relevant variables (experience, gender, and region) in a cross-sectional survey of each Latin American country.

To compute the regional averages, we simply average across countries the coefficients of the Mincerian equations. Figure 2.6, panel a, is an example that also presents the average wage returns by educational group, which is a rougher approximation of the returns to skill.

An important concern in estimating the skill premiums is how to deal with endogeneity. Endogeneity can arise because of (1) sample selection (that is, we can observe only the wages of workers who perform work in a given period); or (2) omitted-variable bias. Classically, unobserved ability has been the most studied source of omitted-variable bias.

The literature has suggested two main approaches to mitigate endogeneity. The first is a correction to account for sample selection (Heckman 1977). This procedure computes, in a first stage, the probability of labor market participation according to workers' observable characteristics and includes a function of this probability in the returns-to-skill estimation to correct for selection bias. Applying this method to Latin America, the premiums decline (as expected), but the trajectory is similar to what had been estimated using Mincerian ordinary least squares (OLS) regressions for the region (figure 2B.1).

The second approach to address endogeneity—in this case, to address omitted-variable bias—uses worker-level panel data to account for unobserved workers' characteristics that are fixed over time (Abowd, Creecy, and Kramarz 2002). The available

FIGURE 2B.1: **Wage Premium from Education, Correcting for Selection Bias, Latin America, 1993–2013**

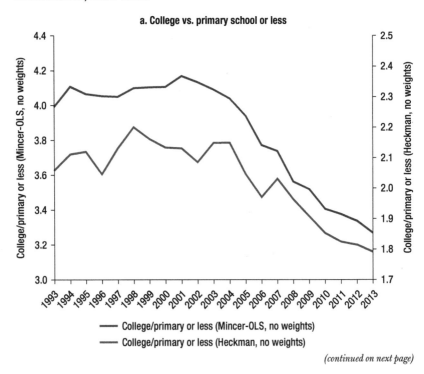

a. College vs. primary school or less

— College/primary or less (Mincer-OLS, no weights)
— College/primary or less (Heckman, no weights)

(continued on next page)

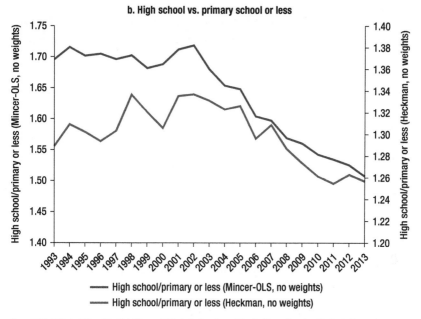

b. High school vs. primary school or less

— High school/primary or less (Mincer-OLS, no weights)
— High school/primary or less (Heckman, no weights)

Sources: World Bank, Office of the Chief Economist for Latin America and the Caribbean, based on the Socio-Economic Database for Latin America and the Caribbean (SEDLAC), Universidad Nacional de la Plata (CEDLAS) and the World Bank (http://sedlac.econo.unlp.edu.ar/eng/).

Note: The reported wage premiums are defined as the exponential of the ratio of the coefficient of the respective levels of education. For example, the premium for college versus primary education or less is the exponential of the ratio of the coefficient of a complete college dummy and a complete secondary dummy. We have estimated the Mincerian equation using ordinary least squares (OLS) and no weights. We have also estimated this equation using Heckman (1977) full maximum likelihood, with no weights, where the dependent variable is the logarithm of the hourly wage from the primary job of individuals ages 25–55. The explanatory variables are a male dummy (only in the equation for "all workers"), educational dummies, age, age squared, regional dummies, and an urban/rural dummy. The selection equation includes the same variables plus number of children and school attendance. Note that the Heckman regressions were done without weights to facilitate the convergence of the maximum likelihood estimation. (We did a two-step process, and it does not allow weights.) Hence, for comparison with the Heckman estimation, the Mincer-OLS estimates also do not use weights and therefore differ slightly from those reported in figure 2.6, panel a.

evidence for Latin American countries also agrees with our estimates (Frías, Kaplan, and Verhoogen 2009; Gonzaga, Menezes-Filho, and Terra 2006).

More recently, refinements to the worker fixed-effect setup have been proposed. Frías, Kaplan, and Verhoogen (2009) allow the individual-specific component in wages to vary over time, and therefore, in this model, experience can affect individual ability differently across workers. Another strand of the literature is concerned with the extent to which firm-level unobserved characteristics are related to the skill premium

(Card, Heining, and Kline 2013; Gruetter and Lalive 2009). Other approaches consist of instrumental variables, natural experiments, or randomized controlled trials (for example, studies using the date of birth as an instrument for education) (Angrist and Krueger 1991).

Another important methodological aspect in estimating returns to skill is how to measure educational attainment. To produce estimates for Latin America, we need to make the data consistent across countries. In this book, we rely mostly on the Socio-Economic Database for Latin America and the Caribbean (SEDLAC), the harmonized Latin American and Caribbean household survey data set for estimations. Several countries in the region do not capture years of education in their household surveys but instead capture a detailed categorical variable for the last educational level attained. Because the conversion of years of education into educational levels is more precise than the opposite conversion, we relied on this categorical variable in our estimates. But to compare "skilled" and "unskilled" workers, we have to choose whether to include in a given educational level the people who dropped out of that

FIGURE 2B.2: **Wage Premium Estimations by Educational Group, with and without Dropouts, 1993–2013**

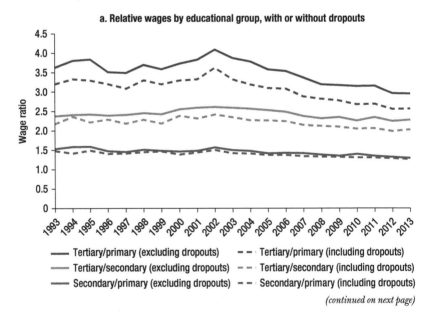

a. Relative wages by educational group, with or without dropouts

Tertiary/primary (excluding dropouts) – – Tertiary/primary (including dropouts)
Tertiary/secondary (excluding dropouts) – – Tertiary/secondary (including dropouts)
Secondary/primary (excluding dropouts) – – Secondary/primary (including dropouts)

(continued on next page)

FIGURE 2B.2: **Wage Premium Estimations by Educational Group, with and without Dropouts, 1993–2013** *(continued)*

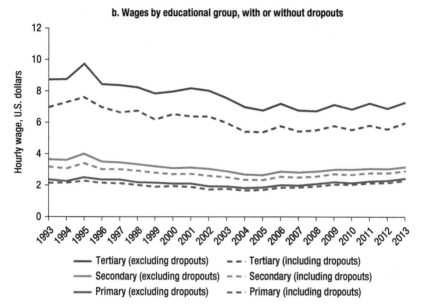

b. Wages by educational group, with or without dropouts

— Tertiary (excluding dropouts)   – – Tertiary (including dropouts)
— Secondary (excluding dropouts)   – – Secondary (including dropouts)
— Primary (excluding dropouts)   – – Primary (including dropouts)

Sources: Authors' calculations based on data from the Socio-Economic Database for Latin America and the Caribbean (SEDLAC), Universidad Nacional de la Plata (CEDLAS) and the World Bank (http://sedlac.econo.unlp.edu.ar/eng/).
Note: The continuous lines show the average hourly wage of workers in the educational group indicated, excluding dropouts. The dashed lines include dropouts. Earnings figures include both wage and self-employed full-time workers ages 15–65.

educational level—that is, people who started but did not finish a given educational level. This question is particularly important concerning high school dropouts in Latin America, because they represent a large share of total adult workers (16.7 percent of workers in 2012).

Figure 2B.2, panel a, shows the wages of educational groups including and not including dropouts. Panel b complements this evidence and shows the evolution of wages of each educational group including and not including dropouts. We see that even though the inclusion of dropouts slightly decreases skill premiums, the trends are parallel.

Annex 2C. Robustness of Employment and Skill-Use Growth in Tradable and Nontradable Industries to a Different Definition

FIGURE 2C.1: Employment and Skill-Use Growth, by Sector Type, in South America

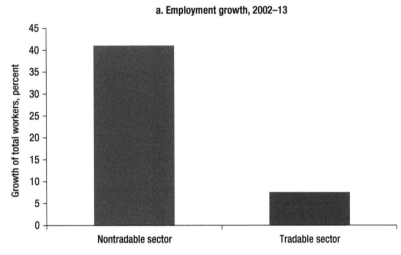

a. Employment growth, 2002–13

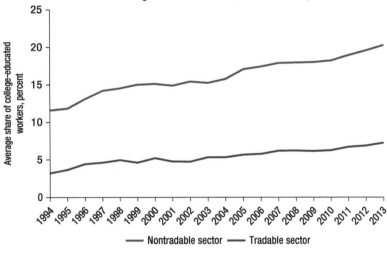

b. Share of college-educated workers within each sector, 1994–2013

— Nontradable sector ——— Tradable sector

Source: World Bank, Office of the Chief Economist for Latin America and the Caribbean, based on the Socio-Economic Database for Latin America and the Caribbean (SEDLAC), Universidad Nacional de la Plata (CEDLAS) and the World Bank (http://sedlac .econo.unlp.edu.ar/eng/).

Note: The tradable sector includes agriculture and mining (primary sector) and manufacturing. The nontradable sector includes restaurants and hotels, financial services, construction, public administration and domestic work, electricity and gas, transport and communications, real estate, education and health, and other business activities. The panels plot the average across countries including Argentina, Brazil, Chile, Colombia, Ecuador, Mexico, Peru, and Uruguay.

Annex 2D. Country-by-Country Changes in Inequality-Related Indicators and Correlations between the Key Variables

TABLE 2D.1: Changes in Inequality-Related Indicators, Selected Latin American Countries, 1995–2003, 2003–13, and 1995–2013
(annualized change, percentage points)

Country	Change in total income Gini	Change in labor income Gini	Change in returns to skill (completed tertiary vs. primary or less)	Change in returns to skill (completed tertiary vs. high school)	Change in ratio of skilled to unskilled workers (completed tertiary vs. primary or less)	Change in ratio of skilled to unskilled workers (completed tertiary vs. high school)	Change in aggregate domestic demand	Change in real exchange rate	Change in Gini not due to observables
				a. 1995–2003					
South America									
Argentina	0.6	0.3	-1.6	-2.3	3.2	1.0	-0.2	-8.8	2.0
Bolivia	-0.1	0.0	9.2	1.9	-1.3	-1.9	3.2	0.8	2.4
Brazil	-0.2	-0.4	-4.9	2.5	0.6	-0.6	1.2	-4.7	-0.9
Chile	-0.1	-0.1	-3.2	0.3	3.5	0.6	4.4	-1.6	-1.1
Ecuador	0.1	0.0	3.9	1.9	-0.8	-1.8	2.5	1.7	1.6
Peru	0.0	0.5	4.5	2.5	1.7	0.5	1.3	-0.7	-0.6
Uruguay	0.4	0.4	5.4	3.3	1.7	0.2	-1.3	-1.8	0.5
Central America and Mexico									
Costa Rica	0.5	0.4	3.8	1.6	1.7	1.0	3.7	-0.3	-0.2
Dominican Republic	0.6	0.1	6.3	2.3	0.3	-0.2	5.5	-2.6	-0.8

(continued on next page)

TABLE 2D.1: Changes in Inequality-Related Indicators, Selected Latin American Countries, 1995–2003, 2003–13, and 1995–2013

(continued)

(annualized change, percentage points)

Country	Change in total income Gini	Change in labor income Gini	Change in returns to skill (completed tertiary vs. primary or less)	Change in returns to skill (completed tertiary vs. high school)	Change in ratio of skilled to unskilled workers (completed tertiary vs. primary or less)	Change in ratio of skilled to unskilled workers (completed tertiary vs. high school)	Change in aggregate domestic demand	Change in real exchange rate	Change in Gini not due to observables
				a. 1995–2003 *(continued)*					
Central America and Mexico (continued)									
El Salvador	−0.4	−0.4	−6.3	3.4	0.8	1.4	2.7	1.8	0.2
Honduras	0.4	0.5	4.0	2.6	0.2	0.2	4.8	3.4	1.3
Mexico	−0.4	−0.2	−8.5	1.1	1.4	0.3	4.6	5.7	−1.2
Nicaragua	−0.2	−0.2	−6.1	−1.1	0.8	1.2	4.7	−1.1	−1.1
Panama	−0.2	0.3	2.5	−0.5	−0.6	0.0	6.2	0.6	1.3
				b. 2003–13					
South America									
Argentina	−1.1	−0.8	−10.1	−3.0	4.6	0.3	10.8	11.0	−1.4
Bolivia	−1.0	−0.9	−20.8	−5.8	3.8	0.0	6.5	1.8	−2.4
Brazil	−0.5	−0.5	−20.7	−3.8	1.9	0.6	6.1	5.9	−0.7
Chile	−0.4	−0.6	−11.0	−3.3	4.6	0.9	8.8	2.2	0.9

(continued on next page)

TABLE 2D.1: **Changes in Inequality-Related Indicators, Selected Latin American Countries, 1995–2003, 2003–13, and 1995–2013**

(continued)

(annualized change, percentage points)

Country	Change in total income Gini	Change in labor income Gini	Change in returns to skill (completed tertiary vs. primary or less)	Change in returns to skill (completed tertiary vs. high school)	Change in ratio of skilled to unskilled workers (completed tertiary vs. primary or less)	Change in ratio of skilled to unskilled workers (completed tertiary vs. high school)	Change in aggregate domestic demand	Change in real exchange rate	Change in Gini not due to observables
Colombia	−0.1	−0.3	−3.6	0.7	0.8	−0.6	7.5	5.3	0.5
Ecuador	−0.8	−0.9	−7.9	−0.7	2.9	2.1	7.1	−0.9	−1.2
Peru	−0.9	−0.9	−10.0	−3.6	3.7	0.4	10.9	0.9	−0.2
Uruguay	−0.4	−0.8	−10.3	−1.8	4.3	0.7	10.3	5.9	−0.9
Central America and Mexico									
Costa Rica	−0.1	0.3	8.6	1.7	0.3	−0.7	5.7	3.3	0.4
Dominican Republic	−0.5	−0.3	−0.4	1.8	0.9	0.1	7.8	3.7	−0.4
El Salvador	−0.7	−0.2	−2.3	0.4	0.1	−0.7	1.9	−0.3	0.4
Honduras	−0.5	−0.3	−11.4	−3.9	0.5	0.6	5.2	1.9	1.9
Mexico	−0.2	−0.2	−5.8	−0.5	1.9	0.2	3.6	−0.4	0.8
Nicaragua	−0.9	−0.6	−4.6	−1.1	0.5	0.0	7.8	−0.2	−2.3
Panama	−0.5	−0.6	−10.8	−2.0	4.2	0.9	5.6	−0.4	−1.3

(continued on next page)

TABLE 2D.1: Changes in Inequality-Related Indicators, Selected Latin American Countries, 1995–2003, 2003–13, and 1995–2013

(continued)

(annualized change, percentage points)

Country	Change in total income Gini	Change in labor income Gini	Change in returns to skill (completed tertiary vs. primary or less)	Change in returns to skill (completed tertiary vs. high school)	Change in ratio of skilled to unskilled workers (completed tertiary vs. primary or less)	Change in ratio of skilled to unskilled workers (completed tertiary vs. high school)	Change in aggregate domestic demand	Change in real exchange rate	Change in Gini not due to observables
					c. 1995–2013				
South America									
Argentina	-0.4	-0.3	-6.3	-2.7	4.0	0.6	5.8	-2.1	0.1
Bolivia	-0.6	-0.5	-7.5	-2.3	1.5	-0.8	6.0	1.4	-0.2
Brazil	-0.4	-0.5	-13.6	-1.0	1.4	0.1	4.3	-0.1	-0.8
Chile	-0.3	-0.4	-7.5	-1.7	4.1	0.8	8.6	0.3	0.0
Ecuador	-0.4	-0.5	-2.7	0.5	1.3	0.4	5.8	0.2	0.0
Peru	-0.5	-0.3	-3.5	-0.9	2.8	0.4	7.3	0.2	-0.4
Uruguay	0.0	-0.3	-3.3	0.5	3.1	0.5	4.6	2.0	-0.2

(continued on next page)

TABLE 2D.1: **Changes in Inequality-Related Indicators, Selected Latin American Countries, 1995–2003, 2003–13, and 1995–2013**

(continued)

(annualized change, percentage points)

Country	Change in total income Gini	Change in labor income Gini	Change in returns to skill (completed tertiary vs. primary or less)	Change in returns to skill (completed tertiary vs. high school)	Change in ratio of skilled to unskilled workers (completed tertiary vs. primary or less)	Change in ratio of skilled to unskilled workers (completed tertiary vs. high school)	Change in aggregate domestic demand	Change in real exchange rate	Change in Gini not due to observables
Central America and Mexico									
Costa Rica	0.2	0.3	6.5	1.7	0.9	0.0	5.7	1.7	0.1
Dominican Republic	0.0	−0.1	2.6	2.0	0.6	0.0	8.7	0.4	−0.6
El Salvador	−0.6	−0.3	−4.1	1.7	0.4	0.2	2.5	0.6	0.3
Honduras	−0.1	0.0	−4.5	−1.0	0.4	0.4	6.1	2.9	1.6
Mexico	−0.3	−0.2	−7.0	0.2	1.7	0.3	4.7	2.2	−0.1
Nicaragua	−0.6	−0.4	−5.3	−1.1	0.6	0.6	8.1	−0.6	−1.8
Panama	−0.3	−0.2	−4.9	−1.3	2.0	0.5	7.4	0.0	−0.2

Sources: Gini coefficients from Rodríguez-Castelán et al. (2016). Other data from World Bank, Office of the Chief Economist for Latin America and the Caribbean, based on data from the Socio-Economic Database for Latin America and the Caribbean (SEDLAC), Universidad Nacional de la Plata (CEDLAS) and the World Bank (http://sedlac.econo.unlp.edu.ar/eng/). Aggregate domestic demand data from the World Bank's World Development Indicators (http://data.worldbank.org/data-catalog/world-development-indicators). Real exchange rates from the Internal Revenue Service, U.S. Treasury.

Note: The Gini coefficient measures the equality of income distribution, ranging from zero (perfect equality) to 100 (maximal inequality). "Domestic demand" includes private consumption, public consumption, and gross capital formation. For all information regarding wages, the 1st and 99th percentiles for every country-year, gender, and education level are trimmed. "Gini attributable to observables" refers to the contribution to the variance of log of hourly wage of a set of 16 education dummies and 39 potential experience dummies. Countries include Argentina, Bolivia, Brazil, Chile, Costa Rica, the Dominican Republic, Ecuador, El Salvador, Honduras, Mexico, Nicaragua, Panama, Peru, and Uruguay.

79

TABLE 2D.2: Correlations of Inequality-Related Indicators, Selected Latin American Countries, 1995–2003, 2003–13, and 1995–2013

Indicator	Change in Gini total income	Change in Gini labor income	Change in returns to skill (completed tertiary vs. primary or less)	Change in returns to skill (completed tertiary vs. high school)	Change in labor supply (completed tertiary vs. primary or less)	Change in labor supply (completed tertiary vs. high school)	Change in aggregate domestic demand	Change in real exchange rate	Change in Gini not due to observables
				a. 1995–2003					
Change in Gini total income	1								
Change in Gini labor income	0.5130*	1							
	(0.0000)								
Change in returns to skill (completed tertiary vs. primary or less)	0.2543*	0.6014*	1						
	(0.0068)	(0.0000)							
Change in returns to skill (completed tertiary vs. high school)	0.2353*	0.4404*	0.7187*	1					
	(0.0210)	(0.0000)	(0.0000)						
Change in labor supply (completed tertiary vs. primary or less)	0.2489*	0.1384	−0.1582*	0.0344	1				
	(0.0081)	(0.1457)	(0.0957)	(0.7392)					
Change in labor supply (completed tertiary vs. high school)	0.2326*	0.1327	−0.1264	0.0198	0.6720*	1			
	(0.0136)	(0.1631)	(0.1840)	(0.8480)	(0.0000)				
Change in aggregate domestic demand	−0.0783	−0.0850	−0.1868*	−0.1170	0.0048	0.0082	1		
	(0.4121)	(0.3730)	(0.0486)	(0.2563)	(0.9598)	(0.9315)			

(continued on next page)

TABLE 2D.2: Correlations of Inequality-Related Indicators, Selected Latin American Countries, 1995–2003, 2003–13, and 1995–2013 *(continued)*

Indicator	Change in Gini total income	Change in Gini labor income	Change in returns to skill (completed tertiary vs. primary or less)	Change in returns to skill (completed tertiary vs. high school)	Change in labor supply (completed tertiary vs. primary or less)	Change in labor supply (completed tertiary vs. high school)	Change in aggregate domestic demand	Change in real exchange rate	Change in Gini not due to observables
Change in real exchange rate	−0.0344	−0.0534	−0.1607*	−0.0886	−0.0954	−0.0274	0.5262*	1	
	(0.7189)	(0.5759)	(0.0905)	(0.3905)	(0.3171)	(0.7746)	(0.0000)		
Change in Gini not due to observables	0.3068*	0.3343*	0.1797*	0.1557	−0.0022	−0.0149	−0.2238*	−0.0638	1
	(0.0024)	(0.0009)	(0.0797)	(0.1299)	(0.9834)	(0.8856)	(0.0284)	(0.5366)	
b. 2003–13									
Change in Gini total income	1								
Change in Gini labor income	0.6731*	1							
	(0.0000)								
Change in returns to skill (completed tertiary vs. primary or less)	0.3528*	0.5839*	1						
	(0.0000)	(0.0000)							
Change in returns to skill (completed tertiary vs. high school)	0.3045*	0.4565*	0.6454*	1					
	(0.0002)	(0.0000)	(0.0000)						
Change in labor supply (completed tertiary vs. primary or less)	0.1287	−0.0305	−0.1916*	−0.0921	1				
	(0.1116)	(0.7074)	(0.0173)	(0.2741)					

(continued on next page)

TABLE 2D.2: Correlations of Inequality-Related Indicators, Selected Latin American Countries, 1995–2003, 2003–13, and 1995–2013 (continued)

Indicator	Change in Gini total income	Change in Gini labor income	Change in returns to skill (completed tertiary vs. primary or less)	Change in returns to skill (completed tertiary vs. high school)	Change in labor supply (completed tertiary vs. primary or less)	Change in labor supply (completed tertiary vs. high school)	Change in aggregate domestic demand	Change in real exchange rate	Change in Gini not due to observables
b. 2003–13 (continued)									
Change in labor supply (completed tertiary vs. high school)	0.2161*	0.0474	−0.2121*	−0.0074	0.6675*	1			
	(0.0071)	(0.5592)	(0.0083)	(0.9302)	(0.0000)				
Change in aggregate domestic demand	−0.0683	−0.0118	−0.0682	−0.0470	0.0648	0.0448	1		
	(0.4001)	(0.8841)	(0.4009)	(0.5776)	(0.4248)	(0.5813)			
Change in real exchange rate	−0.1812*	−0.0920	−0.1770*	−0.1476*	−0.0350	−0.1155	0.2029*	1	
	(0.0245)	(0.2566)	(0.0281)	(0.0786)	(0.6667)	(0.1538)	(0.0116)		
Change in Gini not due to observables	0.2790*	0.3993*	0.0925	0.1397*	−0.1167	−0.1341	0.1500*	0.0154	1
	(0.0007)	(0.0000)	(0.2719)	(0.0961)	(0.1652)	(0.1102)	(0.0737)	(0.8550)	
c. 1995–2013									
Change in Gini total income	1								
Change in Gini labor income	0.6313*	1							
	(0.0000)								
Change in returns to skill (completed tertiary vs. primary or less)	0.3610*	0.6197*	1						
	(0.0000)	(0.0000)							

(continued on next page)

TABLE 2D.2: Correlations of Inequality-Related Indicators, Selected Latin American Countries, 1995–2003, 2003–13, and 1995–2013 (continued)

Indicator	Change in Gini total income	Change in Gini labor income	Change in returns to skill (completed tertiary vs. primary or less)	Change in returns to skill (completed tertiary vs. high school)	Change in labor supply (completed tertiary vs. primary or less)	Change in labor supply (completed tertiary vs. high school)	Change in aggregate domestic demand	Change in real exchange rate	Change in Gini not due to observables
Change in returns to skill (completed tertiary vs. high school)	0.3012*	0.4650*	0.6592*	1					
	(0.0000)	(0.0000)	(0.0000)						
Change in labor supply (completed tertiary vs. primary or less)	0.1156*	−0.0137	−0.1833*	−0.0408	1				
	(0.0670)	(0.8281)	(0.0035)	(0.5423)					
Change in labor supply (completed tertiary vs. high school)	0.1961*	0.0735	−0.1753*	0.0082	0.6600*	1			
	(0.0018)	(0.2452)	(0.0053)	(0.9021)	(0.0000)				
Change in aggregate domestic demand	−0.1145*	−0.0960	−0.1318*	−0.0894	0.0703	0.0322	1		
	(0.0695)	(0.1286)	(0.0365)	(0.1816)	(0.2662)	(0.6114)			
Change in real exchange rate	−0.1158*	−0.1008	−0.1811*	−0.1184*	−0.0471	−0.0770	0.3431*	1	
	(0.0665)	(0.1103)	(0.0039)	(0.0763)	(0.4568)	(0.2230)	(0.0000)		
Change in Gini not due to observables	0.2944*	0.3672*	0.1767*	0.1759*	−0.0695	−0.0762	−0.0791	−0.0548	1
	(0.0000)	(0.0000)	(0.0079)	(0.0082)	(0.2994)	(0.2552)	(0.2376)	(0.4136)	

Sources: Gini coefficients adapted from Rodríguez-Castelán et al. (2016); World Bank, Office of the Chief Economist for Latin America and the Caribbean, based on data from the Socio-Economic Database for Latin America and the Caribbean (SEDLAC), Universidad Nacional de la Plata (CEDLAS) and the World Bank (http://sedlac.econo.unlp.edu.ar/eng/). Aggregate domestic demand data from the World Bank's World Development Indicators (http://data.worldbank.org/data-catalog/world-development-indicators). Real exchange rate data from the Internal Revenue Service, U.S. Treasury.

Note: The Gini coefficient measures the equality of income distribution, ranging from zero (perfect equality) to 100 (maximal inequality). "Domestic demand" includes private consumption, public consumption, and gross capital formation. For all information regarding wages, the 1st and 99th percentiles for every country-year, gender, and education level are trimmed. "Gini attributable to observables" refers to the contribution to the variance of log of hourly wage of a set of 16 education dummies and 39 potential experience dummies. Countries include Argentina, Bolivia, Brazil, Chile, Costa Rica, the Dominican Republic, Ecuador, El Salvador, Honduras, Mexico, Nicaragua, Panama, Peru, and Uruguay.

Significance level: * = at least 10 percent.

Annex 2E. Supplementary Informality Figures and Correlations

TABLE 2E.1: **Changes in Informality Measures, Selected Latin American Countries, 1995–2003, 2003–13, and 1995–2013**
(annualized change, percentage points)

Country	Change in share of informal workers (definition 1)[a]	Change in share of informal workers (definition 2)[b]	Change in share of informal workers (definition 3)[c]
a. 1995–2003			
South America			
Argentina	1.0	1.3	0.5
Bolivia	0.4	1.0	0.1
Brazil	−0.5	−0.4	−0.3
Chile	n.a.	n.a.	n.a.
Ecuador	−0.3	−0.6	0.2
Peru	−0.5	−0.9	0.3
Uruguay	n.a.	n.a.	−4.6
Central America and Mexico			
Costa Rica	0.1	0.2	−0.2
Dominican Republic	n.a.	n.a.	0.5
El Salvador	0.1	0.1	−0.1
Honduras	n.a.	n.a.	0.1
Mexico	0.0	0.1	0.1
Nicaragua	0.1	0.6	−0.5
Panama	n.a.	n.a.	0.9
b. 2003–13			
South America			
Argentina	−0.9	−1.0	−0.6
Bolivia	−0.8	−1.3	−0.3
Brazil	−1.1	−1.1	−0.8
Chile	−0.7	−0.5	−0.9
Ecuador	−1.6	−2.2	−0.4
Peru	−1.5	−1.8	−0.8
Uruguay	−1.2	−1.0	−0.9

(continued on next page)

TABLE 2E.1: **Changes in Informality Measures, Selected Latin American Countries, 1995–2003, 2003–13, and 1995–2013** *(continued)*
(annualized change, percentage points)

Country	Change in share of informal workers (definition 1)[a]	Change in share of informal workers (definition 2)[b]	Change in share of informal workers (definition 3)[c]
Central America and Mexico			
Costa Rica	−0.4	−0.4	−0.3
Dominican Republic	n.a.	n.a.	0.1
El Salvador	0.3	0.6	0.2
Honduras	n.a.	n.a.	−0.1
Mexico	0.2	0.5	−0.4
Nicaragua	−1.0	−1.0	n.a.
Panama	n.a.	n.a.	−1.1
c. 1995–2013			
South America			
Argentina	−0.1	0.0	−0.1
Bolivia	−0.3	−0.3	−0.1
Brazil	−0.8	−0.8	−0.6
Chile	n.a.	n.a.	n.a.
Ecuador	−1.0	−1.5	−0.1
Peru	−1.0	−1.4	−0.3
Uruguay	n.a.	n.a.	−2.5
Central America and Mexico			
Costa Rica	−0.2	−0.2	−0.2
Dominican Republic	n.a.	n.a.	0.3
El Salvador	0.2	0.4	0.1
Honduras	n.a.	n.a.	0.0
Mexico	0.1	0.3	−0.2
Nicaragua	−0.5	−0.3	n.a.
Panama	n.a.	n.a.	−0.2

Sources: World Bank, Office of the Chief Economist for Latin America and the Caribbean, based on the Socio-Economic Database for Latin America and the Caribbean (SEDLAC), Universidad Nacional de la Plata (CEDLAS) and the World Bank (http://sedlac.econo.unlp.edu.ar/eng/). n.a. = not available.

a. "Share of informal workers" definition 1: self-employed plus employees not contributing to social security as a proportion of self-employed and employees.

b. "Share of informal workers" definition 2: only employees contributing to social security as a proportion of total employees.

c. "Share of informal workers" definition 3: self-employed without complete tertiary plus employees and employers in small firms as a proportion of total employment.

TABLE 2E.2: **Correlations of Changes in Formality Measures with Changes in Inequality-Related Indicators, Selected Latin American Countries, 1995–2003, 2003–13, and 1995–2013**

Indicator	Change in the share of informal workers (definition 1)[a]	Change in the share of informal workers (definition 2)[b]	Change in the share of informal workers (definition 3)[c]
	a. 1995–2003		
Change in Gini total income	−0.1451	−0.2119*	0.0191
	(0.2452)	(0.0877)	(0.8500)
Change in Gini labor income	0.0400	−0.1518	0.0732
	(0.7501)	(0.2238)	(0.4669)
Change in returns to skill (completed tertiary vs. primary or less)	−0.1039	−0.2191*	0.0227
	(0.4066)	(0.0771)	(0.8216)
Change in returns to skill (completed tertiary vs. high school)	−0.1339	−0.1877	−0.0664
	(0.3206)	(0.1620)	(0.5297)
Change in the labor supply (completed tertiary vs. primary or less)	−0.3957*	−0.3105*	−0.1562
	(0.0010)	(0.0112)	(0.1189)
Change in the labor supply (completed tertiary vs. high school)	−0.3243*	−0.2638*	−0.1597
	(0.0079)	(0.0324)	(0.1106)
Change in aggregate domestic demand	0.1012	0.1918	0.0745
	(0.4187)	(0.1229)	(0.4593)
Change in real exchange rate	0.0209	0.1154	−0.0386
	(0.8678)	(0.3561)	(0.7017)
Change in Gini not due to observables	−0.1327	−0.2522*	0.0308
	(0.3252)	(0.0584)	(0.7709)
Change in the share of informal workers (definition 1)[a]	1		
Change in the share of informal workers (definition 2)[b]	0.8917*	1	
	(0.0000)		
Change in the share of informal workers (definition 3)[c]	0.5848*	0.3865*	1
	(0.0000)	(0.0013)	
	b. 2003–13		
Change in Gini total income	−0.1012	−0.1142	0.1141
	(0.2537)	(0.1976)	(0.1812)

(continued on next page)

TABLE 2E.2: **Correlations of Changes in Formality Measures with Changes in Inequality-Related Indicators, Selected Latin American Countries, 1995–2003, 2003–13, and 1995–2013** *(continued)*

Indicator	Change in the share of informal workers (definition 1)[a]	Change in the share of informal workers (definition 2)[b]	Change in the share of informal workers (definition 3)[c]
Change in Gini labor income	−0.0347	−0.0913	0.1344
	(0.6965)	(0.3037)	(0.1146)
Change in returns to skill (completed tertiary vs. primary or less)	−0.0656	−0.1255	−0.0341
	(0.4603)	(0.1564)	(0.6901)
Change in returns to skill (completed tertiary vs. high school)	0.0109	−0.0422	−0.0588
	(0.9040)	(0.6403)	(0.4932)
Change in the labor supply (completed tertiary vs. primary or less)	−0.1041	−0.0614	−0.0876
	(0.2406)	(0.4892)	(0.3053)
Change in the labor supply (completed tertiary vs. high school)	−0.1132	−0.0829	−0.0502
	(0.2015)	(0.3504)	(0.5571)
Change in aggregate domestic demand	−0.2491*	−0.1907*	−0.1510*
	(0.0044)	(0.0304)	(0.0760)
Change in real exchange rate	−0.0482	−0.0101	0.0366
	(0.5879)	(0.9099)	(0.6689)
Change in Gini not due to observables	0.2185*	0.2099*	0.1328
	(0.0143)	(0.0188)	(0.1204)
Change in the share of informal workers (definition 1)[a]	1		
Change in the share of informal workers (definition 2)[b]	0.9593*	1	
	(0.0000)		
Change in the share of informal workers (definition 3)[c]	0.3405*	0.2093*	1
	(0.0001)	(0.0218)	
c. 1995–2013			
Change in Gini total income	−0.0705	−0.1067	0.0560
	(0.3415)	(0.1494)	(0.4024)
Change in Gini labor income	0.0487	−0.0485	0.0895
	(0.5115)	(0.5134)	(0.1801)

(continued on next page)

TABLE 2E.2: **Correlations of Changes in Formality Measures with Changes in Inequality-Related Indicators, Selected Latin American Countries, 1995–2003, 2003–13, and 1995–2013** *(continued)*

Indicator	Change in the share of informal workers (definition 1)[a]	Change in the share of informal workers (definition 2)[b]	Change in the share of informal workers (definition 3)[c]
c. 1995–2013 *(continued)*			
Change in returns to skill (completed tertiary vs. primary or less)	−0.0118	−0.0834	0.0004
	(0.8735)	(0.2603)	(0.9953)
Change in returns to skill (completed tertiary vs. high school)	0.0201	−0.0219	−0.0522
	(0.7945)	(0.7764)	(0.4457)
Change in the labor supply (completed tertiary vs. primary or less)	−0.1892*	−0.1377*	−0.1106*
	(0.0101)	(0.0623)	(0.0972)
Change in the labor supply (completed tertiary vs. high school)	−0.1680*	−0.1353*	−0.0929
	(0.0227)	(0.0670)	(0.1639)
Change in aggregate domestic demand	−0.1982*	−0.1329*	−0.0367
	(0.0070)	(0.0720)	(0.5830)
Change in real exchange rate	−0.0388	0.0232	−0.0216
	(0.6007)	(0.7546)	(0.7468)
Change in Gini not due to observables	0.0338	−0.0063	0.0461
	(0.6609)	(0.9344)	(0.5003)
Change in the share of informal workers (definition 1)[a]	1		
Change in the share of informal workers (definition 2)[b]	0.9426*	1	
	(0.0000)		
Change in the share of informal workers (definition 3)[c]	0.4347*	0.2797*	1
	(0.0000)	(0.0002)	

Sources: Gini coefficients adapted from Rodríguez-Castelán et al. (2016). Other data from World Bank, Office of the Chief Economist for Latin America and the Caribbean, based on the Socio-Economic Database for Latin America and the Caribbean (SEDLAC), Universidad Nacional de la Plata (CEDLAS) and the World Bank (http://sedlac.econo.unlp.edu.ar/eng/). Aggregate domestic demand data from the World Bank's World Development Indicators (http://data.worldbank.org/data-catalog/world -development-indicators). Real exchange data from the Internal Revenue Service, U.S. Treasury. Minimum wages from official country data.

Note: "Domestic demand" includes private consumption, public consumption, and gross capital formation. For all information regarding wages, the 1st and 99th percentiles for every country, year, gender, and education levels are trimmed. Gini not attributable to observables controls log of hourly wage with a set of 16 education dummies and 39 potential experience dummies. Mean wages for full-time employers, employees, and self-employed workers ages 15–65. 0 and 99th percentile income trimmed.

a. "Share of informal workers" definition 1: self-employed plus employees not contributing to social security as a proportion of self-employed and employees.

b. "Share of informal workers" definition 2: only employees contributing to social security as a proportion of total employees.

c. "Share of informal workers" definition 3: self-employed without complete tertiary plus employees and employers in small firms as a proportion of total employment.

Significance level: * = at least 10 percent.

Notes

1. Note, however, that international comparisons of inequality are problematic, and hence should be treated with caution. Most surveys in developed countries inquire about *income*, while those in developing countries more commonly ask households about *consumption*. However, Latin American countries are the exception, because households are generally asked to report their different income sources; in only a few countries do the surveys inquire about consumption patterns. Even when income is asked about, differences in questionnaire design have been shown to lead to non-negligible differences in reported measures of household income. For example, some surveys capture net income while others capture gross income. See Alvaredo and Gasparini (2015) for a discussion.

2. The 10 most-unequal Latin American countries are (in order of greatest inequality) Haiti, Honduras, Colombia, Brazil, Guatemala, Panama, Chile, Paraguay, Mexico, and Bolivia (data from the World Bank's World Development Indicators database, http://data.worldbank.org /data-catalog/world-development-indicators). The most recent inequality data vary from 2007 to 2014, depending on the country.

3. The Gini coefficient is a measure of statistical dispersion representing the income distribution of a nation's residents. A coefficient of zero expresses perfect equality (every resident has the same income), whereas a coefficient of one (or 100 points) expresses maximal inequality (one person has all the income, and all others have none).

4. The reported differences are not conditional on the average income level of the countries in the region. However, these results are robust if the level of income is taken into account. In that case, the mean Gini coefficient among countries in Latin America is approximately 2.6 points lower than the average Gini coefficient among countries in Sub-Saharan Africa but almost 12 Gini points higher than the average Gini among countries in Eastern Europe and Central Asia. Measured by this procedure, the countries of Eastern Europe and Central Asia exhibit the narrowest average income inequality in the world. Moreover, the average level of total income inequality among the countries of East Asia and the Pacific is 3.4 Gini points below the corresponding average across Latin America, while the countries of the Middle East and North Africa show a differential of −6.4 Gini points, and the countries of South Asia show a differential of −7.7 Gini points. These differences are statistically significant except in the cases of Sub-Saharan Africa and East Asia and the Pacific.

5. Despite the change since 2010 in the official methodology to measure income in Costa Rica, there is no evidence of inequality reduction. Both the previous and current methodologies show an increase.

6. Although less commonly used than the Gini coefficient, the Theil index measures income inequality based on a generalized entropy measure. It is decomposable, unlike the Gini index, and can be used to measure within-group and between-group inequality (Theil 1967).

7. The 90–10 percentile ratio is another measure of overall wage inequality frequently used by labor economists. It can be further decomposed in separate trends for bottom inequality (defined by the log(p50/p10) ratio) and top inequality (defined by log(p90/p50)).

8. This decline is also robust to different aggregations. For instance, both the weighted and unweighted average of Latin American countries show similar declines in the 2000s.

9. This book uses earnings to identify workers' payments. Unless otherwise noted, earnings include the wages of the dependent employees and the pay of the self-employed obtained for the services performed in their jobs. With a few exceptions noted in the text, earnings are reported monthly and have been harmonized across surveys by the Socio-Economic Database for Latin America and the Caribbean (SEDLAC), Universidad Nacional de la Plata (CEDLAS) and the World Bank (http://sedlac.econo.unlp.edu.ar/eng/).

10. This average for non-Latin American countries hides important differences. Although earnings inequality increased in most developed countries, it was relatively stable in most developing countries (Milanovic 2016). Only a relatively small set of countries exhibited similar patterns to Latin America (for example, Italy, the Kyrgyz Republic, New Zealand, Poland, and the United Kingdom). However, in all of those countries, the change in earnings inequality was of a much smaller magnitude than in Latin America.

11. Cord et al. (2014) expanded the previous analysis using a nonparametric decomposition technique based on Lerman and Yitzhaki (1985).

12. Based on a sample of workers in urban areas of Argentina, Brazil, Chile, Colombia, and Mexico.

13. This same study classified as countries that did not benefit from the commodity boom the Dominican Republic, El Salvador, Guatemala, Honduras, Mexico, Paraguay, and Uruguay, while excluding from its analysis Costa Rica, Nicaragua, and Panama because of data limitations.

14. Returns to specific skills, including cognitive and socioemotional skills, are much harder to measure. The only data source available that measures one cognitive ability (reading scores) and a subset of noncognitive skills (personality traits) in Latin America that would allow for an exploration of their importance for wage determination are the Skills Toward Employment and Productivity (STEP) Surveys conducted in urban areas in Bolivia, Colombia, and El Salvador. These are cross-sectional studies carried out between 2012 and 2014. Hence, they do not allow for drawing implications for the evolution of wage inequality. The relationship of noncognitive skills (measured in the three Latin American countries) and wages is not as strong as the association between cognitive reading skills and earnings (Cunningham, Acosta, and Muller 2016). Cognitive skills are strongly associated with education, but they explain a smaller share of the variance of wages (Messina 2017). Considering data constraints and the fundamental role of education in the provision of skills, this book focuses on the returns to education and their implications for inequality.

15. As discussed in the previous section, the reduction in returns to education in Latin America was paralleled by a reduction in the returns to labor market experience, approximated by the potential experience defined as the worker's age minus years of education minus 6 (Fernández and Messina 2017). Hence, returns to "skill" in this section refers to returns to both education and experience.

16. Both "between-group" wage differences (for example, linked to education) and "within-group" differences in workers' characteristics contribute to labor earnings inequality. The relative importance of between- and within-group inequality is an area of active research. The calculations presented were obtained by decomposing log-wage variance into observable and residual components. This decomposition was done by regressing log earnings on a full set of dummies for years of experience (0–39 years), years of education (0–16 years), state of residence (27 states), race (white dummy), and location (urban dummy). It is important to note that the exact contribution of the within-group components decreases as the set of dummies included increases. Using a similar specification, Adão (2015) finds similar results for Brazil for the 1981 to 2009 period.

17. "Observed skills" are defined as being those that the econometrician can observe in the data. Note that some skills of workers may be unobservable in the data (such as interpersonal skills, motivation, specific skills for a job, or IQ) even though they are observable by employers.

18. Considering an alternative decomposition methodology based on the Theil index (an information-theoretic inequality measure) for wages across subperiods and country-by-country in Latin America, the results are similar. Within-group components account for around 55 percent of the total change in wage inequality. Although this value is sensitive to the number of

groups considered, even in detailed experience and education groups, the within-group component seems to account for a larger share of total wage inequality than the between-group component.

19. As expected, the within-group component of log-wage variance presents a lower contribution to log-wage variance when a more comprehensive set of dummies for sector of employment is included. However, even in the case when detailed sector dummies are included, the within-group component contributes to more than 50 percent of the overall level of wage inequality (table 2A.2).

20. Note that, although high, this share is below that of, for example, the United States, where the increased premium associated with schooling in general and postsecondary education in particular accounts for an estimated 60–70 percent of the overall rise of earnings dispersion between 1980 and 2005 (Autor 2014; Goldin and Katz 2007). Notably, however, inequality in the United States increased during this period, as did the returns to schooling (principally postsecondary education), in sharp contrast with Latin American trends in the 2000s.

21. We use 1997 as the first year in this analysis because, for earlier years, we have data for significantly fewer countries.

22. Table 2.2 covers 1994–2012 data. For results from the 1986–95 period, see Helpman, Itskhoki, and Redding (2010).

23. The large difference between the weighted and unweighted measure comes mainly from the spectacular performance of Brazil, where the share of the working-age population that completed secondary education more than doubled during the period, from 13 percent in 1990 to 31 percent in 2009 (De la Torre et al. 2014).

24. Figures cited in this paragraph and the preceding one are based on calculations from data from the Socio-Economic Database for Latin America and the Caribbean (SEDLAC), Universidad Nacional de la Plata (CEDLAS) and the World Bank (http://sedlac.econo.unlp.edu.ar/eng).

25. The growth rate of domestic demand is measured by the sum of consumption and investment averaged over all Latin American countries.

26. The G-7 countries include Canada, France, Germany, Italy, Japan, the United Kingdom, and the United States.

27. For a detailed discussion of the link between informality and inequality, see Amarante, Arim, and Yapor (2016).

28. The analysis focuses on men to avoid issues regarding differences in labor market participation between men and women.

29. Wage differences across skill groups in formal and informal sectors may also be driven by unobserved skills. If for a given skill cell workers in the informal sector have lower levels of other skills that are unobserved, the importance of informality for inequality would be overstated.

30. This analysis requires panel data on employment that were available only for Argentina, Bolivia, and Brazil.

31. These values were obtained in Mincerian equations, controlling for characteristics including gender, age, experience, and whether the family lives in an urban or rural area.

References

Abowd, J. M., R. H. Creecy, and F. Kramarz. 2002. "Computing Person and Firm Effects Using Linked Longitudinal Employer-Employee Data." Report No. 2002–06, Center for Economic Studies, U.S. Census Bureau, Washington, DC.

Abowd, J. M., F. Kramarz, and D. N. Margolis. 1999. "Minimum Wages and Employment in France and the United States." NBER Working Paper No. 6996, National Bureau of Economic Research, Cambridge, MA.

Abowd, J. M., F. Kramarz, D. N. Margolis, and K. R. Troske. 2001. "The Relative Importance of Employer and Employee Effects on Compensation: A Comparison of France and the United States." *Journal of the Japanese and International Economies* 15 (4): 419–36.

Acemoglu, D. 2002. "Technical Change, Inequality, and the Labor Market." *Journal of Economic Literature* 60 (March): 7–72.

Adão, R. 2015. "Worker Heterogeneity, Wage Inequality, and International Trade: Theory and Evidence from Brazil." Job Market Paper, Massachusetts Institute of Technology, Cambridge, MA.

Alvaredo, F., A. B. Atkinson, T. Piketty, and E. Saez. 2013. "The Top 1 Percent in International and Historical Perspective." *Journal of Economic Perspectives* 27 (3): 3–20.

Alvaredo, F., and L. Gasparini. 2015. "Recent Trends in Inequality and Poverty in Developing Countries." In *Handbook of Income Distribution*, Vol. 2, edited by A. B. Atkinson and F. Bourguignon. Amsterdam: Elsevier.

Amarante, V., R. Arim, and M. Yapor. 2016. "Decomposing Inequality Changes in Uruguay: The Role of Formalization in the Labor Market." *IZA Journal of Labor & Development*: 5–13.

Angrist, J., and A. Krueger. 1991. "Does Compulsory School Attendance Affect Schooling and Earnings?" *Quarterly Journal of Economics* 106 (4): 979–1014.

Autor, D. H. 2014. "Skills, Education, and the Rise of Earnings Inequality among the 'Other 99 Percent.'" *Science* 344 (6186): 843–51.

Autor, D. H., L. F. Katz, and M. S. Kearny. 2008. "Trends in U.S. Wage Inequality: Revising the Revisionists." *Review of Economics and Statistics* 90 (2): 300–23.

Barro, R. J., and J. W. Lee. 2013. "A New Data Set of Educational Attainment in the World, 1950–2010." *Journal of Development Economics* 104: 184–98.

Barros, R., M. De Carvalho, S. Franco, and R. Mendonca. 2010. "Markets, the State and the Dynamics of Inequality in Brazil." In *Declining Inequality in Latin America: A Decade of Progress?* edited by L. F. López-Calva and N. Lustig. Washington, DC: Brookings Institution; New York: United Nations Development Programme.

Battistón, D., C. García-Domench, and L. Gasparini. 2014. "Could an Increase in Education Raise Income Inequality? Evidence for Latin America." *Latin American Journal of Economics* 51 (1): 1–39.

Bourguignon, F., F. H. Ferreira, and N. Lustig, eds. 2005. *The Microeconomics of Income Distribution Dynamics in East Asia and Latin America*. Washington, DC: World Bank.

Campos-Vázquez, R. M., L. F. López-Calva, and N. Lustig. 2016. "Declining Wages for College-Educated Workers in Mexico: Are Younger or Older Cohorts Hurt the Most?" Policy Research Working Paper 7546, World Bank, Washington, DC.

Card, D., J. Heining, and P. Kline. 2013. "Workplace Heterogeneity and the Rise of West German Wage Inequality." *Quarterly Journal of Economics* 128 (3): 967–1105.

Card, D., T. Lemieux, and W. C. Riddell. 2003. "Unionization and Wage Inequality: A Comparative Study of the U.S., the U.K., and Canada." NBER Working Paper 9473, National Bureau of Economic Research, Cambridge, MA.

Cord, L. J., O. B. Cabanillas, L. Lucchetti, C. Rodríguez-Castelán, L. D. Sousa, and D. Valderrama. 2014. "Inequality Stagnation in Latin America in the Aftermath of the Global Financial Crisis." Policy Research Working Paper 7146, World Bank, Washington, DC.

Cornia, G. A. 2014. "Inequality Trends and Their Determinants: Latin America over 1990–2010." In *Falling Inequality in Latin America: Policy Changes and Lessons*, edited by A. Cornia. UNU-WIDER Studies in Development Economics. Oxford, UK: Oxford University Press.

Cunningham, W., P. Acosta, and N. Muller. 2016. *Minds and Behaviors at Work: Boosting Socioemotional Skills for Latin America's Workforce*. Directions in Development: Human Development Series. Washington, DC: World Bank.

Davis, S. J. and J. Haltiwanger. 1991. "Wage Dispersion between and within U.S. Manufacturing Plants, 1963-1986." NBER Working Paper 3722, National Bureau of Economic Research, Cambridge, MA.

De Ferranti, D., G. Perry, F. Ferreira, and M. Waltin. 2004. *Inequality in Latin America: Breaking with History?* Washington, DC: World Bank.

De la Torre, A., G. Beylis, and A. Ize. 2015. *Jobs, Wages and the Latin American Slowdown: Latin America and the Caribbean Semiannual Report* (October). Washington, DC: World Bank.

De la Torre, A., and A. Ize. 2016. "Employment, Wages, Distribution, and the Latin American Deceleration." Background paper, World Bank, Washington, DC.

De la Torre, A., J. Messina, and S. Pienknagura. 2012. "The Labor Market Story Behind Latin America's Transformation." Semiannual Report (October). Office of the Regional Chief Economist, Latin America and the Caribbean, World Bank, Washington, DC.

De la Torre, A., E. Yeyati, G. Beylis, T. Didier, C. Rodríguez-Castelán, and S. Schmukler. 2014. *Inequality in a Lower Growth Latin America.* Semiannual Report (October). Office of the Regional Chief Economist, Latin America and the Caribbean. Washington, DC: World Bank.

Fernández, M., and J. Messina. 2017. "Skill Premium, Labor Supply and Changes in the Structure of Wages in Latin America." IDB Working Paper 786, Inter-American Development Bank, Washington, DC.

Ferreira, F. H. G., S. P. Firpo, and J. Messina. 2017. "Ageing Poorly? Accounting for the Decline in Earnings Inequality in Brazil, 1995-2012." Policy Research Working Paper 8018, World Bank, Washington, DC.

Ferreyra, M. M., C. Avitabile, J. Botero Alvarez, F. Haimovich Paz, and S. Urzúa. 2016. *At a Crossroads: Higher Education in Latin America and the Caribbean.* Directions in Development: Human Development Series. Washington, DC: World Bank.

Frías, J. A., D. S. Kaplan, and E. A. Verhoogen. 2009. "Exports and Wage Premia: Evidence from Mexican Employer-Employee Data." Columbia University. Unpublished.

Gasparini, L., and G. Cruces. 2013. "Poverty and Inequality in Latin America: A Story of Two Decades." *Journal of International Affairs* 66 (2): 51-63.

Gasparini, L., and N. Lustig. 2011. "The Rise and Fall of Income Inequality in Latin America." Working Paper 1110, Tulane University, New Orleans.

Goldin, C., and L. F. Katz. 2007. "Long-Run Changes in the U.S. Wage Structure: Narrowing, Widening, Polarizing." NBER Working Paper 13568, National Bureau of Economic Research, Cambridge, MA.

Gonzaga, G., N. O Menezes-Filho, and C. Terra. 2006. "Trade Liberalization and the Evolution of Skill Earnings Differentials in Brazil." *Journal of International Economics* 68 (2): 345-67.

Gruetter, M., and R. Lalive. 2009. "The Importance of Firms in Wage Determination." *Labour Economics* 16 (2): 149-60.

Heckman, J. J. 1977. "Sample Selection Bias as a Specification Error (with an Application to the Estimation of Labor Supply Functions)." NBER Working Paper 172, National Bureau of Economic Research, Cambridge, MA.

Helpman, E., O. Itskhoki, and S. Redding. 2010. "Inequality and Unemployment in a Global Economy." *Econometrica* 78 (4): 1239-83.

ILO (International Labour Organization). 2010/11. *Global Wage Report 2010/11: Wage Policies in Times of Crisis.* Geneva: International Labour Office.

Karabarbounis, L., and B. Neiman. 2014. "The Global Decline of the Labor Share." *Quarterly Journal of Economics* 129 (1): 61-103.

Katz, L., and K. Murphy. 1992. "Changes in Relative Wages, 1963-1987: Supply and Demand Factors." *Quarterly Journal of Economics* 107 (1): 35-78.

Lakner, C., and B. Milanovic. 2013. "Global Income Distribution: From the Fall of the Berlin Wall to the Great Recession." Policy Research Working Paper 6719, World Bank, Washington, DC.

Lemieux, T. 2006. "Increasing Residual Wage Inequality: Composition Effects, Noisy Data, or Rising Demand for Skill?" *American Economic Review* 96 (3): 461-98.

Lerman, R. I., and S. Yitzhaki. 1985. "Income Inequality Effects by Income Source: A New Approach and Applications to the United States." *Review of Economics and Statistics* 67 (1): 151–56.

Levy, S., and L. F. López-Calva. 2016. "Labor Earnings, Misallocation, and the Returns to Education." World Bank, Washington, DC.

López-Calva, L., and N. Lustig, eds. 2010. *Declining Inequality in Latin America: A Decade of Progress?* Washington, DC: Brookings Institution and United Nations Development Programme.

Manacorda, M., C. Sánchez-Páramo, and N. Schady. 2010. "Changes in Returns to Education in Latin America: The Role of Demand and Supply of Skills." *Industrial & Labor Relations Review* 63 (2): 307–26.

Messina, J. 2017. "The Market for Skills: Beyond Supply and Demand." In *Learning Better: Public Policy for Skills Development,* edited by M. J. Busso, M. J. Cristia, D. Hincapié, J. Messina, and L. Ripani. Washington, DC: Inter-American Development Bank.

Milanovic, B. 2016. *Global Inequality: A New Approach for the Age of Globalization.* Cambridge, MA: Harvard University Press.

Ñopo, H., N. Daza, and J. Ramos. 2012. "Gender Earnings Gaps in the World: A Study of 64 Countries." *International Journal of Manpower* 33 (5): 464–513.

Paes de Barros, R., M. Foguel, and G. Ulyssea. 2007. *Desigualdade de Renda do Brasil: Uma análise de queda recente.* Brasilia: Institute for Applied Economic Research (IPEA).

Piketty, T. 2014. *Capital in the Twenty-First Century.* Cambridge, MA: Harvard University Press.

Rodríguez-Castelán, C., L. F. López-Calva, N. Lustig, and D. Valderrama. 2016. "Understanding the Dynamics of Labor Income Inequality in Latin America." Policy Research Working Paper 7795, World Bank, Washington, DC.

Székely, M., and M. Hilgert. 1999. "The 1990s in Latin America: Another Decade of Persistent Inequality." Working Paper No. 410, Inter-American Development Bank, Washington, DC.

Székely, M., and P. Mendoza. 2015. "Is the Decline in Inequality in Latin America Here to Stay?" *Journal of Human Development and Capabilities* 16 (3): 397–419.

Theil, H. 1967. *Economics and Information Theory.* Chicago: Rand McNally and Company.

Williamson, J. G. 2015. "Latin American Inequality: Colonial Origins, Commodity Booms, or a Missed 20th Century Leveling?" NBER Working Paper 20915, National Bureau of Economic Research, Cambridge, MA.

World Bank. 2011. "A Break with History: Fifteen Years of Inequality Reduction in Latin America." LCSPP Poverty and Labor Brief No. 2, World Bank, Washington, DC.

———. 2015a. "Social Protection for the Harder Road Ahead: Containing the Social Costs of Lower Growth in Latin America and the Caribbean." Working Paper 100298, World Bank, Washington, DC.

———. 2015b. "Working to End Poverty in Latin America and the Caribbean: Workers, Jobs, and Wages." LAC Poverty and Labor Brief (June). World Bank, Washington, DC.

3

The Role of Labor Supply in Wage Inequality Trends

Introduction

As chapter 2 has outlined, labor supply trends evolve differently across levels of schooling. The share of the workforce that had completed high school increased steadily during the past two decades, while the share of potential workers with only basic skills, as proxied by primary education or less, declined. Expanded access to education across Latin America increased the skilled (highly educated) labor supply, which in turn exerted downward pressure on wage inequality by decreasing the earnings premium for skill (Azevedo, Inchauste, and Sanfelice 2013; Cornia 2014; Gasparini et al. 2011; Gasparini and Lustig 2011; López-Calva and Lustig 2010; Lustig, López-Calva, and Ortiz-Juárez 2013).

This chapter contributes to this literature by discussing how expanded access to education helped reduce wage inequality in Latin America. It also offers new hypotheses on the determinants of changes in the skill premium as well as the channels through which such determinants were transmitted. Specifically, it seeks to answer the following questions: What is the relative importance of the increasing supply of education (skills), including tertiary education, in determining the trajectory of labor income inequality since the mid-1990s? And through which channels have such factors operated?

Changes in the structure of wages can be linked to (1) changes in the distribution of the observable characteristics of workers (such as age, years of schooling, race, gender, working in formal or informal markets, earnings above or below minimum wages, and geographic location); and (2) changes in returns to those characteristics.[1]

An important finding of existing studies is that changes in the distribution in education, keeping constant the returns to schooling, have tended to be unequalizing. This is the case in spite of the fact that the distribution of educational attainment has become more equal.[2] This means that, had the pay structure by education level remained unchanged, the more-equal distribution of the education endowment would have resulted in an *increase* in labor income inequality. Because this sounds counter-intuitive, this finding is known as the "paradox of progress,"[3] which is, essentially, a by-product of the convexity of returns: when returns to education are convex, there can be an inverse relationship between inequality of education and income inequality. Eventually, as the dispersion of years of schooling becomes smaller and smaller, this paradoxical result will disappear.

In contrast, available evidence suggests that a fall in the returns to human capital—or, more precisely, in the returns to education—is a common factor in explaining the decline in hourly labor income inequality (Azevedo, Inchauste, and Sanfelice 2013; Barros et al. 2010; Campos-Vázquez, López-Calva, and Lustig 2016; Cornia 2014; De la Torre, Messina, and Pienknagura 2012; Fernández and Messina 2017; Ferreira, Firpo, and Messina 2017; Gasparini and Cruces 2010). In particular, during the 2000s, wherever overall inequality declined, the returns to primary, secondary, and tertiary education versus no schooling or incomplete primary schooling also declined. In Brazil, Ecuador, Nicaragua, and Paraguay, the returns declined for all levels of education relative to no schooling or incomplete primary education, while in Costa Rica a decline was reported only for the return to primary education versus no schooling or incomplete primary, and in Uruguay only for the return to tertiary education (Lustig, López-Calva, and Ortiz-Juárez 2013).

In addition to focusing on the impact of changes in the *quantity* of education on the wage structure, this chapter will analyze other supply-side hypotheses based on the *quality* and the *composition* of the supply of education. One such hypothesis, the "degraded tertiary" hypothesis (Campos-Vázquez, López-Calva, and Lustig 2016), posits that the notable expansion of coverage in postprimary education could have been accompanied by increasing variation in the quality of education centers, pushing the average quality of postprimary education downward, especially at the tertiary level. If this were true, the reduction in the education premium would show up predominantly for younger workers. Alternatively, Campos-Vázquez, López-Calva, and Lustig (2016) consider that the reduction in returns to tertiary education could have been fueled by an acceleration of skill obsolescence among older workers as they get displaced by technology or by younger workers who are less costly and also more adroit at using the new technologies. Based on results by Camacho, Messina, and Uribe (2016) for Colombia; Campos-Vázquez, López-Calva, and Lustig (2016) for Mexico; and Wang (2015) for Brazil, this section discusses and presents new evidence on the validity of the degraded tertiary hypothesis and the magnitude and importance of this effect for inequality dynamics.

Another supply-side hypothesis concerns the composition of the supply of educated workers. Demographic changes have increased the share of older workers whose skills might have depreciated more rapidly as new technologies have been adopted, and this effect could very well outweigh the wage premium of work experience. The next section presents new results on this phenomenon in Mexico (Campos-Vázquez, López-Calva, and Lustig 2016) and Brazil (Wang 2015) and discusses whether the relative decline of older workers' wages has been widespread in Latin America (Fernández and Messina 2017).

Skill Supply and Demand in the Determination of Relative Wages

As mentioned above, existing studies suggest that one of the main factors underlying the decline in earnings inequality was the reduction of the education premium (the wage returns for college education, equating here to "skill"). In a basic labor supply-and-demand framework, increases in the supply of skilled workers translate into reductions in the skill premium unless the demand for skills is increasing as well. This process will reduce the inequality of earnings, because differences in education are the main observed factor behind earnings inequality.

The supply-and-demand framework has been useful in explaining the evolution of the education premium in the United States (Autor, Katz, and Krueger 1998; Katz and Murphy 1992). In Latin America during the 1990s, the college premium increased in spite of a rapid increase of college graduates. Hence, demand for high skills must have outpaced shifts in supply (Manacorda, Sánchez-Páramo, and Schady 2010).

López-Calva and Lustig (2010) posit that the most important factor behind the decline in the returns to education has been a relative increase of workers with completed secondary and tertiary education—a result of the significant educational upgrading in the region during the 1990s (Cruces, Domench, and Gasparini 2012). In Brazil and Mexico, there have been notable changes in the composition of the labor supply, and an increase in the relative supply of skilled workers seems to be the dominant factor explaining the decline in the skill premium (Barros et al. 2010; Campos-Vázquez, López-Calva, and Lustig 2016; Esquivel, Lustig, and Scott 2010). In Argentina, the reduction in the skill premium appears to be related not just to the change in the composition of labor by skills but also to the employment effects of a booming economy (Gasparini and Cruces 2010).

However, Gasparini et al. (2011) use a partial equilibrium framework to study the supply and demand for labor in 16 countries in Latin America during 1989–2009, and they reach a different conclusion. They assume a production function with an elasticity of substitution between skilled and unskilled labor for different values and find that, more often than not, demand-side factors dominate supply-side explanations for the decline in skill premiums.[4]

From a methodological point of view, it is not an easy task to determine whether demand or supply factors were predominant. A comparison of the results for Mexico between Gasparini et al. (2011) and Campos-Vázquez, López-Calva, and Lustig (2016), for example, reveals that the results are sensitive to the age cohorts of workers, the period under study, and above all, the elasticity of substitution between skilled and unskilled workers. Our analysis in the next section will shed more light on this discussion.

Comovement of Labor Supply, Skill Premium, and Relative Wage Changes

A less-well-known fact is that, in many countries, both the skill premium and relative wages have evolved quite differently across birth cohorts in the past two decades (Fernández and Messina 2017). Figure 3.1, panel a, shows the evolution in Argentina, Brazil, Chile, and Mexico of the high school premium (relative to workers with primary education or less) for three potential work experience groups: those with 0–4 years, 15–19 years, and 25–29 years of work experience. In all four countries it is quite evident that the skill premium (in this case, for a high school education) declined during the 1990–2010 period. However, this trend is far from homogeneous across workers born in different years. In Argentina, Brazil, and Mexico, the wage premium for highly experienced workers (25–29 years of potential experience in the labor market) declined much more rapidly than the wage premium for young workers (0–4 years of potential experience in the labor market).[5]

The relative skill supply across workers in different birth cohorts has also evolved at different speeds (figure 3.1, panel b). In Mexico, for example, the share of high school graduates in the workforce increased relative to the share of workers with less than secondary education among all experience groups, but the changes were much more abrupt across those workers with more experience. Thus, relative supply changes appear to be connected to relative wages. In the case of Mexico, it was precisely the wages of the more-experienced workers that fell more than proportionally as well (Campos-Vázquez, López-Calva, and Lustig 2016).

If we concentrate on college graduates, the share of workers who were highly experienced (25–29 years of experience) increased much more rapidly than the share of those who were inexperienced (0–4 years of experience) in Brazil, Chile, and Mexico (figure 3.2). As predicted by the supply-demand model, earnings across experience groups appear to respond to changes in labor supply. The earnings of college-educated workers with more experience increased more slowly (or declined faster, depending on the country) than the earnings of those with little experience (figure 3.2).

The role of experience is not explicitly considered in the Katz and Murphy (1992) framework, which Gasparini et al. (2011) applied to several Latin American countries. The underlying assumption in this framework is that all workers within an educational group are perfect substitutes—an assumption supported by the evidence discussed in Manacorda, Sánchez-Páramo, and Schady (2010) for selected Latin American countries during the 1990s. However, our previous discussion suggests that the 2000s may have been different, and changes in relative supply within birth cohorts may have changed the evolution of relative wages.

FIGURE 3.1: **Wage Premium and Relative Labor Supply for High School vs. Primary Education, by Work Experience Level, Selected Latin American Countries**

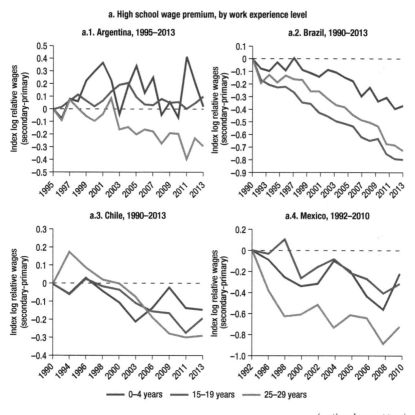

a. High school wage premium, by work experience level

a.1. Argentina, 1995–2013

a.2. Brazil, 1990–2013

a.3. Chile, 1990–2013

a.4. Mexico, 1992–2010

—— 0–4 years —— 15–19 years —— 25–29 years

(continued on next page)

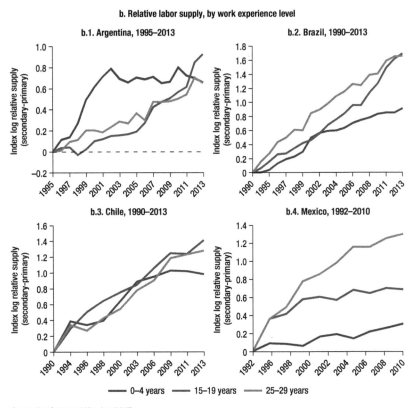

b. Relative labor supply, by work experience level

b.1. Argentina, 1995–2013

b.2. Brazil, 1990–2013

b.3. Chile, 1990–2013

b.4. Mexico, 1992–2010

— 0–4 years — 15–19 years — 25–29 years

Source: Fernández and Messina (2017).

The Supply-Demand Framework at Work

In investigating the role of labor supply changes in the skill premium, we explicitly take into account differences across education levels and cohorts. In what follows, firms are assumed to use a production technology that requires two labor inputs: skilled and unskilled workers. In a background paper for this study, Fernández and Messina (2017), building on previous work by Manacorda, Sánchez-Páramo, and Schady (2010), assume that high school graduates and workers with primary education or less are "unskilled," although the former may be more productive. By contrast, "skilled" workers are those with postsecondary education.

FIGURE 3.2: **Change in the Share of the Workforce and Wages of College-Educated Workers, by Country and Experience Level, Selected Latin American Countries**

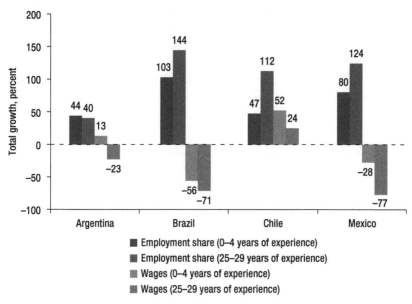

■ Employment share (0–4 years of experience)
■ Employment share (25–29 years of experience)
■ Wages (0–4 years of experience)
■ Wages (25–29 years of experience)

Source: Fernández and Messina (2017).
Note: Data periods are as follows: Argentina, 1995–2013; Brazil, 1990–2013; Chile, 1990–2013; and Mexico, 1992–2012.

Moreover, workers with different levels of labor market experience within each subgroup are imperfect substitutes. Hence, within each skill category, firms may choose to produce with more-inexperienced workers, for example, but those workers are neither as equally productive as, nor perfect substitutes for, more-experienced employees. This may be the case because the less-experienced workers need to be trained and supervised on their jobs while they acquire the necessary on-the-job knowledge. Both the relative productivity and the extent of substitutability between more- and less-experienced workers are estimated in the model.[6]

The Supply Inequality Framework at Work

Using this model, the results show that changes in labor supply are important but not sufficient to explain the declining inequality trends in Latin America. The "observed" line in figure 3.3 shows the evolution of the skill premium in Argentina, Brazil, Chile, and Mexico. The figure also shows the goodness of fit of two models. The first model builds a counterfactual evolution of the skill premium as predicted by changes in the relative *supply* of skilled and unskilled workers. The second shows the model's predictions once changes in labor *demand* are allowed for.

As figure 3.3 shows, the model that limits the variation of the skill premium to changes in the labor *supply* tends to overpredict the reduction of the skill premium. This model fails to predict the increase in the skill premium during the first half of the period (approximately up to 2002). It then subsequently understates the decline in the wage premium in the four countries after 2002. This is a marked pattern in Argentina, Chile, and Mexico. Changes in the labor supply do a better job of tracking the decline in the skill premium in Brazil than in the other countries, because there is no increase in Brazil's wage premium during the 2000s.

FIGURE 3.3: Skill Premium in Selected Latin American Countries: Observed and Simulated Data

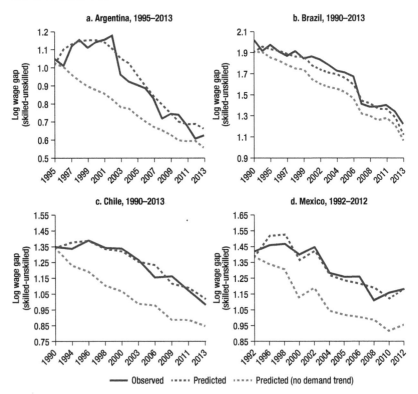

Source: Authors' estimates based on Fernández and Messina (2017).
Note: "Skilled" refers to workers with postsecondary education. "Unskilled" refers to workers with primary education or less. "Predicted (no demand trend)" refers to a simulation based only on changes in the relative supply of skilled and unskilled workers. "Predicted" refers to a simulation that also takes into account changes in labor demand.

By contrast, the model in which *demand* changes are introduced produces a much better fit of the data.

The importance of the shifting demand for skilled labor to account for changes in the skill premium is better illustrated in figure 3.4, which shows the evolution of the demand for skill as predicted by the model. In the four countries, the demand for skill increased up to a turning point around 2000–03, after which demand declined in all four countries. By the end of the period, the level of relative demand for skilled labor in Brazil and Mexico was only 10 percent above its level of the 1990s. In Argentina and Chile, the reduction of demand for skilled labor was smaller, and by 2012 the level of relative demand was around 20 percent above the level predicted for the early 1990s.

Thus, we conclude that it is hard to square the evolution of the skill premium with changes in the labor supply alone. A slowdown in the *demand* for skilled labor also appears to be an important driver of falling inequality in Latin America during the 2000s.

What's the role of the supply of experience in the evolution of the experience premium? As we saw in chapter 2, the experience premium fell during the 2000s. The model of Fernández and Messina (2017) attributes an important role to population aging in the observed decline in the premiums, in particular among low-skilled workers.

FIGURE 3.4: **Changes in Demand for Skill, Selected Latin American Countries, 1990–2013**

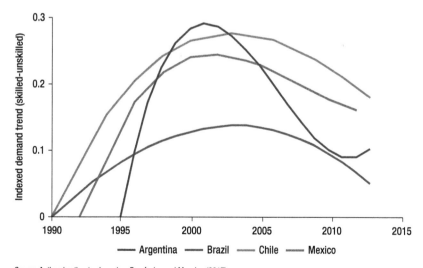

Source: Authors' estimates based on Fernández and Messina (2017).
Note: "Skill" refers to workers with postsecondary education.

In the case of high-skilled workers the model can't reject perfect substitution among experience groups, although the estimates are very imprecise. As we shall see in the next section, there are reasons to believe demand for labor market experience among college-educated workers may be changing too.

Falling Wages of Recent Cohorts of College-Educated Workers: Degraded Tertiary versus Skill Obsolescence

In the context of high economic growth during the 2000s in Latin America, the reduction of the education premium was expected because the wages of unskilled workers grew faster than the wages of skilled workers. However, this was not the case in all Latin American countries. As discussed in chapter 2, the wages of unskilled workers (those with primary education or less) grew strongly in virtually all countries. By contrast, the wages of skilled workers (defined in this section as college graduates) fell in real terms in Chile and Mexico. These trends contrast sharply with those in the developed world, where the wages of skilled individuals have grown much faster than the wages of the unskilled.

A possible explanation for the decline of real wages of college graduates is that the rapid expansion of the region's education systems may have degraded the value of higher-education diplomas for any of the following reasons:

- Stress on the system generates congestion in the classrooms and lowers the average quality of all new graduates.

- The system has problems adapting the curricula to rapidly changing demand for skills, resulting in increasing mismatches of skills to jobs.

- The increase in demand for higher education has triggered an unorderly expansion of higher-education institutions, and some new institutions offer diplomas with lower value added, resulting in lower market premiums.

- Expansion of the system implies that marginal students accessing higher education are of lower ability. If the higher education system does not play a levelling role, the implication is that some graduates will exit the system with a lower skill set.

All of these proposed reasons relate to some form of the "degraded tertiary" hypothesis, to use the term proposed by Campos-Vázquez, López-Calva, and Lustig (2016). The average (relative) returns to tertiary education could have fallen because, as its coverage expanded, either the quality of the marginal institutions, the quality of the marginal students, or both, decreased. This hypothesis has received some attention in the literature. Carneiro and Lee (2011) show that increases in enrollment of college graduates in the United States between 1960 and 2000 led to a decline in the average quality, resulting in a decrease of 6 percentage points in the college premium.

Castro and Yamada (2012) find evidence that the "convexification" of the wage-education profile (as a consequence of the low quality of basic education and the better quality of tertiary education) began reversing starting in the 2000s. The authors argue that this finding is consistent with the decreasing quality of tertiary education observed during the past 10 years.

Using a completely different approach, Reyes, Rodríguez, and Urzúa (2013) find that a significant proportion of college graduates (35–42 percent, depending on the degree and the institution) obtain negative net economic returns from their investments. These findings—complemented with income data that show that the gap between the cost and the benefits of tertiary education depends on the quality of that education (World Bank 2011)—suggest that the quality of certain types of tertiary education has reduced the skill premium in Chile.

The increasing mismatch between the supply of and demand for skills has also been recently documented. In the case of secondary education, a study of Argentina, Brazil, and Chile finds that the skill premium for secondary education declined because of a mismatch between (1) the skills acquired by workers who go directly from secondary education to the labor market, and (2) the skills required by the labor market that hires these workers (Bassi et al. 2012).

It is worth noting that declines in the quality of graduates as a result of rapid expansion of the education system are not exclusive to postsecondary education and have been noted in other contexts. Filmer and Schady (2011) show evidence suggesting that the expansion of high school enrollment induced by conditional cash transfers (CCTs) has reduced the quality of education for these students, since there is no evidence that test scores or wages of the "CCT generation" are higher.

An alternative to the "degraded tertiary" hypothesis suggests that, in a context of rapid technological change, the college wage premium may fall for those individuals whose skills are either rapidly depreciating or being replaced by machines. Chapter 4 will further discuss skill-biased technological change and search for direct evidence of skill redundancies. For now, it is enough to say that some skills may become obsolete as a consequence of technological change. In this context, workers who have a harder time readapting their skills to the new market demands would see their labor market prospects deteriorate. We call this the "skill obsolescence effect," following Campos-Vázquez, López-Calva, and Lustig (2016).

The "degraded tertiary" and "skill obsolescence" hypotheses have different predictions. The "degraded tertiary" hypothesis suggests that the wages of young college graduates should be negatively affected, either against younger workers with lower education or against older workers who attended university. "Skill obsolescence" can occur in workers of all ages, but older workers are more likely to be affected. Workers gain a mix of general and occupation- or sector-specific skills as they acquire experience in the labor market. If occupation- or sector-specific skills depreciate rapidly—for example, because of the introduction of computers in the workplace—the more-experienced workers are more likely to see their skills depreciate.

Mean Log Hourly Wages of College-Educated Males in Mexico, by Birth Cohort, 2000–15
(2014 local currency units)

Birth year	2000	2002	2004	2006	2008	2010	2012	2014	2015
1985–89	n.a.	n.a.	n.a.	n.a.	n.a.	3.56	3.54	3.59	3.68
1980–84	n.a.	n.a.	n.a.	3.74	3.74	3.72	3.77	3.77	3.74
1975–79	3.75	3.83	3.86	3.92	3.92	3.86	3.89	3.87	3.87
1970–74	3.96	4.06	4.01	4.05	4.05	3.98	3.96	3.93	3.92
1965–69	4.12	4.14	4.08	4.13	4.13	3.97	3.95	3.93	3.97
1960–64	4.11	4.13	4.11	4.16	4.16	4.03	3.96	3.96	3.94
1955–59	4.17	4.22	4.18	4.16	4.16	4.01	4.00	3.89	3.95
1950–54	4.29	4.28	4.19	4.25	4.25	4.14	3.99	3.93	3.85

Source: Campos-Vázquez, López-Calva, and Lustig (2016).
Note: Earnings are obtained from labor force surveys and are expressed in 2014 local currency units. Earnings refer to full-time workers (at least 30 weekly hours of work) with a valid wage. The table includes workers with a college education: salaried, self-employed, and employers. Earnings below and above the 1st and 99th percentile (within gender and education group) are dropped. Sample restricted to male workers between 23–65 years old. n.a. = not available.

Using Mexican data for 2000–15, Campos-Vázquez, López-Calva, and Lustig (2016) investigate which of the two channels—degraded tertiary value or skill obsolescence—carries more weight. Table 3.1, reproduced from that work, shows the wage evolution of college-educated males in Mexico over the 15-year period for workers born in different cohorts.

The first interesting finding is that the wages of the oldest cohort (born 1950–54) decline by 10 percent. Similar patterns are observed for cohorts born between 1955 and 1969. In contrast, wages of the youngest cohort (1985–89) show modest gains (3 percent).

These results are in line with the skill obsolescence hypothesis. However, entry wages for the youngest cohorts decline relative to those of their immediate predecessors, perhaps suggesting degraded tertiary effects. Unfortunately, the youngest cohort we can observe in the data entered the labor market in 2010 and was thus affected by the global financial crisis that hit Mexico particularly hard. As usual with cohort analyses, disentangling time, age, and cohort effects is challenging, particularly when the temporal dimension is relatively short.

We extend the analysis to include the Mexican sample back to 1986 using an alternative data set (from the National Household Income and Expenditure Survey, ENIGH) as well as data for Argentina and Brazil. In the case of Mexico, the decline in entry wages of young college-educated workers appears to be a long-term trend dating to the 1990s, a feature that suggests degraded tertiary effects (table 3.2).

TABLE 3.2: **Mean Log Hourly Wages of College-Educated Males in Selected Latin American Countries, by Birth Cohort, 1986–2011** *(2005 local currency units)*

Birth year	a. Argentina						b. Brazil						c. Mexico					
	1986	1991	1996	2001	2006	2011	1986	1991	1996	2001	2006	2011	1986	1991	1996	2001	2006	2011
1982–86	n.a	n.a	n.a	n.a	n.a	2.43	n.a	n.a	n.a	n.a	n.a	2.09	n.a	n.a	n.a	n.a	n.a	3.35
1977–81	n.a	n.a	n.a	n.a	1.85	2.77	n.a	n.a	n.a	n.a	2.05	2.36	n.a	n.a	n.a	n.a	3.54	3.69
1972–76	n.a	n.a	n.a	1.85	2.06	2.70	n.a	n.a	n.a	2.09	2.33	2.53	n.a	n.a	n.a	3.66	3.85	3.85
1967–71	n.a	n.a	2.30	2.28	2.18	2.72	n.a	n.a	2.30	2.39	2.46	2.50	n.a	n.a	3.50	3.92	3.90	3.98
1962–66	n.a	2.13	2.16	2.31	2.10	2.79	n.a	1.80	2.61	2.57	2.67	2.57	n.a	3.86	3.81	3.94	4.01	3.89
1957–61	2.39	2.63	2.42	2.42	2.21	2.76	2.53	1.94	2.76	2.68	2.69	2.83	3.95	4.20	3.80	4.06	3.97	3.79
1952–56	2.59	2.36	2.69	2.41	2.30	2.83	2.93	2.02	2.94	2.70	2.75	2.90	3.99	4.34	3.95	4.17	4.05	4.00
1947–51	2.86	2.61	2.43	2.53	2.32	2.74	3.09	2.12	3.01	2.85	2.75	2.84	4.29	4.30	4.14	4.09	4.02	3.60
1942–46	3.17	2.24	2.63	2.48	2.24	2.28	3.19	2.08	3.06	2.88	2.81	3.09	4.18	4.63	4.13	4.51	3.79	2.73
1937–41	3.08	2.54	2.45	2.45	2.07	n.a	3.04	1.97	3.11	3.13	2.53	n.a	4.00	4.63	4.03	4.38	4.16	n.a
1932–36	3.07	2.58	2.73	2.57	n.a	n.a	3.16	1.87	3.16	3.13	n.a	n.a	4.42	4.35	4.30	4.74	n.a	n.a
1927–31	2.84	2.77	3.21	n.a	n.a	n.a	3.25	1.95	2.76	n.a	n.a	n.a	4.23	4.71	3.35	n.a	n.a	n.a
1924–26	2.62	2.79	n.a	n.a	n.a	n.a	3.18	1.61	n.a	n.a	n.a	n.a	4.36	n.a	n.a	n.a	n.a	n.a

Source: Calculations based on Socio-Economic Database for Latin America and the Caribbean (SEDLAC), Universidad Nacional de la Plata (CEDLAS) and the World Bank (http://sedlac.econo.unlp.edu.ar/eng/) and the National Household Income and Expenditure Survey (ENIGH).

Note: Sample includes college-educated males who are 25–65 years old and are full-time workers (employers, self-employed, or salaried). n.a = not available.

The results for Argentina and Brazil suggest a mixed picture, with signs of both skill obsolescence and degraded tertiary effects. As in Mexico, the wages of older cohorts in Argentina declined more rapidly than the wages of younger workers over the 1986–2011 period, although the decline in Argentina is not as marked as in Mexico if we exclude the first year of observation (1986), when average wages are very unreliable because of hyperinflation. Even so, entry wages for college graduates in Argentina have gradually declined over time—except for the most recent cohort. As for Brazil, the wages of college graduates have remained relatively stable across cohorts. However, Wang (2015) finds that the variance of wages of young Brazilian cohorts increased during the past decade, a feature consistent with a degraded tertiary hypothesis.

The Degraded Tertiary Effect

Disentangling the causes behind either a degraded tertiary effect or skill obsolescence is not straightforward. The policy implications are naturally very different depending on which factor carries more weight in explaining the change in the skill premium. Chapter 4 will describe possible sources of skill obsolescence, presenting evidence of technological change and how it has affected the demand for tasks performed in the workplace. The remainder of this section instead sheds further light on the possible sources of a degraded tertiary effect.

As discussed earlier, a decline in the value added of a higher education diploma may be related to both supply and demand factors. A decline in the quality of demand for college education (stemming from lower-ability students accessing the system) would require very different remedies than a deterioration of supply (which may require direct action to improve the quality of higher education institutions). Results from a case study in Colombia can help to separate the key forces underlying a possible degraded tertiary effect.

Camacho, Messina, and Uribe (2016) exploit rich administrative data in Colombia to tease out supply and demand factors in a possible degradation of the higher education diploma. Colombia constitutes a good case study because the country experienced a rapid expansion in the demand for higher education and a deterioration of the college degree. In fact, high school graduation rates increased more in Colombia than anywhere else in Latin America—rising from 20 percent in the early 1990s to 47 percent in the late 2000s, thus boosting the demand for higher education (figure 3.5, panel a).

As expected given the expansion of demand, the quality of the marginal student accessing higher education declined during the 2001–11 period, as suggested by the high school exit tests that provide access to higher education (currently the standardized Saber 11 test, administered before high school graduation in Colombia). The mean Saber 11 score percentile among the students accessing higher education declined by 10 percentage points between 1998 and 2010 (figure 3.5, panel b).

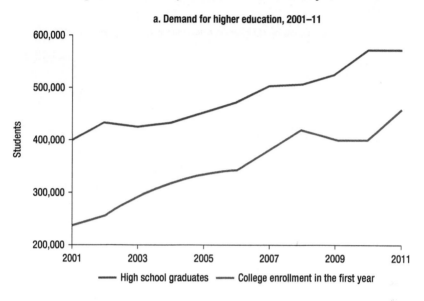

a. Demand for higher education, 2001–11

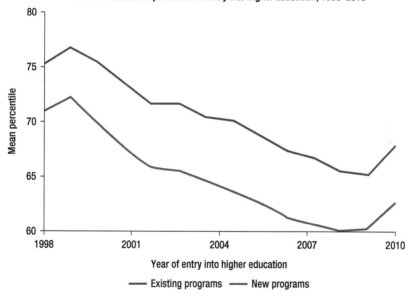

b. Mean test score percentile at entry into higher education, 1998–2010

(continued on next page)

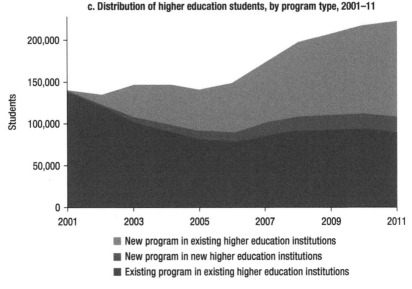

c. Distribution of higher education students, by program type, 2001–11

◼ New program in existing higher education institutions
◼ New program in new higher education institutions
◼ Existing program in existing higher education institutions

Source: Camacho, Messina, and Uribe (2016).
Note: "New programs" are those whose first graduate finished school in 2002 or after.

Moreover, the increase in demand was fundamentally accommodated by the creation of new programs. In response to the dramatic rise in the number of students, the number of higher education programs almost doubled during the 2000s—from 3,600 programs in 2001 to 6,276 programs in 2011 (figure 3.5, panel c).

Were these new programs of lower quality than existing programs? Answering this question requires taking into account that students are not randomly allocated to higher education institutions and programs. Instead, they self-sort according to (1) their preferred areas of study; (2) the availability or not of those studies in their region of residence (unless they have the means to commute); and (3) the expected wage returns, which may depend on their prospects of succeeding in each program, the reputation of the institution offering the program, and so on. At the same time, institutions and programs may be more or less selective of the students they choose to enroll. This warns against assessing programs' relative merits based on either simple comparisons of the average standardized-exam exit scores or the first-job wages of graduates from new and existing programs.

Consistent with the public concern raised by new higher education programs in Colombia, the students of newly created programs score worse on the college exit exams (Saber Pro) than do students of more-established programs. The differences in test scores between these groups of students range from 0.22 standard deviations (in written communication) to 0.33 standard deviations (in quantitative reasoning). Similarly, graduates from new programs have worse labor market outcomes. Their probability of having a formal job in the first 1-4 years after graduation is 4 percentage points lower (71 percent) than that of graduates from traditional programs (75 percent). They also earn about 15 percent less.

However, the students attending the newly created programs in Colombia are different from those attending traditional programs. In particular, more of them come from families of lower socioeconomic status. The share of high-income students (from families making five times the minimum wage or more) in the new programs is 13 percent, compared with 22 percent among those who attend traditional programs. The share of students of new programs with college-educated parents is 28 percent, 11 percentage points lower than the share of those who attended traditional programs.

Figure 3.6 shows the impact of attending one of Colombia's newly created higher education programs on test scores (Saber Pro), on wages, and on the probability of being a formal worker after graduation:

- *Effect on test scores.* The exit test scores of graduates from traditional programs are 0.32 standard deviations higher than the scores of graduates from new programs (red bar). However, those differences virtually disappear once we consider that students from disadvantaged backgrounds are likelier to attend the new programs and that these new programs are concentrated in degrees with low returns.[7] The impact of attending a new program declines to −0.06 standard deviations after controlling for a full set of student characteristics including socioeconomic background, the high school attended, and the standardized exam scores upon entry into higher education (blue bar). Adding a full set of higher education institution characteristics (most notably, the area of study) further reduces the impact to −0.04 (yellow bar).

- *Effect on entry wage.* Graduates from new programs earn, on average, 14 percent less in their first jobs than graduates of traditional programs. However, the difference declines to 3 percent once graduates with similar characteristics who graduate from the same area of studies are compared.

- *Effect on formal employment.* The probability of being a formal worker is virtually the same between the graduates of old and new programs once students from similar backgrounds and attending similar areas of study are compared.

Impact of Attending a Newly Created Higher Education Program in Colombia, 2008–11

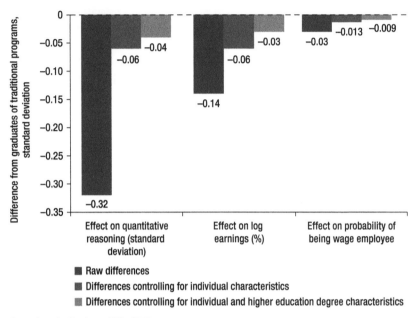

Source: Camacho, Messina, and Uribe (2016).
Note:. "Newly created" higher education programs are those whose first graduate finished school in 2002 or after.

We conclude that the recent expansion in the demand for higher education in Colombia does not seem to have been accompanied by a degraded supply. Once we compare similar students in similar areas of study, the returns of attending a newly created program do not differ much from the returns of attending traditional, well-established programs. This is perhaps surprising, considering the rapid expansion of Colombia's higher education system. More than 50 percent of the 2011 graduates graduated from a program introduced during the previous decade.

However, Colombia was an early adopter of quality controls in the higher education system. Starting in 2003, minimum quality standards were required to set up a new program. In addition, a certification of excellence was put in place. Camacho, Messina, and Uribe (2016) provide further evidence that these accreditation systems were effective. This, in turn, should put caution into extrapolating these results to other countries in the region, particularly those countries where quality controls are not in place. More research is needed to understand how the quality of higher education institutions has evolved in other countries of the region.

Conclusions

This chapter has focused on supply-side factors (such as the relative supply of workers by education and experience levels) and their association with wage inequality trends. The channels through which these factors operate are, in the first instance, pure changes in endowments (that is, in the composition of the labor force), and changes in the wage structure (that is, in the returns to observable characteristics of workers). Fernández and Messina (2017) show that the endowment effects for experience are small, but for education are strongly unequalizing, while the wage-structure effects (the returns to education and experience) are equalizing. If the endowment effects are unequalizing, this suggests that the region is still experiencing what Bourguignon, Ferreira, and Lustig (2005) called the "paradox of progress"—that is, because of the convexity of returns, an upgrading of education and a reduction in its distribution can be unequalizing during part of the upgrading period. More important, the paradox of progress implies that changes in the composition of the labor force, per se, cannot be the driving force of inequality dynamics in the region. If the wage-structure effects are equalizing, this opens the question of what factors may be behind recent changes in the returns to observable skills. This chapter has offered a detailed discussion of the array of forces that may have driven the decline in the skills premium.

The chapter finds that, although the expansion of the supply of workers with more education plays a systematic role in pushing down the education premium, this explanation is not enough to account for the full dynamics of relative wages observed during the past two decades. In particular, supply-side trends fail to capture the increase of the education premium observed in most Latin American countries during the 1990s. By contrast, it underpredicts the sharp decline of the 2000s. In conclusion, demand-side forces cannot be disregarded.

The chapter then concentrates on a particular stylized fact: the much slower growth (and, in some countries, declining growth) of earnings among college-educated workers during the 2000s. Two alternative hypotheses are discussed. First, if wages of college graduates are stagnant or declining because of a "degraded tertiary" effect, the relative losses should concentrate among the younger cohorts. Second, if instead rapid technological change is rendering obsolete some of the skills of college-educated workers, the losses are more likely to concentrate among the older cohorts. The evidence of these two channels is mixed. In Mexico, wage declines among college-educated workers are concentrated among older cohorts. In Argentina and Brazil, there are signs of falling demand for both older workers and very young college graduates.

The chapter ended with a discussion of the role of quality in higher education. The analysis for Colombia suggests that part of the decline in the education premium may be related to a deterioration of quality among the marginal students graduating from college. Such deterioration, in turn, is more associated with the expansion of the system (which has increasingly allowed students from less-favorable backgrounds to attend college) than with a decline in the quality of the postsecondary education programs offered by the higher education sector.

Notes

1. See the seminal paper by Oaxaca (1973) and all the rich literature that followed.

2. See Campos-Vázquez, López-Calva, and Lustig (2016); Fernández and Messina (2017); and Ferreira, Firpo, and Messina (2017).

3. The term was introduced by Bourguignon, Ferreira, and Lustig (2005). For a formal explanation, see the section entitled "Education and Inequality: The Paradox of Progress" in chapter 10 of that work.

4. This study uses the methodology developed by Katz and Murphy (1992) and Goldin and Katz (2007), who formalized the Tinbergen (1975) framework. A summary of these results can be found in Lustig, López-Calva, and Ortiz-Juárez (2013, table 1).

5. We refer to "potential experience" because the experience level is inferred based on schooling and age.

6. Highly educated workers (college) and less-educated workers (high school graduates and high school dropouts) are modeled as imperfect substitutes in a constant elasticity of substitution production function. Similarly, low- and high-experience workers are imperfect substitutes within the high- and low-education groups. A three-step procedure estimates the elasticities of substitution to construct measures of the supply of high- and low-skill workers. The estimated elasticities of substitution across schooling groups (around 2.3) and experience groups among low-educated workers (around 3.5) suggest imperfect substitutability across groups. The model uses the same elasticities in all three countries (Fernández and Messina 2017).

7. More than 60 percent of the programs offered in areas such as education, performing arts, and design were created in the 2000s. The returns in these areas rank among the lowest of all college degrees.

References

Autor, D., L. Katz, and A. Krueger. 1998. "Computing Inequality: Have Computers Changed the Labor Market?" *Quarterly Journal of Economics* 113 (4): 1169–214.

Azevedo, J., G. Inchauste, and V. Sanfelice. 2013. "Decomposing the Recent Inequality Decline in Latin America." Policy Research Working Paper 6715, World Bank, Washington, DC.

Barros, R., M. De Carvalho, S. Franco, and R. Mendonca. 2010. "Markets, the State and the Dynamics of Inequality in Brazil." In *Declining Inequality in Latin America: A Decade of Progress?* edited by L. F. López-Calva and N. Lustig. Washington, DC: Brookings Institution Press; New York: United Nations Development Programme.

Bassi, M., M. Busso, S. Urzúa, and J. Vargas. 2012. *Disconnected: Skills, Education and Employment in Latin America.* Washington, DC: Inter-American Development Bank.

Bourguignon, F., F. H. Ferreira, and N. Lustig, eds. 2005. *The Microeconomics of Income Distribution Dynamics in East Asia and Latin America.* Washington, DC: World Bank.

Camacho, A., J. Messina, and J. P. Uribe. 2016. "The Expansion of Higher Education in Colombia: Bad Students or Bad Programs?" IDB Discussion Paper 452, Inter-American Development Bank, Washington, DC. Available at: http://www.jsmessina.com/assets/papers/CMU.pdf.

Campos-Vázquez, R. M., L. F. López-Calva, and N. Lustig. 2016. "Declining Wages for College-Educated Workers in Mexico: Are Younger or Older Cohorts Hurt the Most?" Policy Research Working Paper 7546, World Bank, Washington, DC.

Carneiro, P., and S. Lee. 2011. "Trends in Quality-Adjusted Skill Premia in the US, 1960–2000." CEPR Discussion Paper No. DP8108, Centre for Economic Policy Research, London.

Castro, J., and G. Yamada. 2012. "'Convexification' and 'Deconvexification' of the Peruvian Wage Profile: A Tale of Declining Education Quality." Working Paper 12-02, Department of Economics, Universidad del Pacífico, Lima, Peru.

Cornia, G.A. 2014. "Inequality Trends and Their Determinants: Latin America over 1990–2010." In *Falling Inequality in Latin America: Policy Changes and Lessons*, edited by A. Cornia. UNU-WIDER Studies in Development Economics. Oxford, UK: Oxford University Press.

Cruces, G., C. García Domench, and L. Gasparini. 2012. "Inequality in Education: Evidence for Latin America." Working Paper 0135, Center for Distributive, Labor and Social Studies (CEDLAS), Universidad Nacional de La Plata, Argentina.

De la Torre, A., J. Messina, and S. Pienknagura. 2012. "The Labor Market Story Behind Latin America's Transformation." Semiannual Report (October). Office of the Regional Chief Economist, Latin America and the Caribbean, World Bank, Washington, DC.

Esquivel, G., N. Lustig, and J. Scott. 2010. "Mexico: A Decade of Falling Inequality—Market Forces or State Action?" In *Declining Inequality in Latin America: A Decade of Progress?* edited by Luis F. López-Calva and Nora Lustig. Washington, DC: Brookings Institution Press; New York: United Nations Development Programme.

Fernández, M., and J. Messina. 2017. "Skill Premium, Labor Supply and Changes in the Structure of Wages in Latin America." IDB Working Paper 786, Inter-American Development Bank, Washington, DC.

Ferreira, F. H. G, S. P. Firpo, and J. Messina. 2017. "Ageing Poorly? Accounting for the Decline in Earnings Inequality in Brazil, 1995–2012." Policy Research Working Paper 8018, World Bank, Washington, DC.

Filmer, D., and N. Schady. 2011. "Does More Cash in Conditional Cash Transfer Programs Always Lead to Larger Impacts on School Attendance?" *Journal of Development Economics* 96 (1): 150–57.

Gasparini, L., and G. Cruces. 2010. "A Distribution in Motion: The Case of Argentina." In *Declining Inequality in Latin America: A Decade of Progress?* edited by L. F. López-Calva and N. Lustig, 100–33. Washington, DC: Brookings Institution Press; New York: United Nations Development Programme.

Gasparini, L., S. Galiani, G. Cruces, and P. Acosta. 2011. "Educational Upgrading and Returns to Skills in Latin America: Evidence from a Supply-Demand Framework, 1990–2010." Policy Research Working Paper 5921, World Bank, Washington, DC.

Gasparini, L., and N. Lustig. 2011. "The Rise and Fall of Income Inequality in Latin America." Working Paper 1110, Tulane University, New Orleans.

Goldin, C., and L. F. Katz. 2007. "The Race between Education and Technology: The Evolution of U.S. Educational Wage Differentials, 1890 to 2005." Working Paper 12984, National Bureau of Economic Research, Cambridge, MA.

Katz, L., and K. Murphy. 1992. "Changes in Relative Wages, 1963–1987: Supply and Demand Factors." *Quarterly Journal of Economics* 107 (1): 35–78.

López-Calva, L. F., and N. Lustig, eds. 2010. *Declining Inequality in Latin America: A Decade of Progress?* Washington, DC: Brookings Institution Press; New York: United Nations Development Programme.

Lustig, N., L. F. López-Calva, and E. Ortiz-Juárez. 2013. "Declining Inequality in Latin America in the 2000s: The Cases of Argentina, Brazil, and Mexico." *World Development* 44 (C): 129–41.

Manacorda, M., C. Sánchez-Páramo, and N. Schady. 2010. "Changes in Returns to Education in Latin America: The Role of Demand and Supply of Skills." *Industrial & Labor Relations Review* 63 (2): 307–26.

Oaxaca, R. 1973. "Male-Female Wage Differentials in Urban Labor Markets." *International Economic Review* 14: 693–703.

Reyes, L., J. Rodríguez, and S. Urzúa. 2013. "Heterogeneous Economic Returns to Postsecondary Degrees: Evidence from Chile." NBER Working Paper 18817, National Bureau of Economic Research, Cambridge, MA.

Tinbergen, J. 1975. "Substitution of Academically Trained by Other Manpower." *Review of World Economics* 111 (3): 466–76.

Wang, Y. 2015. "Education Expansion and Decline in Tertiary Premium in Brazil: 1995–2013." Tulane Economics Working Paper 1525, Tulane University, New Orleans.

World Bank. 2011. "A Break with History: Fifteen Years of Inequality Reduction in Latin America." LCSPP Poverty and Labor Brief No. 2, World Bank, Washington, DC.

4

The Role of Labor Demand Conditions in Wage Inequality Trends

Introduction

The expansion in educational attainment and other human capital dimensions has played a significant role in the changing trajectory of earnings inequality in Latin America since the mid-1990s. However, chapter 3 also broadly concluded that the region's trends toward growing or stagnant earnings inequality in the 1990s and reduced inequality in the first decade of the 2000s cannot be explained solely by the increasing number of skilled (college-educated and high-experience) workers. In particular, the shift in earnings inequality trends between the 1990s and the 2000s is not consistent with the constant improvement in the supply of education throughout the period.

In what follows, we discuss the role of changes in labor demand conditions. These changes—and how they translate into demand for different types of labor—reduced wage inequality. We will focus on three different demand shocks: (1) shifts in domestic demand, (2) exchange rate appreciation from the commodity boom, and (3) trade liberalization and technological change. The latter is considered to be the primary driver of wage inequality in developed countries.[1]

The chapter will first discuss the role of *shifts in aggregate domestic demand.* In Latin America—where macroeconomic fluctuations are much more pronounced than in high-income countries and external shocks play a major role in explaining aggregate demand behavior (De la Torre, Beylis, and Ize 2015)—demand-driven fluctuations may affect inequality differently than they do elsewhere in the world.

This chapter argues that aggregate demand fluctuations (together with the underlying supply-side trends) have been an important driver of the fall in wage inequality during the boom period in South America because of asymmetries between the labor markets for skilled and unskilled labor.[2] In general, an increase in domestic aggregate demand (say, one driven by a major improvement in the terms of trade) falls on both the tradable and nontradable sectors, but the demand for tradable goods can be satisfied through imports at prices that are set exogenously (from the small open economy point of view) in international markets. A real exchange rate appreciation attracts labor to the nontradable sector. However, it leads to a decline in the skill premium (and therefore a reduction in earnings inequality) only if there is some form of asymmetry between the markets for skilled and unskilled labor.

This chapter discusses two possible asymmetries. First, asymmetry in skill intensities, whereby the nontradable sector is less-skilled-labor-intensive than the tradable sector. This would lead to a decline in the skilled wage premium as domestic demand rises. But it is not clear whether this asymmetry had a first-order effect in practice. As chapter 2 showed, the nontradable sector, at least on average, does not seem to be more intensive in unskilled labor than the tradable sector. To be sure, one of the sectors that expanded considerably during the 2000s when aggregate domestic demand surged was construction, and this sector is intensive in unskilled labor. Other sectors that expanded included restaurants and hotels and retail trade, which are also low-skill-intensive. However, skill-intensive sectors within nontradable sectors also expanded. A second possible asymmetry could concern labor supply elasticities, whereby unskilled labor supply is less responsive than the skilled labor supply to wage changes. This is the explanation explored theoretically and illustrated empirically by De la Torre and Ize (2016) and discussed in some detail later in this chapter in the subsection entitled "Differential Supply Elasticities between Skilled and Unskilled Workers."

The chapter discusses the role of a second change in labor demand conditions: *the exchange rate appreciation from the commodity boom* and the associated shift to the nontradable sector that changed interfirm wage differentials. This demand-side force explains the fall in wage inequality through its effects on the *within*-group wage inequality rather than *between*-group wage inequality. This is in sharp contrast with the effects of education expansion and shifts in aggregate domestic demand. These forces reduced inequality *between* workers with different observable characteristics (in terms of skill, including education and experience, occupation, or sector of employment). However, they cannot explain the fall in *within*-group wage inequality, that is, across workers with similar levels of education and labor market experience and who are employed in the same sector and occupation. Chapter 2 documented that falling within-group wage inequality accounted for more than half of the decline in total wage inequality and that this decline occurred inter firms (as opposed to intra firms) of the same sector.

We therefore discuss in this chapter the factors that could drive falling interfirm wage differences among similar workers and, in particular, the role of the exchange rate appreciation in South America during the commodity boom.

This chapter concludes by discussing the reasons why *skill-biased technological change and trade liberalization*, the two forces on which the literature for developed countries focus the most, cannot explain the observed fall in wage inequality in Latin America. Major changes in technology affect the wage gap between skilled and unskilled workers, and thus earnings inequality, by changing the demand for unskilled labor relative to skilled labor.[3] In what follows we discuss and provide new evidence on key questions for Latin America: How is skill-biased technological change affecting the region's occupational structure? Is the region undergoing job polarization (a relative contraction of employment in routine and middle-skilled occupations)? What is the role of trade liberalization in changing wage inequality in Latin America?

Shifts in Domestic Demand and Rising Wages for Unskilled Workers

The 1990s and 2000s were periods of pronounced domestic demand fluctuations and labor demand developments. After a decade of disappointing growth, the region grew rapidly in the 2000s. Terms of trade improved in South American countries but deteriorated in Central America and Mexico during this period (De la Torre, Beylis, and Ize 2015). Through spending effects, changes in the terms of trade affected aggregate domestic demand more than supply. The terms-of-trade changes and associated demand fluctuations were associated with differentiated aggregate wage and employment dynamics in these two country subgroups—that is, employment and average wages grew faster in South America than in Central America and Mexico.

In general, an increase in domestic aggregate demand (driven, for example, by a major improvement in the terms of trade) affects both the tradable and nontradable sectors, but the demand for tradable goods can be satisfied through imports at prices that are set exogenously (from the small open economy point of view) in international markets. Hence, the real exchange rate appreciates as the price of nontradables (which is set locally) rises in response to demand pressures, while the price of tradables remains fixed. This change in relative prices would attract labor to the nontradable sector, which may affect the skill premium to the extent that the skill content differs across tradable and nontradable sectors.

It is interesting to note the strong correlations between the region's decreasing wage inequality and the surge in domestic demand and associated real exchange rate appreciation during the commodity boom (2003–11) (figure 4.1, panel a). In fact, during this period, the ratio of unskilled to skilled wages rose in the nontradable sectors of the countries for which detailed labor data are available, and this ratio moved in close correlation with the expansion of aggregate demand in the nontradable sectors of these countries (figure 4.1, panel b). A similar link does not seem to exist in the case of the tradable sectors (figure 4.1, panel c), arguably because imports rose to satisfy the excess demand in these sectors. Moreover, there is a clear correlation between the expansion in demand and the rise in unskilled workers' wages in the nontradable sector relative to those in the tradable sector (figure 4.1, panel d).[4]

FIGURE 4.1: **Domestic Demand and Labor Income Distribution Trends during the Economic Boom in Selected Latin American Countries, 2003–11**

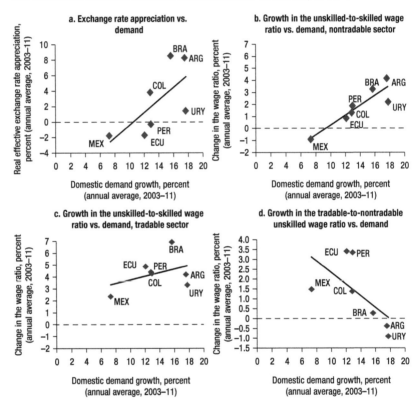

Sources: Labor Database for Latin America and the Caribbean (LABLAC) (http://lablac.econo.unlp.edu.ar/eng/index.php); Socio-Economic Database for Latin America and the Caribbean (SEDLAC), Universidad Nacional de la Plata (CEDLAS) and the World Bank (http://sedlac.econo.unlp.edu.ar/eng/); World Bank, World Development Indicators Database (http://data. worldbank.org/data-catalog/world-development-indicators; and International Monetary Fund, International Financial Statistics. *Note:* Annual average growth rates are the arithmetic mean of the accumulated growth between 2002 and 2011, except for Ecuador, which takes 2003 as a starting point (and is annualized accordingly). Because of inconsistencies in the data, domestic demand growth for Argentina was replaced by the projection of a cross-sectional regression of domestic demand growth on GDP growth, which was run on the observations for the rest of the countries. ARG = Argentina; BRA = Brazil; COL = Colombia; ECU = Ecuador; MEX = Mexico; PER = Peru; URY = Uruguay.

This book emphasizes the role of the tightness or softness of market conditions on wage inequality in the region. In the 2000s, aggregate domestic demand trends were radically different in South America than in Central America and Mexico. In South America, the period was marked by a strong increase in domestic demand that reflected the spending effect of positive terms-of-trade improvements, which responded to the commodity price boom but also to large capital flows to the region. In turn, South America witnessed its largest decline in returns to skill and thus the largest decline in wage inequality. The observed surge in demand was associated with a larger employment expansion in the nontradable sector than in the tradable sector, as shown in chapter 2. This could have reduced the skill premium for two distinct reasons: (1) differential skill intensities between sectors, or (2) differential supply elasticities between skilled and unskilled workers, discussed below.

Differential Skill Intensities between Sectors

The conventional wisdom, particularly in South America, posits that the demand expansion brought about by real exchange rate appreciation in the 2000s led to a larger expansion in labor demand for nontradable than tradable sectors, favoring relatively less-skill-intensive sectors. The underlying assumption was that the nontradable sector is more intensive in unskilled labor than the tradable sector in Latin America. Hence, increases in the demand for nontradable goods and services would benefit less-educated workers the most. This could be the case, for example, if growth in nontradables were accounted for by growth in the construction sector, which is less skill-intensive than most sectors.

Evidence for the region, however, contradicts this assumption. In South America, on average, the nontradable sector is more skill-intensive than the tradable sector, as shown in chapter 2. Some relatively less-skill-intensive nontradable sectors—particularly construction—expanded considerably, and the level of education of workers in that sector is below average. Yet, construction has a relatively small employment share (around 7 percent in most countries), and other nontradable sectors that are high-skill-intensive expanded as well—business services, for example. Moreover, the extent of sectoral reallocation to nontradable sectors was relatively small (De la Torre, Beylis, and Ize 2015).

This overall picture for the region is confirmed for most countries using detailed data at the subsector level and is robust to including services such as restaurants and hotels and financial services in the tradable sector (definition 1) or nontradable sector (definition 2). Specifically, tables 4A.1–4A.4 in annex 4A summarize the skill intensities and employment expansion in the various subindustries of the tradable and nontradable sectors in Argentina (2003–11), Brazil (2002–12), Chile (2003–11), and Peru (2002–12). Results can be summarized as follows:

- *In Argentina,* where workers in the nontradable sector had an average of 11.2 years of schooling and workers in the tradable sector had 10.8 years, the fastest-growing industries were construction, other business activities, and hotels and restaurants (table 4A.1). The average years of education in these sectors, at baseline, were 8.7, 12.9, and 10.9, respectively.

- *In Brazil,* where workers in the nontradable sector had an average of 7.9 years of schooling and workers in the tradable sector had 5.7 years, the fastest-growing industries were other business activities, hotels and restaurants, construction, and land transport via pipelines (table 4A.2). The average years of education in these sectors, at baseline, were 9.9, 6.6, 5.1, and 6.6, respectively.

- *In Chile,* where workers in the nontradable sector had an average of 11.3 years of schooling and workers in the tradable sector had 9.8 years, the fastest-growing industries were wholesale and retail, mining of metal ores, and other business activities (table 4A.3). The average years of education in these sectors, at baseline, were 10.7, 13.5, and 13.2, respectively.

- *In Peru,* where workers in the nontradable sector had an average of 10.5 years of schooling and workers in the tradable sector had 6.8 years, the fastest-growing industries were construction, public administration, and hotels and restaurants (table 4A.4). While public administration is a high-paying and relatively skilled sector (with average worker education of 12.1 years), the average wages and years of education are low in construction (8.9 years) and hotels and restaurants (8 years).

Overall, evidence for Brazil, Chile, and Peru indicates that (1) employment grew faster in the nontradable than in the tradable sector, and (2) skill intensity, measured by the mean years of education, is higher in the nontradable sector. In contrast, in Argentina, employment grew faster in the tradable than in the nontradable sector. As skill intensity is still higher in the nontradable than in the tradable sector, the aggregate evidence is not consistent with Dutch disease type of effects. Looking at subsectors within tradable and nontradable sectors, the picture is less clear. Some nontradable low-skill-intensive sectors grew strongly (for example, construction, retail) in most countries. However, neither the skill gap of these subsectors with respect to average years of education in tradable sectors nor the magnitude of cross-sectoral flows suggest the traditional Dutch disease channel to be a dominant one.

Differential Supply Elasticities between Skilled and Unskilled Workers

De la Torre, Beylis, and Ize (2015) explore an alternative hypothesis. Using a simple model, they establish that asymmetric supply elasticities—whereby the supply of unskilled labor is less responsive to wage changes than the supply of skilled labor—would produce an outcome that fits the stylized facts of the 2000s.

Framework for a Shift in Aggregate Demand and Expansion in the Skilled-Labor Supply Leading to a Decline in Wage Inequality

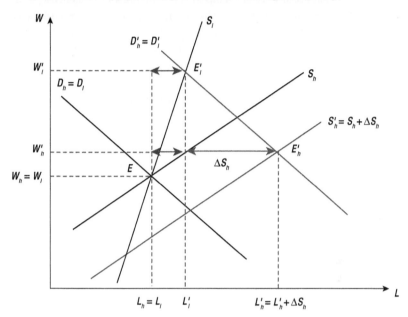

Source: De la Torre, Beylis, and Ize (2015).

The framework is illustrated in figure 4.2, which depicts the case of a parallel shift in demand (D) for unskilled and skilled workers (that is, $D'_l - D_l = D'_h - D_h$) in a context where—in keeping with the stylized facts—the supply of skilled labor expands more (from S_h to S'_h) than the supply of unskilled labor (for simplicity, S_l does not shift).

As shown in the figure and more formally in De la Torre, Beylis, and Ize (2015), a less-wage-elastic supply of unskilled labor is a necessary and sufficient condition for the symmetric demand expansion to have a differential impact across wages of skilled and unskilled workers. Unskilled workers, who have become relatively scarcer, take advantage of the demand push to ask for higher wages (W'_l), while the wages of skilled workers increase moderately (W'_h). Of course, a necessary condition is that skilled workers do not compete with unskilled workers for unskilled jobs. This may be the case if mobility costs across sectors are large (Artuc, Lederman, and Porto 2015) or if the wage gap between skilled and unskilled jobs is sufficiently large that, even after unskilled wages increase, skilled workers have no incentives to take unskilled jobs. Needless to say, this process can be sustained only for a limited period of time, while barriers to worker mobility limit skilled workers from entering unskilled labor sectors.

Eventually, if the wages of unskilled workers continue to grow, skilled workers would start competing for those jobs.

Does the empirical evidence support the hypothesis of asymmetric supply wage elasticities across skill groups? Most of the literature in this regard focuses on Europe and the United States and tends to show that the supply of unskilled labor is more elastic to wage changes than that of skilled labor, which is contrary to the mechanism postulated by De la Torre, Beylis, and Ize (2015). Bargain, Orsini, and Peichl (2014) compare these elasticities between selected European countries (the Euro 17)[5] and the United States and present new estimates of the elasticity of labor supply for workers in the lower earnings quintile of the wage distribution and workers in the top earnings quintile. They find that in the Euro 17 countries, the supply elasticity of those in the top quintile of the wage distribution (most likely, skilled workers) tends to be lower than the supply elasticity of those in the bottom quintile of the wage distribution (most likely unskilled workers) (figure 4.3, panel b).

However, Latin American labor markets differ considerably from those in Europe and the United States, not least because of the absence of significant unemployment insurance schemes and the presence of high informality in Latin America. Estimating labor supply elasticities for Argentina, Brazil, Chile, and Mexico with data covering 2000–14, Bargain and Silva (forthcoming) find evidence of a less wage-elastic supply of unskilled than skilled labor, at least in the largest labor force reservoir of married women (figure 4.3, panel a).[6]

Perhaps a lower elasticity among unskilled workers was a specific feature of the 2000s. In a context of rapidly increasing skilled-labor supply and strong demand growth, the lower reservoir of unskilled workers may have increased their bargaining power. An alternative hypothesis is that the reservoir of unskilled workers is always lower in developing countries than in developed countries where unemployment insurance systems are more comprehensive. Indeed, the unemployment rate among unskilled workers tends to be lower than among skilled workers in Latin American countries, which is in sharp contrast with what happens in high-income countries such as the United States (De La Torre and Ize 2016). Thus, while better-educated (hence wealthier) workers can afford to be temporarily unemployed, less-educated (hence poorer) workers cannot.

Thus, we conclude that the domestic demand push in South America, coupled with declining supply of less-educated workers, may have contributed to the observed strong wage growth among low-skilled workers. This, in turn, is a candidate explanation for the much stronger wage growth among the less skilled observed in South America than in Central America and Mexico, where the domestic demand push did not take place.

FIGURE 4.3: Labor Supply Elasticity in Latin America and Selected High-Income Countries

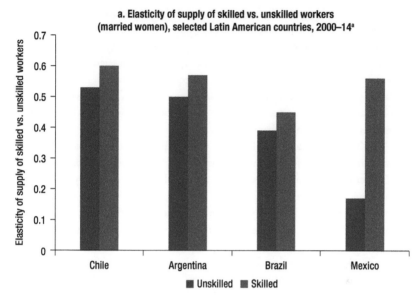

a. Elasticity of supply of skilled vs. unskilled workers (married women), selected Latin American countries, 2000–14[a]

b. Elasticity of supply of workers in top vs. bottom wage quintiles, Euro 17 countries and the United States, 1998–2005[b]

Sources: Bargain, Orsini, and Peichl (2014); Bargain and Silva (forthcoming).
a. "Unskilled" refers to completed primary education or less. "Skilled" refers to completed tertiary education or more. Estimates of elasticities use repeated cross-sections for Argentina, Brazil, Chile, and Mexico over the 2000–14 period.
b. Euro 17 refers to the 17 European Union (EU) member states that are full members of the European Economic and Monetary Union. Estimates used data for the 1998–2005 period.

Exchange Rate Appreciation from the Commodity Boom and Interfirm Wage Differentials

Education expansion and shifts in domestic demand explain changes in wage inequality between skilled and unskilled workers in Latin America. However, they cannot explain the large fall in within-group wage inequality, that is, pay differentials among workers with similar education, labor market experience, and sector of employment. This matters, as the fall in within-group wage inequality accounts for more than half of the fall in overall wage inequality in the 2000s (see chapter 2). Hence, we now turn to factors that could explain changes in wage inequality among workers who are similar in terms of their observable characteristics.

Two types of factors could explain wage differences across observably similar workers in terms of education and experience but also occupation and sector: (1) differences in skills across workers that are not observable in employment surveys (for example, differences in socioemotional skills), and (2) interfirm differences in wages (for workers in the same sector and with the same occupation or skill level) or intrafirm differences (across departments or areas of the same firm). Results in chapter 2 show that most initial wage inequality between workers and its fall in the 21st century in Latin America has primarily been an interfirm (as opposed to an intrafirm) phenomenon. Using data from Brazil, this book finds that from 2003 to 2012, over two-thirds of the fall in wage inequality for workers in the same sector and occupation can be accounted for by a declining variance of wages between firms and only one-third by a declining variance within firms. This result is also confirmed using data for developed countries. For example, virtually all of the rise in wages in U.S. inequality from 1981 to 2013 is due to interfirm as opposed to intrafirm dispersion (Song et al. 2015). These findings point toward a framework that explicitly considers interfirm heterogeneity as the relevant framework for understanding wage inequality across workers with similar observable characteristics.

This section investigates whether falling interfirm wage dispersion was a source of declining wage inequality in Latin America and discusses its potential drivers.

Falling Interfirm Wage Dispersion as a Source of Declining Wage Inequality

Changes in wage inequality resulting from changes in interfirm pay differentials for observationally similar workers of the same sector can arise from three sources: (1) changes in pay heterogeneity across firms, (2) changes in heterogeneity among workers, and (3) changes in the degree to which the most desirable workers and the most desirable firms find each other ("assortativity" in the matching of workers to plants).[7]

Separating these three sources of variation is complicated and requires rich data that allow for identifying and following workers and firms over time. This analysis was possible only in Costa Rica (the only Latin American country where wage inequality increased in the 2000s) and Brazil (where wage inequality fell, in line with the rest of the region). More research is needed to understand whether the conclusions for these two countries can be extended elsewhere. In these two countries, we follow Card, Heining, and Kline (2013) and estimate models with additive fixed effects for workers and firms, as further discussed in box 4.1. We find that in Costa Rica, where wage inequality increased, the main component behind this trend was increasing heterogeneity in pay across firms (variance of firm fixed effects) (figure 4.4, panel a). In a similar vein, in Brazil, where wage inequality fell significantly in the 2000s, the heterogeneity in pay across firms was the component of the total wage variance that declined the most (see yellow portion of the bars in figure 4.4, panel b).

In Costa Rica, the rise in the variance of firm effects accounts for 33 percent of the total increase in wage inequality, and the rise in the variance of worker effects accounts for 21 percent, with the rise in their covariance and the residual explaining the remainder. In Brazil, the fall in the variance of firm effects accounts for 41 percent of the total decline in wage inequality, and the fall in the variance of worker effects accounts for 20 percent, with the fall in their covariance and the residual explaining the remainder. Importantly, in both countries, the contribution of assortativity in the matching of workers to plants (covariance of worker and firm effects) did not change, despite high increases in the minimum wages in Brazil usually linked to improvements in assortativity in the matching.

BOX 4.1: **Estimating the Role of Firm Heterogeneity**

This book follows Card, Heining, and Kline (2013) and estimates a model with additive fixed effects for workers and firms. This model disentangles the contribution to interfirm pay differentials of three factors:

- Dispersion in quality across employers (firm fixed effects)
- Dispersion in ability across workers (worker fixed effects)
- Degree to which the most desirable workers are paired with the most productive firms (covariance of worker and firm effects).

Results for Costa Rica and Brazil are presented in figure 4.4. In Costa Rica, dispersion in firm effects accounts for 33 percent of the total increase in wage inequality, and dispersion in worker effects accounts for 21 percent, with a rise in their covariance and the residual explaining the remainder (figure 4.4, panel a). In Brazil, compression in firm effects accounts for 41 percent of the total decline in wage inequality, and compression in worker effects accounts for 20 percent, with a fall in their covariance and the residual explaining the remainder (figure 4.4, panel b).

FIGURE 4.4: Decomposition of Wage Variance among Full-Time Male Workers across Firms in Costa Rica and Brazil

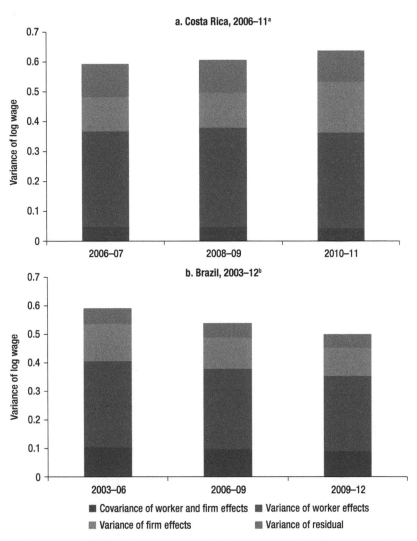

Sources: Authors' calculations based on data from the Costa Rican Department of Social Security (CCSS) and Brazil's Annual Social Information Report (RAIS).
a. Estimations based on male full-time workers in Costa Rica at the individual-firm level. The log wage from every individual-firm observation is regressed by a set of firm and individual fixed effects in the following sets of years: 2006–07, 2008–09, and 2010–11.
b. The sample uses male full-time workers (at least 35 hours per week), ages 20–60. We select the highest wage earned of a person in a firm every year. The log wage from every individual-firm observation is regressed by a set of firm and individual fixed effects in the following sets of years: 2003–06, 2006–09, and 2009–12.

Factors That Could Explain Declining Interfirm Wage Dispersion

Firm heterogeneity provides another angle of the importance of demand-side factors. In what follows, we argue that a decline in interfirm wage dispersion can result from (1) exchange rate appreciation from the commodity boom, (2) narrowing dispersion in firm productivity, and (3) changes in minimum wage policies.

- *Exchange rate appreciation*

The observed exchange rate appreciation in South America relative to several important export destinations negatively affected firms' export participation. This, in turn, decreased wages among the more-productive exporting firms relative to the less-productive firms in the same industry (see annex 4B for a description of the literature on the effects of exchange rate movements on wage inequality "within" an industry). Because more-productive firms also tend to pay higher wages, this process decreases within-sector wage inequality. The converse is true for countries where the exchange rate has depreciated or where trade costs fell.

Moreover, in commodity-boom countries that witnessed a significant exchange rate appreciation, the observed Dutch disease effects were associated with a shift to the nontradable sector (from the tradable sector). Because interfirm wage differentials are lower in the nontradable sector, this process may have reduced interfirm wage dispersion and therefore overall wage inequality. As discussed in chapter 2, employment in South America grew more during the 2000s in the nontradable sector than in the tradable sector. If the nontradable sector has lower employer heterogeneity (as observed in other countries) and employs a larger share of workers than the tradable sector, wage inequality falls. However, this process can be slower in the presence of obstacles to worker mobility.

In sum, the exchange rate appreciation in South America may have reduced inequality by reducing interfirm wage dispersion through two channels. First, it may reallocate labor away from the most productive firms operating in the tradable sector, which are also the high-paying firms. Second, it may have pushed workers into the nontradable sector, where interfirm wage dispersion is lower.

- *Narrowing dispersion in firm productivity*

Many developed countries have experienced widening dispersion in labor productivity, leading to an increase in earnings inequality. The specific link between widening dispersion in the firm productivity distribution and increasing earnings inequality was found for the United Kingdom by Faggio, Salvanes, and Van Reenen (2010) and for the United States by Dunne et al. (2004). These authors linked the observed growth of within-group inequality with increased firm-level productivity dispersion due to new technologies. When a new technology such as information and communication technology (ICT) becomes available, firms adopt it and translate it into rising productivity at different rates, increasing firm-level productivity dispersion. Alternative explanations include an increase in transitory shocks or a more volatile environment for firms, greater sorting for firms, or firm entry and exit dynamics.

The available data from Costa Rica do not allow for an analysis of this indicator, but if global trends also occurred there, this phenomenon could have been a source of the country's rising wage inequality.

Evidence for Brazil does not suggest that firms' labor productivity distribution became less dispersed (Alvarez, Engbom, and Moser 2016).[8] Instead, value added per worker appears to have become increasingly delinked from worker pay during this period (Alvarez, Engbom, and Moser 2016; Silva, Almeida, and Strokova 2015). This process could result in lower wage inequality even if workers' and firms' fundamentals are not altered. Hence, more research is needed, but the available evidence does not confirm that the fall in inequality resulted from narrowing dispersion in firm productivity.

- *Changes in minimum wage policies*

Latin American countries differed markedly in their institutional wage policies such as the minimum wage. How economic rents are split between capital and labor can be affected by the dynamics of the minimum wage. More specifically, a larger share of a firm's profits is likely to fall into workers' hands when the minimum wage becomes more binding. If remuneration policies across firms become less heterogeneous—for example, because a higher but more similar share of the benefits from the employment relationship is distributed to workers—wage inequality falls.

This channel is a plausible cause of falling interfirm wage dispersion and may have operated to varying degrees across countries. However, its importance depends on how high the minimum wage is and by how much it increased. The country-specific role that changes in minimum wage policies played in the observed changes in interfirm wage differentials and their impact on overall wage inequality is an important topic for further research. Note that minimum wage policies are expected to have a broader effect on wage inequality beyond the specific effect on interfirm wage dispersion, as discussed in the next section.

Why Skill-Biased Technological Change, Job Polarization, and Traditional Trade Channels Do Not Explain the Decline in Wage Inequality

The literature usually focuses on skill-biased technological change as the key demand force that can raise the relative demand for unskilled labor. In countries such as the United States, research and opinion surveys suggest that these forces—particularly technological change—are the primary drivers of changes in wage inequality (Autor, Katz, and Krueger 1998; Berman, Bound, and

Griliches 1994; Feenstra and Hanson 1999; Goldin and Katz 2007; Krueger 2012). Polarization of occupations in the labor market—a more recent version of the technological change hypothesis—had an important impact on the compensation of U.S. workers and, through this channel, on wage inequality (Autor et al. 2014; Autor and Dorn 2013). We devote the last section of this chapter to discussion of the role of the traditional trade channels in the decline in wage inequality in Latin America.

Technological Change and Job Polarization

The consequences of technological change on the demand for skills have attracted enormous attention since at least the Second Industrial Revolution.[9] The introduction of rail transport, automobiles, and automated production was believed to be a serious threat to human work because the machines were seen as replacing thousands of jobs. But those gloomy views could not have been less aligned with subsequent changes in the workplace. Although machines did destroy and permanently replace many assembly-line jobs, their use also led to the creation of many new jobs. The machines required a new set of specialized operators, and new forms of production organization demanded more and different types of managers and professionals.

More recently, digital technology and the introduction of computers in the workplace have fundamentally altered the workspace around the world, reawakening fears of job destruction. Many of the tasks traditionally performed by middle-skilled workers are now being fundamentally transformed by machines. In particular, "routinizable" jobs such as bookkeeping and many clerical tasks are now carried out by computers, displacing a large proportion of workers. Much as during the Second Industrial Revolution, the new forms of production are shifting demand, rather than destroying net employment, in favor now of skills that require the abstract reasoning and creativity needed for complex problem-solving, all of which are (as yet) difficult to replace by computers.

The ICT revolution differs from the Second Industrial Revolution in at least two major ways. First, it affects not only blue-collar jobs but also white-collar jobs. Second, those jobs that are most easily routinizable tend to be in the middle of the skill or wage distribution, not at the bottom. In contrast, many occupations at the bottom of the skill distribution (for example, taxi drivers) require social and interpersonal skills that are difficult to replace by computers. Workers in those occupations seem to have benefited from technological change.

Recent research shows that since 1990 many industrialized countries have experienced, along with increasing wage inequality, employment changes that were strongly U-shaped in skill level, with relative employment declines in the middle of the distribution and relative gains at the tails.[10] For instance, in 15 of 16 European countries for which harmonized labor force survey data were available, high-paying occupations expanded relative to middle-wage occupations in the 1990s and 2000s (Goos, Manning, and Salomons 2009, 2011). In all 16 countries, low-paying occupations expanded relative to middle-wage occupations. The United Kingdom and the United States exhibited similar results (Acemoglu 1999; Autor, Katz, and Kearny 2006, 2008; Goos and Manning 2007).

This phenomenon—illustrated in figure 4.5 for the United States and deemed "polarization"[11]—challenges the standard skill-biased technological change (SBTC) model (Tinbergen 1974, 1975). The SBTC model has been the leading explanation for the increase in inequality during the 1980s because of its ability to (1) account for the evolution of skill premia in the United States (Autor, Katz, and Kearney 2008; Autor, Katz, and Krueger 1998; Carneiro and Lee 2009; Katz and Murphy 1992), and (2) capture major cross-country differences in skill premia among advanced nations (Atkinson 2008; Card and Lemieux 2001; Davis 1992; Fitzenberger and Kohn 2006; Katz, Loveman, and Blanchflower 1995; Murphy, Riddell, and Romer 1998). A key difference between the traditional SBTC hypothesis and the more-nuanced polarization hypothesis is that the latter predicts a non-monotonic impact of technological change on the demand for skill throughout the earnings distribution (Acemoglu and Autor 2011).

FIGURE 4.5: **Employment Share Changes, by Skill Percentile, United States, 1980–2005**

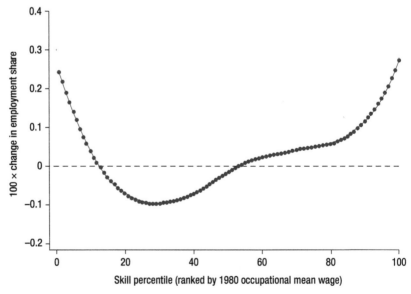

Source: Autor and Dorn (2013).

Polarization can increase or reduce wage inequality, depending on the relative forces that pull demand for skills at different points of the wage distribution. In the United States, the consensus is that occupation polarization has contributed to a deepening of economic inequality. Are there signs of SBTC and job polarization in Latin America? Has this process contributed to the recent inequality decline?

Technology moves fast across countries, and ICT and computers have certainly entered the workplace in developing countries (World Bank 2016). However, barriers to technology adoption as well as the availability of abundant, cheap unskilled labor can slow down the process, because some technologies that are profitable in developed countries may not be so in the developing world. Finally, other forces (for example, the aggregate domestic demand push discussed earlier) may be changing the demand for skills, obscuring the role of technology.

Maloney and Molina (2016) analyze the evolution of employment across broad occupational groups in census data from 21 developing countries, including Brazil, the Dominican Republic, Ecuador, El Salvador, Mexico, Nicaragua, Panama, and Peru, in search of signs of polarization. In contrast with predictions from the polarization hypothesis, they fail to observe a decline in occupations that are easily codifiable, such as operators and assemblers. Moreover, elementary occupations appear to be in decline, and high-skilled occupations such as professionals and technicians exhibited positive employment growth. Overall, changes in the occupational structure appear to be inconsistent with the polarization hypothesis and perhaps more in line with traditional SBTC mechanisms.

In what follows, we try to reproduce figure 4.5 for Latin American countries to look for obvious signs of polarization in the region. An important challenge in reproducing this picture is that most household surveys change the classification of occupations over time, rendering it difficult to make disaggregated comparisons over a long time span. Messina, Pica, and Oviedo (2016) examine changes at the detailed occupation and sector level in Brazil, Chile, Mexico, and Peru—four countries in the region that have household survey data with a homogeneous occupation classification that did not change during the 2000s.

With the exception of Chile, the four countries showed few signs of job polarization. Figure 4.6 organizes occupations by skill percentile, ranked by the mean years of education (dashed line) and mean hourly wage (solid line) of workers in that occupation in 2002 (base year). It shows the smoothed changes in employment across finely defined occupational categories in Brazil, Chile, Mexico, and Peru over the 2000s.[12] In Chile, employment growth was concentrated among high-wage and, to a lesser extent, low-wage occupations. In contrast, the occupations in the middle of the distribution displayed modest employment losses. The other three countries had modest growth of similar magnitude among occupations in the middle- to high-wage range. Only occupations below the 30th percentile of initial wages seem to have lost employment.

Employment Share Changes across Occupations, Ranked by Skill Level, Selected Latin American Countries

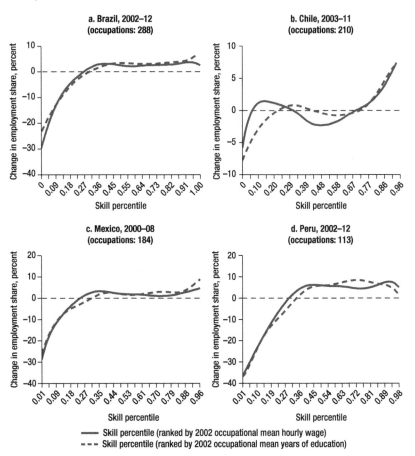

a. Brazil, 2002–12
(occupations: 288)

b. Chile, 2003–11
(occupations: 210)

c. Mexico, 2000–08
(occupations: 184)

d. Peru, 2002–12
(occupations: 113)

——— Skill percentile (ranked by 2002 occupational mean hourly wage)
- - - Skill percentile (ranked by 2002 occupational mean years of education)

Source: Messina, Pica, and Oviedo (2016).

Note: These figures are constructed by using the Socio-Economic Database for Latin America and the Caribbean (SEDLAC), Universidad Nacional de la Plata (CEDLAS) and the World Bank (http://sedlac.econo.unlp.ar/eng/) data to calculate the change between 2002 and 2012 in the share of employment accounted by detailed occupations encompassing all employment in the country. Occupations are ranked by skill level, which is approximated by the mean hourly wage of workers in each occupation in 2002 (base year) (solid line) and in mean years of education in 2002 (base year) (dashed line).

Thus, we find little prima facie evidence of employment polarization in Brazil, Mexico, or Peru. With the exception of Chile (where employment changes were, albeit more moderate, still aligned with those observed in Europe and the United States), employment in the middle and top of the income distribution increased—a pattern that is better aligned with a traditional SBTC hypothesis but not with the more-nuanced polarization hypothesis. This indicates that polarization patterns may not have arrived yet in Latin America, perhaps because of barriers to technology adoption or penetration.

The changes shown in figure 4.6 also suggest a channel through which wage inequality may have declined. The four countries show clear signs of employment moving away from low-paying occupations. To the extent that the workers in low-paying occupations managed to move up the ladder and find better-paying jobs, this pattern of occupational mobility would contribute to overall inequality reduction. Unfortunately, the lack of suitable long panels in the region renders the analysis of job changes difficult, making this a potentially fruitful area for further research.

The decline in low-paying occupations is paralleled by a similar pattern in sectoral employment changes. Figure 4.7 mimics figure 4.6, but the unit of observation now is the sector. Perhaps with the exception of Mexico (where changes in sector classification do not allow for a similar figure), the sector changes suggest that low-paying sectors have been in decline, while high-paying sectors have expanded. Because this is a period of falling unemployment and increasing labor participation, it is fair to expect that most of these changes reflected employment shifts, with workers moving to better-paying sectors or sectors that demand a higher level of education.

The shift away from low-paying sectors and occupations was associated with a rapid increase of wages in those same sectors. Figure 4.8 shows the evolution of average wages across occupations in the four countries studied by Messina, Pica, and Oviedo (2016). There is a clear monotonic relationship, with wages in low-paying occupations increasing much faster than wages in high-paying ones.

The evidence presented thus far is not consistent with skill polarization. With the exception of Chile, where employment changes are more aligned with those observed in Europe and the United States, employment in the middle and top of the distribution increased. Low-paying occupations and sectors declined substantially, suggesting that changes in the composition of employment may help to explain the decline in inequality.

Perhaps more important, average earnings expanded rapidly in low-paying occupations and low-skill-intensive sectors, while wages declined in high-paying occupations and high-skilled sectors, and employment shares fell in those sectors or occupations where wages grew the most (low-paying occupations and low-skill-intensive sectors). This implies that forces other than technology may have been more important to the recent inequality dynamics in Latin America. To be sure, one candidate for such forces is changes in the supply of skills.

Traditional Trade Channels

Several external shocks have shifted demand since the mid-1990s in Latin America, including the commodity boom and China's economic rise (in the 2000s) as well as changing trade patterns due to trade liberalization (in the 1990s).[13] In the literature on Latin America, trade liberalization has been shown to play an important role in wage

Employment Share Changes across Sectors, Ranked by Skill Level, Selected Latin American Countries

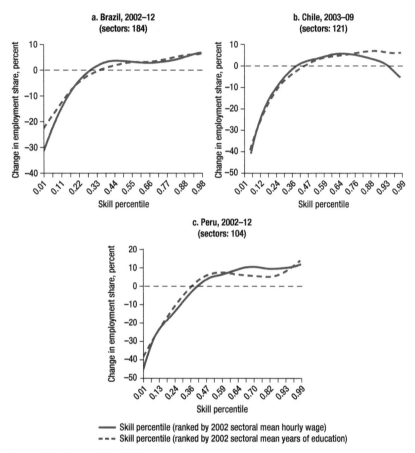

a. Brazil, 2002–12
(sectors: 184)

b. Chile, 2003–09
(sectors: 121)

c. Peru, 2002–12
(sectors: 104)

—— Skill percentile (ranked by 2002 sectoral mean hourly wage)
- - - Skill percentile (ranked by 2002 sectoral mean years of education)

Source: Messina, Pica, and Oviedo (2016).
Note: These figures are constructed by using the Socio-Economic Database for Latin America and the Caribbean (SEDLAC), Universidad Nacional de la Plata (CEDLAS) and the World Bank (http://sedlac.econo.unlp.edu.ar/eng/) data to calculate the change between 2002 and 2012 in the share of employment accounted by detailed sectors encompassing all employment in the country. Sectors are ranked by skill level, which is approximated by the mean hourly wage of workers in each occupation in 2002 (base year) (solid line) and in mean years of education in 2002 (base year) (dashed line).

inequality trends in at least two important cases: (1) following Mexico's 1986 accession to the General Agreement on Tariffs and Trade (GATT) (later the World Trade Organization) (Revenga 1997), and (2) following Brazil's trade liberalization from 1988 to 1995 (Gonzaga, Menezes-Filho, and Terra 2006).

Most neoclassical trade models suggest that changes in output prices drive changes in wage inequality because of reallocation of resources among industries. In fact, the

FIGURE 4.8: **Wage Changes across Occupations, Ranked by Skill Level, Selected Latin American Countries**

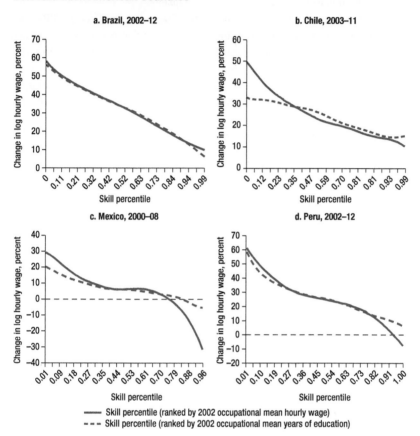

a. Brazil, 2002–12

b. Chile, 2003–11

c. Mexico, 2000–08

d. Peru, 2002–12

—— Skill percentile (ranked by 2002 occupational mean hourly wage)
- - - Skill percentile (ranked by 2002 occupational mean years of education)

Source: Messina, Pica, and Oviedo (2016).

Note: These figures are constructed by using the Socio-Economic Database for Latin America and the Caribbean (SEDLAC), Universidad Nacional de la Plata (CEDLAS) and the World Bank (http://sedlac.econo.unlp.edu.ar/eng/) data to calculate the change between 2002 and 2012 in log hourly wage across detailed occupations. Occupations are ranked by skill level, which is approximated by the mean hourly wage of workers in each occupation in 2002 (base year) (solid line) and in mean years of education in 2002 (base year) (dashed lines).

links between product prices and factor returns are a key element of general equilibrium trade models. Interest in these links was intensified by the "trade and wages" debate, wherein lower prices of unskilled-labor-intensive products were advanced as one explanation for the decline in the relative wage of unskilled workers in advanced, skill-abundant countries (Bastos and Silva 2008; Goldberg and Pavcnik 2007, 2017).

The underlying argument was based on the Stolper-Samuelson theorem, which implies that trade liberalization in countries where unskilled labor is relatively scarce will lead to a fall in both the relative price of unskilled-labor-intensive imports and the relative return to unskilled labor, and therefore to an increase in wage inequality. In contrast, in countries where unskilled labor is abundant, the theory would predict that liberalization would lead to a fall in wage inequality.

In Latin America, although most trade liberalization occurred in the 1990s, wage inequality was stagnant or rising in the region during that period (Goldberg and Pavcnik 2007) while inequality fell only in the 2000s (Halliday, Lederman, and Robertson 2015). Hence, Stolper-Samuelson trade effects cannot explain the timing of the downward trend in wage inequality.[14] Moreover, in this strand of the literature, the mechanism by which trade affects labor markets (and thus wage inequality) is through reallocation between sectors. And, as discussed earlier, employment shifts between sectors in Latin America were limited in the 2000s when inequality fell. Finally, most of this literature focuses on changes in inequality that are *between* demographic groups (defined by education or skill), and therefore they are not well fitted to explain wage inequality *within* demographic groups, which, as shown in chapter 2, accounts for a large share of the overall wage inequality.

Interestingly, Halliday, Lederman, and Robertson (2015) offer new evidence that although variations in the price of skill-intensive goods relative to non-skill-intensive goods contributed to rising wage inequality in Mexico until 1999, the mechanisms based on the traditional models fail to explain the subsequent fall in inequality (figure 4.9, panel a). Replicating this analysis for Chile, we find similar results (figure 4.9, panel b). We plot the relative prices of skill-intensive goods in Mexican manufacturing from 1988 to 2005 (figure 4.9, panel a) and in Chilean manufacturing from 2003 to 2011 (figure 4.9, panel b). As panel a shows, there was a break in the evolution of relative prices of skilled goods that increased after Mexico lowered tariffs upon joining the GATT in

FIGURE 4.9: **Evolution of the Relative Price of Skill-Intensive Goods in Mexico and Chile**

a. Mexico, 1988–2005[a]

Relative skilled goods price — Price break test statistic

(continued on next page)

Evolution of the Relative Price of Skill-Intensive Goods in Mexico and Chile *(continued)*

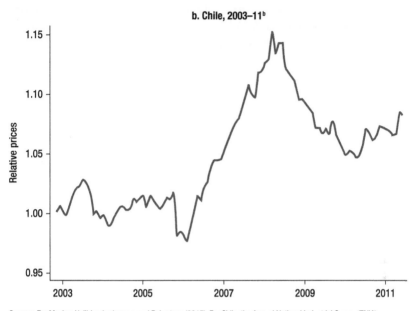

b. Chile, 2003–11[b]

Sources: For Mexico, Halliday, Lederman, and Robertson (2015). For Chile, the Annual National Industrial Survey (ENIA) manufacturer survey for the skilled and unskilled sectors (four-digit CIIU Rev.3) and the 2003–11 Producer Price Index (IPP), National Statistics Institute, by product (six-digit CIIU Rev.3).

a. The series is constructed by taking the ratio of the Fisher output price (unit value) index for skill-intensive goods (measured as the industries in the top third of the manufacturing nonproduction-to-production worker ratio) to less-skill-intensive industries (measured as the industries in the bottom third of the nonproduction-to-production worker ratio). The red line plots the relevant additive outlier test statistic from Vogelsang and Perron (1998). The local extremes of the test statistic indicate a trend break. The maximum appears at June 1997. Note that the relative price falls until around 2001, when China entered the World Trade Organization.

b. The 2003 ENIA covered a total of 5,377 firms and 110 products. Skill intensity is proxied by the ratio of skilled to unskilled workers. (Skilled workers include owners, directors, and specialized workers. Unskilled workers include nonspecialized, auxiliary, services, administrative, and sales workers.) The median skilled-to-unskilled ratio for each firm was used to obtain a single product ratio of skilled to unskilled. The IPP was estimated, by four-digit code, using a Laspeyres index (data are weighted for each product). Values were deflated using a simple average of IPP price indexes on the top and bottom third to compare price movements over time, assuming that firms in the middle third might jump around the middle because of sampling or temporary shocks. Results using an alternative classification of the ratio of skilled to unskilled workers (the ratio of workers specialized in production to workers nonspecialized in production) are similar.

1986, but that direction changed around the mid-1990s after the North American Free Trade Agreement went into effect (with prices initially falling, then either leveling off or rising slightly throughout 2004). In Chile, a country where inequality has been falling since the mid-1990s, there was also a break in the series of relative prices of skill-intensive goods, which fell after 2008 and since then have remained relatively stable, or at least not on an increasing path.

In addition to the analysis of the traditional role of trade, recent papers have expanded this literature by reexamining the consequences of a trade shock on wage inequality using structural models. The broad conclusion is that even when shocks have been large, their impact on wage inequality has been limited. Specifically, using data for Brazil, Adão (2015) finds that the shocks to world commodity prices accounted for only 5–10 percent of the fall in Brazilian wage inequality between 1991 and 2010. Similarly, using data for 33 countries, Lee (2015) finds that changes in trade costs decreased the skill premium in Brazil by only about 0.1 percent with a near-linear production function and, with different production functions, would even have contributed to an increase in the skill premium. However, it is important to note that this literature focuses only on the *direct effects* of the commodity boom on wage inequality in the region—that is, those effects that result from the sectoral responses of employment and wages to observable sector-level demand shifters. In the previous sections we discussed the *indirect effects* resulting from the spending expansion associated with terms-of-trade improvements and concluded they may be important.

Another strand of literature assesses the importance of trade shocks on inequality by focusing on differentiated effects in local labor markets.[15] If we concentrate on the emergence of China as a major trading partner (and competitor) of Latin American countries, we immediately realize that Chinese growth is likely to affect countries asymmetrically across regions. Some regions may be negatively affected by Chinese import competition, perhaps because they specialized in manufacturing goods that China now produces, while others may benefit from growing Chinese demand for commodities. Costa, Garred, and Pessoa (2016) use this identification strategy to study the impact of China on inequality in Brazil and find that the commodity boom effect increased both local wage inequality (in regions affected by import competition) and wage growth (in positively affected locations) during the 2000s.

Conclusions

Since the 1990s, the region had many important changes in labor demand conditions. This chapter discussed the role of these changes—and how they translate into demand for different types of labor—in the reduction of wage inequality in Latin America. It focused on two key factors: shifts in domestic demand and exchange rate appreciation from the commodity boom. It also discusses the reasons why skill-biased technological change, job polarization, and the traditional trade channels do not explain the decline in wage inequality in Latin America in the 2000s.

• *Shifts in domestic demand*

This book emphasizes the role of the tightness or softness in market conditions on wage inequality in the region. In Latin America—where business cycles are much more pronounced than in high-income countries and external shocks play a major role in explaining aggregate demand behavior (De la Torre, Beylis, and Ize 2015)—demand-driven inequality may have a different nature than it does elsewhere in the world.

This chapter argued that demand fluctuations (together with the underlying supply-side trends) have been an important driver of the fall in wage inequality during the boom period in South America. The chapter argued that the aggregate domestic demand push favored the nontradable sector, including some industries (such as construction or restaurants and hotels) which are unskilled-labor-intensive. However, neither the skill gap of these subsectors with respect to average years of education in tradable sectors nor the magnitude of cross-sectoral flows suggest the traditional Dutch disease channel could explain a significant fraction of the inequality decline.

An alternative channel through which the domestic demand push can affect relative wages across skilled and unskilled workers works through their labor supply elasticities. If the elasticity (responsiveness) of labor supply to changes in wages is lower among unskilled workers than among skilled workers, then a shift in aggregate demand, even if symmetric in skill intensity, may lead to a decrease in the relative wage of skilled labor. Estimates of supply elasticities show small differences across worker groups, but are in line with a lower elasticity for unskilled labor.

- *Exchange rate appreciation from the commodity boom*

The domestic demand hypothesis emphasizes movements in relative wages across education groups. However, more than half of the decline in inequality observed during the 2000s took place among workers with similar observable characteristics (such as education, labor market experience, and occupation), what we label within-group inequality. Hence, this chapter analyzed factors that could explain falling within-group inequality and, in particular, the effect of rising heterogeneity across firms on wage inequality.

This chapter presented new evidence on how heterogeneity of employers plays a large role in wage inequality (level and growth). It showed that falling variance in firm unobserved characteristics (that is, firm fixed effects) might be a factor behind falling wage inequality, following Card, Heining, and Kline (2013). Applying the same methodology for Costa Rica and Brazil—the only two Latin American countries for which matched employer-employee panel data were available—the current study found that in Costa Rica, where wage inequality increased, the component of wage variance that increased the most was the variance of firm effects. On the other hand, in Brazil, where wage inequality fell significantly in the 2000s, the variance of firm effects was the component that fell the most.

This chapter has argued that the fall in interfirm wage dispersion in South America could be the result of exchange rate appreciation. The exchange rate appreciation in South America may have reduced inequality by reducing interfirm wage dispersion through two channels. First, it may have reallocated labor away from the most productive firms operating in the tradable sector, which are also the high-paying firms. Second, it may have pushed workers into the nontradable sector, in which interfirm wage dispersion is lower.

- *Technological change and traditional trade channels*

Our findings indicate that technological change and traditional trade channels appear *not* to be the main drivers of wage inequality trends in Latin America. Wages expanded rapidly in low-paying occupations relative to high-paying occupations. Skill-biased technological change would have caused the opposite effect. Also, there is little evidence of labor market polarization. In fact, the evidence of occupational polarization is weak for most countries of the region and for other developing countries (Maloney and Molina 2016; Messina, Pica, and Oviedo 2016).

Regarding the role of trade liberalization, the Stolper-Samuelson theorem suggests that in countries where unskilled labor is relatively abundant it will lead to an increase in both the relative price of unskilled-labor-intensive sectors and the relative return to unskilled labor, and therefore to a reduction in wage inequality. Although most trade liberalization occurred in the 1990s, wage inequality was stagnant or rising in Latin America during that period (Goldberg and Pavcnik 2007) while inequality fell only in the 2000s (Halliday, Lederman, and Robertson 2015). Hence, Stolper-Samuelson trade effects cannot explain the timing of the downward trend in wage inequality. Other trade shocks could have been at play, such as the commodity boom triggered by the emergence of China as a major consumer of commodities. Recent studies indicate that the direct effects of the commodity boom on wage inequality in the region can account for only a small share of the fall in wage inequality in the 2000s (Adão 2015). However, the commodity boom also had indirect (spending) effects of terms-of-trade improvements, which were analyzed in the chapter.

While this chapter, like the preceding one, focuses on the causes of the reduction of wage inequality in the 2000s, it also sheds light on the factors behind the inequality trends in the 1990s. As discussed in chapter 2, wage inequality was stagnant or increased during the 1990s, in sharp contrast to trends in the 2000s. The wage changes behind these trends were markedly different in the respective periods. In fact, wages at the top, middle, and bottom of the wage distribution did not change much in the 1990s. During this period returns to skills increased despite the rapid expansion of education. The divergent patterns between education expansion and returns to education suggest that the changes in labor supply alone are unlikely to explain the changes in wage inequality in the 1990s. Demand factors are likely to have played an important role. As discussed in chapter 2, domestic aggregate demand was falling and exchange rates depreciating. In addition, trade liberalization has been shown to have played an important role in wage inequality trends in at least two important cases: (1) following Mexico's accession in 1986 to the GATT (later the World Trade Organization) (Revenga 1997), and (2) following Brazil's trade liberalization from 1988 to 1995 (Gonzaga et al. 2006). Hence, the trend in wage inequality in the 1990s and 2000s matches up well with that of aggregate demand. The effect of aggregate demand on wage inequality is likely to have been mitigated by the expansion of education.

Annex 4A. Skill Intensities and Employment Expansion during the Commodity Boom in Selected Latin American Countries

TABLE 4A.1: **Employment Changes in Tradable and Nontradable Industries in Argentina, 2003–11**

Sector	Mean log hourly wage, 2003 (1)	Mean years of education, 2003 (2)	Employment share, 2003 (%) (3)	Employment share, 2011 (%) (4)	Change in employment share, 2003–11 (%) (4)–(3)
Tradables (definition 1)	0.88	10.84	19.77	21.02	1.25
Nontradables (definition 1)	0.97	11.19	80.23	78.98	−1.25
Tradables (definition 2)	0.83	10.45	15.17	15.41	0.24
Nontradables (definition 2)	0.97	11.24	84.83	84.59	−0.24
Fast-growing sectors					
Construction (NT)	0.75	8.69	7.34	9.21	1.87
Other business activities (NT)	1.36	12.94	5.46	6.33	0.87
Hotels and restaurants (T/NT)	0.74	10.93	2.80	3.48	0.68
Extraterritorial organizations and bodies (NT)	1.39	12.09	0.33	0.63	0.30
Manufacture of fabricated metal products (T)	0.79	9.42	1.26	1.56	0.30
Fast-declining sectors					
Health and social work (NT)	1.05	12.30	7.38	5.5	−1.88
Wholesale and retail trade and commission trade (NT)	0.63	10.73	16.44	15.11	−1.33
Education (NT)	1.34	14.42	8.67	7.89	−0.78
Agriculture, hunting, and related service activities (T)	0.34	8.15	1.53	1.01	−0.52
Manufacture of chemicals and chemical products (T)	1.34	12.16	1.27	0.91	−0.36

Source: Authors' calculations from National Household Surveys.
Note: Definition 1: tradables are agriculture, fishing, mining, manufacturing, financial intermediation, and hotels and restaurants; nontradables refers to all the other industries. Definition 2: tradables are agriculture, fishing, mining, and manufacturing; nontradables are all other sectors of the economy. NT = nontradable; T = tradable. Listed industries correspond to two-digit sector codes from the International Standard Industrial Classification of All Economic Activities, Rev.3. The total number of two-digit sector codes is 60.

TABLE 4A.2: **Employment Changes in Tradable and Nontradable Industries in Brazil, 2002–12**

Sector	Mean log hourly wage, 2002 (1)	Mean years of education, 2002 (2)	Employment share, 2002 (%) (3)	Employment share, 2012 (%) (4)	Change in employment share, 2002–12 (%) (4)–(3)
Tradables (definition 1)	0.74	5.74	33.34	30.14	−3.20
Nontradables (definition 1)	1.11	7.92	66.66	69.86	3.20
Tradables (definition 2)	0.69	5.30	28.28	24.04	−4.24
Nontradables (definition 2)	1.11	7.94	71.72	75.96	4.24
Fast-growing sectors					
Other business activities (NT)	1.57	9.88	4.25	6.10	1.85
Construction (NT)	0.82	5.11	7.77	9.28	1.51
Hotels and restaurants (T/NT)	0.63	6.55	3.62	4.67	1.05
Land transport; transport via pipelines (NT)	1.15	6.66	3.96	4.67	0.71
Health and social work (NT)	1.59	10.53	3.84	4.36	0.52
Fast-declining sectors					
Agriculture, hunting, and related service activities (T)	0.31	2.80	12.31	8.77	−3.54
Private households with employed persons (NT)	0.31	5.06	9.19	7.59	−1.60
Manufacture of wood and products of wood and cork (T)	0.73	5.45	0.75	0.36	−0.39
Manufacture of textiles (T)	0.62	6.60	1.20	0.83	−0.37
Tanning and dressing of leather; manufacture of luggage (T)	0.62	6.89	0.99	0.69	−0.30

Source: Authors' calculations from National Household Surveys.
Note: Definition 1: tradables are agriculture, fishing, mining, manufacturing, financial intermediation, and hotels and restaurants; nontradables are the rest of the economy. Definition 2: tradables are agriculture, fishing, mining, and manufacturing; nontradables are all other sectors of the economy. NT = nontradable; T = tradable. Listed industries correspond to two-digit sector codes from the International Standard Industrial Classification of All Economic Activities, Rev.3. The total number of two-digit sector codes is 60.

TABLE 4A.3: **Employment Changes in Tradable and Nontradable Industries in Chile, 2003–11**

Sector	Mean log hourly wage, 2003 (1)	Mean years of education, 2003 (2)	Employment share, 2003 (%) (3)	Employment share, 2011 (%) (4)	Change in employment share, 2003–11 (%) (4)–(3)
Tradables (definition 1)	7.01	9.35	28.41	22.50	−5.91
Nontradables (definition 1)	7.31	11.38	71.59	77.50	5.91
Tradables (definition 2)	7.06	9.75	33.18	27.79	−5.39
Nontradables (definition 2)	7.30	11.33	66.82	72.21	5.39
Fast-growing sectors					
Wholesale and retail trade and commission trade (NT)	7.16	10.74	16.37	19.22	2.85
Mining of metal ores (T)	7.69	13.47	0.02	2.52	2.50
Other business activities (NT)	7.78	13.15	3.88	5.31	1.43
Sale, maintenance, and repair of motor vehicles (NT)	7.12	10.68	1.21	2.37	1.16
Construction (NT)	7.26	9.73	8.60	9.48	0.88
Fast-declining sectors					
Agriculture, hunting, and related service activities (T)	6.71	7.32	10.72	8.02	−2.70
Mining of uranium and thorium ores (T)	7.81	12.26	1.31	0.00	−1.31
Private households with employed persons (NT)	6.65	8.48	8.10	6.87	−1.23
Manufacture of food products and beverages (T)	7.00	10.53	3.60	2.72	−0.88
Sewage and refuse disposal, sanitation (NT)	6.76	9.23	1.06	0.30	−0.76

Source: Authors' calculations from National Household Surveys.
Note: Definition 1: tradables are agriculture, fishing, mining, manufacturing, financial intermediation, and hotels and restaurants; nontradables are the rest of the economy. Definition 2: tradables are agriculture, fishing, mining, and manufacturing; nontradables are all other sectors of the economy. NT = nontradable; T = tradable. Listed industries correspond to two-digit sector codes from the International Standard Industrial Classification of All Economic Activities, Rev.3. The total number of two-digit sector codes is 60.

Sector	Mean log hourly wage, 2002 (1)	Mean years of education, 2002 (2)	Employment share, 2002 (%) (3)	Employment share, 2012 (%) (4)	Change in employment share, 2002–12 (%) (4)–(3)
Tradables (definition 1)	0.88	6.83	41.62	39.48	−2.14
Nontradables (definition 1)	1.40	10.49	58.38	60.52	2.14
Tradables (definition 2)	0.79	6.52	35.62	32.24	−3.38
Nontradables (definition 2)	1.40	10.32	64.38	67.76	3.38
Fast-growing sectors					
Construction (NT)	1.44	8.90	4.10	5.99	1.89
Public administration and defense (NT)	1.49	12.06	4.45	5.40	0.95
Hotels and restaurants (T/NT)	1.33	8.01	5.38	6.28	0.90
Land transport; transport via pipelines (NT)	1.20	9.99	5.29	6.11	0.82
Other business activities (NT)	1.98	12.61	3.51	4.15	0.64
Fast-declining sectors					
Agriculture, hunting, and related service activities (T)	0.53	5.06	22.81	19.43	−3.38
Private households with employed persons (NT)	0.88	7.85	4.58	3.28	−1.30
Wholesale and retail trade and commission trade (NT)	1.13	8.81	18.82	17.89	−0.93
Other service activities (NT)	1.21	8.25	2.49	1.76	−0.73
Manufacture of textiles (T)	0.61	6.36	1.74	1.30	−0.44

Source: Authors' calculations from National Household Surveys.
Note: Definition 1: tradables are agriculture, fishing, mining, manufacturing, financial intermediation, and hotels and restaurants; nontradables are the rest of the economy. Definition 2: tradables are agriculture, fishing, mining, and manufacturing; nontradables are all other sectors of the economy. NT = nontradable; T = tradable. Listed industries correspond to two-digit sector codes from the International Standard Industrial Classification of All Economic Activities, Rev.3. The total number of two-digit sector codes is 60.

Annex 4B. Why Exchange Rate Appreciation Should Reduce Wage Inequality within an Industry

There is great heterogeneity across firms regarding export participation. In fact, only a minority of firms export, and the exporters are larger, more productive, and pay higher wages than nonexporters, contributing to within-sector wage inequality (Bernard and Jensen 1995; Greenaway and Kneller 2007; Roberts and Tybout 1996). Moreover, in response to trade liberalization, sector-level productivity rises, but this appears to be mainly because of reallocation within sectors toward more efficient firms: more-productive firms grow and less-productive firms shrink or die, but not because trade raises productivity within particular firms (Bernard and Jensen 1999; Clerides, Lach, and Tybout 1998; Pavcnik 2002).[16] In light of this evidence, Melitz (2003) extended the traditional trade framework to incorporate heterogeneous firms. This model became the standard workhorse for analyzing the behavior of firms that are not identical while considering only a single, homogeneous input: labor. In this setting, wage inequality arises from differences between exporting and nonexporting firms for observationally similar workers.

Building on these advances, Eslava et al. (2010, 2013) use data from Colombia to show that trade liberalization (tariff reduction) created compression in the productivity distribution both by reducing the survival of low-productivity firms and increasing the productivity threshold of new entrants.

Focusing specifically on the role of exporting, a new strand in the literature recently emerged showing that exporting can contribute to reducing wage inequality within industries. It links trade and wage inequality though the effect of trade on product quality (Bastos, Silva, and Verhoogen 2014; Brambilla, Lederman, and Porto 2012; Frías, Kaplan, and Verhoogen 2009; Verhoogen 2008). This literature builds on a new mechanism, "quality upgrading," that focuses on reallocation within firms of the product mix (goods of different qualities destined for different markets) as a mechanism linking trade and labor market outcomes. This literature suggests that firms need to upgrade quality to be successful in selling to richer countries. In that setting, a shock that provides a stronger incentive to start or increase exporting (for example, an exchange rate devaluation or a change in trade costs) leads more-productive firms to increase exports, upgrade quality, and raise wages relative to less-productive firms within the same industry. That is because larger, more-productive firms in each industry already tend to be both higher-wage and more likely to export. As the potential for exporting increases, it is the larger, more-productive firms in each industry that can take advantage, which increases wage dispersion across firms in the industry. While this literature focused on the effect of an exchange rate depreciation, an exchange rate appreciation, by reducing the potential for exporting, is likely to have the opposite effect, leading to a fall in wage dispersion across firms in an industry.

This literature found a robust causal effect of export participation on skill utilization within firms, using data, for example, on the Mexican peso crisis of 1994–95 (Verhoogen 2008) or investigating the impact on Argentinian firms of the Brazilian devaluation of 1999 (Brambilla, Lederman, and Porto 2012). This relationship is consistent with several intuitive theoretical mechanisms through which trade increases within-sector wage inequality in developing countries:

- Exporting may require expertise in international business and foreign languages (Brambilla, Lederman, and Porto 2012; Matsuyama 2007).

- Exporting may induce firms to upgrade product quality, which is a skill-intensive activity (Bastos and Silva 2010; Bastos, Silva, and Verhoogen 2014; Kugler and Verhoogen 2012; Verhoogen 2008).

- By leading to an expansion in the scale of operations, entering export markets may make it profitable for firms to pay the fixed costs associated with the adoption of technologies that are more skill-intensive (Bustos 2011; Yeaple 2005).

A linked strand of the literature has emphasized the role of workers' unobserved characteristics in assessing the effects of trade on wage inequality. Helpman, Itskhoki, and Redding (2010) develop a theoretical framework in which (1) production requires workers, (2) workers are heterogeneous in ability, and (3) the labor market is characterized by search-and-matching frictions. In this framework, a firm pays a search cost determined by the tightness of the labor market. When the economy opens to trade and more-productive firms decide to begin exporting, their revenue increases relative to less-productive firms, which further enhances their incentive to screen out workers of lower ability. This mechanism generates a firm-level wage premium and implies that exporting increases the wage paid by more-productive firms.

Building on this framework, Helpman, Itskhoki, and Redding (2010) extend this model by including two additional sources of heterogeneity across firms. The first is the cost of screening workers to allow for variation in wages across firms after controlling for their employment size and export status. The second is the size of the fixed cost of exporting to allow some small, low-wage firms to profitably export and some large, high-wage firms to serve only the domestic market. Using 1984–95 data for Brazil, they show that interfirm wage dispersion is largely related to firm employment size and trade participation.

Although this literature has focused on the period of increased wage inequality, its theoretical and empirical insights can be used to speculate about the subsequent period (2002–13) of declining wage inequality in Latin America. As discussed, this period was characterized by exchange rate appreciations in most countries relative to several important export destinations that are likely to reduce firms' export participation. In light of this literature, such forces could reduce wage inequality. In fact, through this channel, firms' heterogeneity could be a particularly important source of change in wage dispersion in developing countries, where exchange rate fluctuations are more frequent.

Notes

1. See Autor, Katz, and Krueger (1998); Berman, Bound, and Griliches (1994); Feenstra and Hanson (1999); Goldin and Katz (2007); and Krueger (2012).

2. Unless otherwise noted in this chapter, "skilled" labor refers to workers with postsecondary education. "Unskilled" labor refers to workers with a high school education or less.

3. See Autor (2007); Autor, Katz, and Krueger (1998); Autor et al. (2014); Gaston and Trefler (1997); Goldberg and Pavcnik (2007); Goldin and Katz (2007); Revenga (1992); and Wacziarg and Wallack (2004).

4. This suggests that the pockets of high demand in the nontradable sector had a local effect on unskilled workers' wages that was not perfectly arbitraged through labor mobility. On labor market frictions and labor mobility costs across industries, see Artuc, Lederman, and Porto (2015); Hollweg, Lederman, and Mitra (2014); and the references therein.

5. Euro 17 refers to the 17 European Union (EU) member states that are full members of the European Economic and Monetary Union.

6. According to the theoretical framework of De la Torre, Beylis, and Ize (2015), in terms of magnitude, what matters is the ratio of the two elasticities rather than the differences. Their evidence would be consistent with a supply elasticity for skilled workers about 20 percent higher on average than for unskilled workers, in line with Bargain and Silva (forthcoming) once results are averaged over countries, gender, and marital status.

7. An extensive literature in economic theory studies the sorting patterns of heterogeneous agents. According to this literature, the most desirable workers and the most productive firms get together, generating wage differences between firms within the same sector-occupation.

8. Note that more research is needed to draw definitive conclusions because this analysis uses data covering formal employment only.

9. Also called the "Technological Revolution," the Second Industrial Revolution refers to a phase of rapid industrialization from approximately 1870 to 1914 (ending at the start of World War I).

10. In this context, the relative "skill" level is based on occupational mean hourly wage in the initial year.

11. "Polarization" refers to an economic phenomenon whereby the number of jobs requiring routine skills, and corresponding in the United States to the middle of the wage distribution (such as manufacturing production-line jobs), decrease relative to both those at the bottom (requiring few skills) and those at the top (requiring high skill levels due to automation).

12. The period varies depending on idiosyncratic changes in the country-specific classification of occupations.

13. Importantly, other factors linked to globalization also have contributed to inequality trends. These include outsourcing (Acemoglu, Gancia, and Zilibotti 2015; Feenstra and Hanson 1996, 1997); exchange rate movements (Verhoogen 2008); and the rise of China (Chiquiar and Ramos-Francia 2008; Dussel Peters and Gallagher 2013).

14. Note, however, that Stolper-Samuelson trade effects might occur with a lag if labor markets adjust slowly. Moreover, they depend on the relative skill-intensity of the liberalized sectors. Evidence on relative goods prices for Mexico indicates that when the country joined the GATT, it protected less-skill-intensive industries. When Mexico joined the North American Free Trade Agreement, however, the relative price of skill-intensive goods reversed its rise (Robertson 2004).

15. Since the emergence of the work by Autor, Dorn, and Hanson (2013) that has shown that negative effects of trade on unskilled wages have been larger than expected in the United States, globalization has received renewed attention as a driver of wage inequality.

16. For evidence on pro-competitive effects of trade that occur through selection effects across firms in Latin America, see Fernandes (2007) and Ergoeing, Micco, and Repetto (2011) for Chile.

References

Acemoglu, D. 1999. "Changes in Unemployment and Wage Inequality: An Alternative Theory and Some Evidence." *American Economic Review* 89 (5): 1259–278.

Acemoglu, D., and D. Autor. 2011. "Skills, Tasks and Technologies: Implications for Employment and Earning." In *Handbook of Labor Economics*, Vol. 4, edited by O. Ashenfelter and D. E. Card. Amsterdam: Elsevier.

Acemoglu, D., G. Gancia, and F. Zilibotti. 2015. "Offshoring and Directed Technical Change." *American Economic Journal: Macroeconomics* 7 (3): 84–122.

Adão, R. 2015. "Worker Heterogeneity, Wage Inequality, and International Trade: Theory and Evidence from Brazil." Job Market Paper, Massachusetts Institute of Technology, Cambridge, MA.

Alvarez, J., N. Engbom, and C. Moser. 2016. "Firms and the Decline of Earnings Inequality in Brazil." PEDL Research Note, Department for International Development, United Kingdom.

Artuc, E., D. Lederman, and G. Porto. 2015. "A Mapping of Labor Mobility Costs in the Developing World." *Journal of International Economics* 95 (1): 28–41.

Atkinson, A. B. 2008. *The Changing Distribution of Earnings in OECD Countries.* Oxford, UK: Oxford University Press.

Autor, D. H. 2007. "Structural Demand Shifts and Potential Labor Supply Responses in the New Century." Paper prepared for the Federal Reserve Bank of Boston Conference, "Labor Supply in the New Century," June 19–20.

Autor, D. H., and D. Dorn. 2013. "The Growth of Low-Skill Service Jobs and the Polarization of the U.S. Labor Market." *American Economic Review* 103 (5): 1533–597.

Autor, D. H., D. Dorn, and G. H. Hanson. 2013. "The China Syndrome: Local Labor Market Effects of Import Competition in the United States." *American Economic Review* 103 (6): 2121–168.

Autor, D. H., D. Dorn, G. H. Hanson, and J. Song. 2014. "Trade Adjustment: Worker Level Evidence." *Quarterly Journal of Economics* 129 (4): 1799–860.

Autor, D. H., L. F. Katz, and M. S. Kearny. 2006. "The Polarization of the U.S. Labor Market." *American Economic Review Papers and Proceedings* 96 (2): 189–94.

———. 2008. "Trends in U.S. Wage Inequality: Revising the Revisionists." *Review of Economics and Statistics* 90 (2): 300–23.

Autor, D. H., L. F. Katz, and A. B. Krueger. 1998. "Computing Inequality: Have Computers Changed the Labor Market?" *Quarterly Journal of Economics* 113 (4): 1169–214.

Bargain, O., K. Orsini, and A. Peichl. 2014. "Comparing Labor Supply Elasticities in Europe and the United States: New Results." *Journal of Human Resources* 49 (3): 723–838.

Bargain, O., and J. Silva. Forthcoming. "Labor Supply Elasticities: Evidence for Latin America." Policy Research Working Paper, World Bank, Washington, DC. Available at: https://sites.google .com/site/joanasilvaweb/.

Bastos, P., and J. Silva. 2008. "The Wage and Unemployment Impacts of Trade Adjustment." In *Globalization and Labour Market Adjustment*, edited by D. Greenaway, R. Upward, and P. W. Wright. Basingstoke, UK: Palgrave Macmillan.

———. 2010. "The Quality of a Firm's Exports: Where You Export to Matters." *Journal of International Economics* 82 (2): 99–111.

Bastos, P., J. Silva, and E. Verhoogen. 2014. "Export Destinations and Input Prices." NBER Working Paper 20143, National Bureau of Economic Research, Cambridge, MA.

Berman, E., J. Bound, and Z. Griliches. 1994. "Changes in the Demand for Skilled Labor within U.S. Manufacturing: Evidence from the Annual Survey of Manufacturers." *Quarterly Journal of Economics* 109 (2): 367–97.

Bernard, A. B., and J. B. Jensen. 1995. "Exporters, Jobs, and Wages in U.S. Manufacturing: 1976–1987." *Brookings Papers on Economic Activity: Microeconomics*: 67–119.

———. 1999. "Exceptional Exporter Performance: Cause, Effect, or Both?" *Journal of International Economics* 47 (1): 1–25.

Brambilla, I., D. Lederman, and G. Porto. 2012. "Exports, Export Destinations and Skills." *American Economic Review* 102 (7): 3406–488.

Bustos, P. 2011. "Trade Liberalization, Exports and Technology Upgrading: Evidence on the Impact of MERCOSUR on Argentinian Firms." *American Economic Review* 101 (1): 304–40.

Card, D., J. Heining, and P. Kline. 2013. "Workplace Heterogeneity and the Rise of West German Wage Inequality." *Quarterly Journal of Economics* 128 (3): 967–1105.

Card, D., and T. Lemieux. 2001. "Can Falling Supply Explain the Rising Return to College for Younger Men? A Cohort-Based Analysis." *Quarterly Journal of Economics* 116 (2): 705–46.

Carneiro, P., and S. Lee. 2009. "Estimating Distributions of Potential Outcomes Using Instrumental Variables with an Application to Changes in College Enrolment and Wage Inequality." *Journal of Econometrics* 149 (2): 191–208.

Chiquiar, D., and M. Ramos-Francia. 2008. "A Note on Mexico and U.S. Manufacturing Industries' Long-Term Relationship." Working Paper 2008-08, Banco de México, Mexico City.

Clerides, S., S. Lach, and J. Tybout. 1998. "Is Learning by Exporting Important? Micro-Dynamic Evidence from Colombia, Mexico and Morocco." *Quarterly Journal of Economics* 113 (3): 903–47.

Costa, F., J. Garred, and J. Paulo Pessoa. 2016. "Winners and Losers from a Commodities-for-Manufactures Trade Boom." *Journal of International Economics* 102: 50–69.

Davis, N. 1992. "Teaching about Inequality: Student Resistance, Paralysis, and Rage." *Teaching Sociology* 20 (3): 232–38.

De la Torre, A., G. Beylis, and A. Ize. 2015. *Jobs, Wages, and the Latin American Slowdown.* Latin America and the Caribbean Semiannual Report (October). Washington, DC: World Bank.

De la Torre, A., and A. Ize. 2016. "Employment, Wages, Distribution, and the Latin American Deceleration." Background paper, World Bank, Washington, DC.

Dunne, T., L. Foster, J. Haltiwanger, and K. R. Troske. 2004. "Wage and Productivity Dispersion in United States Manufacturing: The Role of Computer Investment." *Journal of Labor Economics* 22 (2): 397–430.

Dussel Peters, E., and K. P. Gallagher. 2013. "NAFTA's Uninvited Guest: China and the Disintegration of North American Trade." *CEPAL Review* 110 (August): 83–108.

Ergoeing, R., A. Micco, and A. Repetto. 2011. "Dissecting the Chilean Export Boom." *CEPAL Review* 105 (December): 87–102.

Eslava, M., J. Haltiwanger, A. Kugler, and M. Kugler. 2010. "Trade Liberalization and Worker Displacement: Evidence from Trade Reforms in Colombia." Unpublished.

———. 2013. "Trade Reforms and Market Selection: Evidence from Manufacturing Plants in Colombia." *Review of Economic Dynamics* 16: 135–58.

Faggio, G., K. G. Salvanes, and J. Van Reenen. 2010. "The Evolution of Inequality in Productivity and Wages: Panel Data Evidence." *Industrial and Corporate Change* 19 (6): 1919–951.

Feenstra, R. C., and G. H. Hanson. 1996. "Foreign Investment, Outsourcing and Relative Wages." In *Political Economy of Trade Policy: Essays in Honor of Jagdish Bhagwati*, edited by R. C. Feenstra and G. Grossman. Cambridge, MA: MIT Press.

———. 1997. "Foreign Direct Investment and Relative Wages: Evidence from Mexico's Maquiladoras." *Journal of International Economics* 42 (3-4): 371–93.

Feenstra, R. C., G. H. Hanson. 1999. "Productivity Measurement and the Impact of Trade and Technology on Wages: Estimates for the U.S., 1972–1990." *Quarterly Journal of Economics* 114 (3): 907–40.

Fernandes, Ana M. 2007. "Trade Policy, Trade Volumes and Plant-Level Productivity in Colombian Manufacturing Industries." *Journal of International Economics* 71 (1): 52–71.

Fitzenberger, B., and K. Kohn. 2006. "Skill Wage Premia, Employment, and Cohort Effects: Are Workers in Germany All of the Same Type?" IZA Discussion Paper 2185, Institute for the Study of Labor (IZA), Bonn.

Frías, J. A., D. S. Kaplan, and E. A. Verhoogen. 2009. "Exports and Wage Premia: Evidence from Mexican Employer-Employee Data." Columbia University. Unpublished.

Gaston, N., and D. Trefler. 1997. "The Labour Market Consequences of the Canada-U.S. Free Trade Agreement." *Canadian Journal of Economics* 30 (1): 18–41.

Goldberg, P., and N. Pavcnik. 2007. "Distributional Effects of Globalization in Developing Countries." *Journal of Economic Literature* 45 (1): 39–82.

———. 2017. "The Effects of Trade Policy." NBER Working Paper 21957, National Bureau of Economic Research, Cambridge, MA.

Goldin, C., and L. F. Katz. 2007. "Long-Run Changes in the U.S. Wage Structure: Narrowing, Widening, Polarizing." NBER Working Paper 13568, National Bureau of Economic Research, Cambridge, MA.

Gonzaga, G., N. Menezes-Filho, and C. Terra. 2006. "Trade Liberalization and the Evolution of Skill Earnings Differentials in Brazil." *Journal of International Economics* 68 (2): 345–67.

Goos, M., and A. Manning. 2007. "Lousy and Lovely Jobs: The Rising Polarization of Work in Britain." *Review of Economics and Statistics* 89 (1): 118–33.

Goos, M., A. Manning, and A. Salomons. 2009. "Job Polarization in Europe." *American Economic Review* 99 (2): 58–63.

———. 2011. "Explaining Job Polarization: The Roles of Technology, Offshoring and Institutions." Working paper, Department of Economics, Katholieke Universiteit (KU), Leuven, Belgium.

Greenaway, D., and R. Kneller. 2007. "Firm Heterogeneity, Exporting and Foreign Direct Investment." *Economic Journal* 117 (517): F134– F161.

Halliday, T., D. Lederman, and R. Robertson. 2015. "Tracking Wage Inequality Trends with Prices and Different Trade Models: Evidence from Mexico." Policy Research Working Paper 7471, World Bank, Washington, DC.

Helpman, E., O. Itskhoki, and S. Redding. 2010. "Inequality and Unemployment in a Global Economy." *Econometrica* 78 (4): 1239–83.

Hollweg, C. H., D. Lederman, and D. Mitra. 2014. "Structural Reforms and Labor Market Outcomes: International Panel Data Evidence." Policy Research Working Paper 7122, World Bank, Washington, DC.

Katz, L., G. Loveman, and D. Blanchflower. 1995. "Changes in the Structure of Wages in Four OECD Countries." In *Differences and Changes in Wage Structures*, edited by R. B. Freeman and L. F. Katz. Chicago: University of Chicago Press.

Katz, L., and K. Murphy. 1992. "Changes in Relative Wages, 1963–1987: Supply and Demand Factors." *Quarterly Journal of Economics* 107 (1): 35–78.

Krueger, A. 2012. *Struggling with Success: Challenges Facing the International Economy.* Singapore: World Scientific.

Kugler, M., and E. Verhoogen. 2012. "Prices, Plant Size and Product Quality." *Review of Economic Studies* 9 (1): 307–39.

Lee, E. 2015. "Trade, Inequality, and the Endogenous Sorting of Heterogeneous Workers." Job Market Paper, Yale University, New Haven, CT.

Maloney, W. F., and C. Molina. 2016. "A Note on Labor Market Polarization in the Developing World." World Bank, Washington, DC. Unpublished.

Matsuyama, K. 2007. "Beyond Icebergs: Toward a Theory of Biased Globalization." *Review of Economic Studies* 74 (1): 237–53.

Melitz, M. J. 2003. "The Impact of Trade on Intra-Industry Reallocations and Aggregate Industry Productivity." *Econometrica* 71 (6): 1695–725.

Messina, J., G. Pica, and A. M. Oviedo. 2016. "Job Polarization in Latin America." Inter-American Development Bank, Washington, DC. Unpublished. Available at: http://www.jsmessina.com.

Murphy, K., W. C. Riddell, and P. Romer. 1998. "Wages, Skills, and Technology in the United States and Canada." NBER Working Paper 6638, National Bureau of Economic Research, Cambridge, MA.

Pavcnik, N. 2002. "Trade Liberalization, Exit and Productivity Improvements: Evidence from Chilean Plants." *Review of Economic Studies* 69: 245–76.

Revenga, A. 1992. "Exporting Jobs? The Impact of Import Competition on Employment and Wages in U.S. Manufacturing." *Quarterly Journal of Economics* 7 (1): 255–84.

———. 1997. "Employment and Wage Effects of Trade Liberalization: The Case of Mexican Manufacturing." *Journal of Labour Economics* 15 (3): 20–43.

Roberts, M. J., and J. R. Tybout, eds. 1996. *Industrial Evolution in Developing Countries: Micro Patterns of Turnover, Productivity, and Market Structure.* Oxford, UK, and New York: Oxford University Press for the World Bank.

Robertson, R. 2004. "Relative Prices and Wage Inequality: Evidence from Mexico." *Journal of International Economics* 64 (2): 387–409.

Silva, J., R. Almeida, and V. Strokova. 2015. *Sustaining Employment and Wage Gains in Brazil: A Skills and Jobs Agenda.* Directions in Development: Human Development Series. Washington, DC: World Bank.

Song, J., D. J. Price, F. Guvenen, N. Bloom, and T. Von Wachter. 2015. "Firming Up Inequality." NBER Working Paper 21199, National Bureau of Economic Research, Cambridge, MA.

Tinbergen, J. 1974. "Substitution of Graduate by Other Labour." *Kyklos* 27 (2): 217–26.

———. 1975. "Substitution of Academically Trained by Other Manpower." *Review of World Economics* 111 (3): 466–76.

Verhoogen, E. A. 2008. "Trade, Quality Upgrading, and Wage Inequality in the Mexican Manufacturing Sector." *Quarterly Journal of Economics* 123 (2): 489–530.

Vogelsang, Timothy J., and Pierre Perron. 1998. "Additional Tests for a Unit Root Allowing for a Break in the Trend Function at an Unknown Time." *International Economic Review* 39 (4): 1073–1100.

Wacziarg, R., and J. Wallack. 2004. "Trade Liberalization and Intersectoral Labor Movements." *Journal of International Economics* 64: 411–39.

World Bank. 2016. *World Development Report 2016: Digital Dividends.* Washington, DC: World Bank.

Yeaple, S. R. 2005. "A Simple Model of Firm Heterogeneity, International Trade, and Wages." *Journal of International Economics* 65 (1): 1–20.

5
Exploring the Role of Minimum Wages and Unions in Recent Inequality Trends

Introduction

Labor market regulations and institutions play an important role in determining outcomes such as wage inequality, and Latin America has witnessed important policy changes during past decades that may explain some of the observed patterns. This chapter discusses the role of minimum wages and unions, two fundamental aspects of the institutional architecture of labor markets that are often cited as crucial determinants of inequality.[1]

During the 2000s, national minimum wages in Latin America increased considerably—both in level and coverage—except in a few countries such as the Dominican Republic, El Salvador, Mexico, Panama, and Paraguay. In some countries, the minimum wage doubled or even tripled, and the bulk of that increase took place in the second subperiod examined here: 2002–12. In addition, unionization of workers between 1986 and 1998 fell from over 30 percent to around 20 percent in Mexico, and from 60 percent to almost 30 percent in both Peru and in Uruguay (Saavedra and Torero 2005). What is the effect of all these changes on wage inequality? This chapter explores these links.

Institutional and regulatory factors are not equally binding in all Latin American countries. This implies a heterogeneous effect on downward wage rigidities of the lowest-skilled workers and thus on reductions in wage inequality.[2] Brazil's minimum wage legislation appears to be the most binding in the region, followed by Peru's and Colombia's.[3] In most countries, the majority of workers are informal.

This chapter identifies factors, based on new evidence (from labor force panels) and the literature, that determine the extent to which labor market institutions—specifically, minimum wages and levels of unionization—equalize (or not) the distribution of wages.

The Role of the Minimum Wage

Effect of Minimum Wage Policy on Wage Inequality

The minimum wage and its effects on wage inequality have been among the most-studied subjects in labor economics. Results are mixed concerning both the magnitude and the direction of such effects. The level of the minimum wage matters. For example, the minimum wage's effects are potentially much larger in Latin America than in the United States because the minimum wage in the former is often much higher (relative to the median wage) and rapidly increasing.[4] However, minimum wage effects are potentially smaller in Latin America than in Europe, where the minimum wage is also high but the enforcement of legislation is much stricter than in Latin America. Similarly, macroeconomic conditions are likely to be important. A rising minimum wage in a rapidly growing economy may help to distribute the fruits of growth more evenly across workers by lifting the earnings of unskilled workers without sizable employment losses. On the other hand, a rising minimum wage in a context of low growth may backfire, because employment losses among unskilled workers may outweigh wage gains.

In Latin America, minimum wages doubled or tripled over roughly a decade in many countries—a noticeable exception being Mexico. In Brazil, the real minimum wage increased by 130 percent from 1995 to 2014,[5] in Chile it doubled over the same period, in Peru it doubled from 1996 to 2013, and in Uruguay it doubled during the 2000s (as shown in figure 5.1). Moreover, although there is some variation among the region's countries, high real rates of minimum wage growth really began to take off around 2002.

Compliance with minimum wage laws is also quite varied throughout the region. Although the percentage of formal workers making less than one minimum wage is small in almost all of Latin America, the existence of an informal sector makes all minimum wage analysis more complex and dependent on the cross-wage elasticity showing how informal sector employment reacts to formal sector wages. In a nutshell, the interplay between the formal and informal sectors as well as imperfect enforcement makes the analysis of the effects of the minimum wage on wage inequality different from that in developed countries.

The effect of these trends on wage inequality depends on whether the new minimum wage level is binding (an indicator of which is the ratio of the minimum wage to the median wage). Minimum wage levels vary considerably by country.

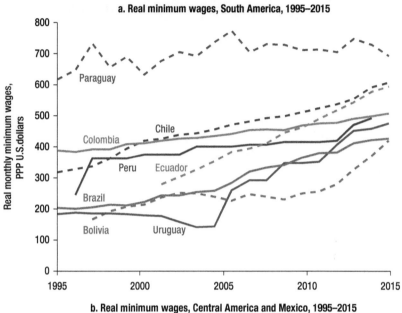

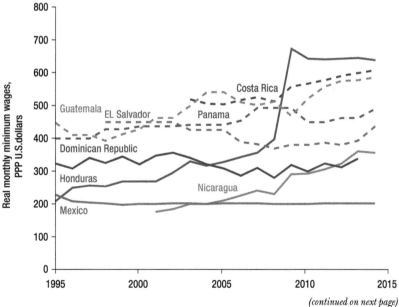

(continued on next page)

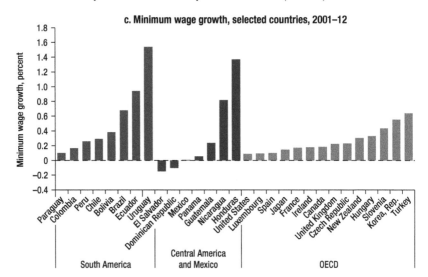

c. Minimum wage growth, selected countries, 2001–12

Sources: OECD.Stat (http://stats.oecd.org/) for OECD minimum wages; official country data for minimum wages in Latin America.

Note: All minimum wages expressed in U.S. dollars, purchasing power parity (PPP). OECD = Organisation for Economic Co-operation and Development. Because a unified minimum wage does not exist in Central American countries, the lowest urban minimum wage in each country is selected as the de facto minimum wage.

This heterogeneity implies differences in the relevance of minimum wage policy that likely affect the impact of the minimum wage on wage inequality. In countries where the minimum wage bite is high, there is a larger risk that further minimum wage increases will either adversely affect employment rates or push vulnerable workers (such as unskilled workers, young people, and women) either into informal-sector jobs or out of the labor force entirely. Annex 5A provides further details on the changes in minimum wages and compliance in the region as well as on the relationship of those wages with inequality measures.

In the literature, the general conclusion is that an increasing minimum wage, despite pervasive incomplete compliance and ever-present but small employment losses, still has a wage-equalizing effect. This effect, however, depends largely upon the level of the minimum wage with respect to the country-specific wage distribution.[6] (Annex 5B further discusses the profile of minimum wage earners.) In much of Latin America, before the large increases of the 21st century, the minimum wage was too low to be binding in the formal sector, and most of the adjustment occurred among informal workers to whom, in principle, the legislation did not apply (Maloney and Nuñez-Mendez 2004; Neri, Gonzaga, and Camargo 2000). The minimum wage also appeared to create numeraire effects that echo higher up the wage distribution.[7] Measured unemployment effects are, for the most part, modest (Bell 1997; Lemos 2004). A recent study shows that the effects on informality instead may be important (Lotti, Messina, and Nunziata 2016).

Considerable studies have been conducted (especially in Brazil but also in Colombia and Central America) on the minimum wage and its effects before most Latin American minimum wages began their ascent at the end of the past century and the first decade of this one. A summary of their findings follows:

- The literature on Brazil analyzing the period before high minimum wage growth, summarized in Ulyssea and Foguel (2006), shows that increases in the minimum wage led to modest reductions in employment and reduced the wage dispersion among those who remained employed. However, in a context of low growth and stagnation of average income during the 1995–2002 period, the rising minimum wage was associated with higher noncompliance with the law, resulting in increasing inequality (Ferreira, Firpo, and Messina 2017; Silva, Almeida, and Strokova 2015).

- Bravo and Contreras (1998) and Saavedra and Torero (2000) find small negative employment effects and reductions in inequality for Chile and Peru, respectively.

- In Mexico and Uruguay, the minimum wage is so low (relative to the median wage) that it is either virtually nonbinding or relevant only in the first decile of the wage distribution. The discussion mirrors that of the United States: the minimum wage has small effects on inequality or poverty because of its low level and variations.

- At the other extreme, in Colombia, the minimum wage is so high that increasing it would have no positive effects on either inequality or poverty, while it would have the usual negative effects on formal employment (Arango and Pachón 2004; Hernández and Pinzon 2006).

- Finally, in the Central American countries—with their multiple minimum wages by industry, region, category, and even educational attainment—the analytical approach has to be different. Nevertheless, in Costa Rica and Honduras, high minimum wages for unskilled workers combined with not-so-high minimum wages for skilled workers may have reduced wage inequality (Gindling and Terrell 2004, 2006).

In sum, the literature on the period before high minimum wage growth largely concludes that the minimum wage has had equalizing effects, perhaps with the exception of Brazil, despite its effects on increasing unemployment, and that much of the wage distribution is unaffected because of noncompliance.

Relatively few studies have been undertaken concerning the minimum wage during the boom years. Those that exist, however, produced the following findings:

- *In Argentina,* the increase of the minimum wage transformed it into a relevant institution not only in the formal sector but also, increasingly, in the informal sector (Maurizio 2014).

- *In Brazil,* a rapid raise of the minimum wage during the boom period had equalizing effects because employers could increase the wages of workers earning near the minimum wage, implying an improvement in the compliance rate of employers and increasing wages for workers near the low end of the distribution (Corseuil, Foguel, and Hecksher 2015; Ferreira, Firpo, and Messina 2017).

- *In Chile,* the minimum wage continues to increase the wages of affected workers, with small unemployment effects, leading unambiguously to an increase in wage equality (Grau and Landerretche 2011).

- *In Uruguay,* the minimum wage increase in the 2000s had insignificant unemployment effects and reduced wage inequality only slightly from 2004 to 2006 (Alves et al. 2012).

In sum, the effects of the minimum wage on wage inequality depend on its level, how much it increases, the extent of noncompliance, and whether it is binding—aspects that the subsections below will further discuss.

Minimum Wage Levels and Paths

The minimum wage has followed different paths in different Latin American countries since 1995, depending on its initial level at the beginning of this period and on the specifics of each country's minimum wage policy. The rules and regulations that govern the process for setting the minimum wage vary greatly by country (box 5.1).

Minimum wage trends in South America differ considerably from those in Central America and the Caribbean (figure 5.1, panels a and b). In Colombia, and especially in Paraguay, the real minimum wage was already quite high in 1995 compared with other Latin American countries.

At the other extreme (in Bolivia, Brazil, and Uruguay), the minimum wage was quite low, whether compared with other Latin American countries or with the countries' own historical levels.

Since 1995, and particularly after the commodity boom that began around 2002, minimum wages increased rapidly in all the South American countries that did not have high minimum wages in 1995. In the countries where the minimum wage had been very low, it increased even faster. In Bolivia, Brazil, Chile, Ecuador, and Uruguay, the minimum wage at least doubled over little more than a decade.

The constitutions of almost all Latin American countries mention the minimum wage. The only exceptions are the constitutions of Chile, Ecuador, Haiti, and Jamaica. The Jamaican constitution is quite minimalist, and the Chilean, Ecuadoran, and Haitian constitutions all mention a "fair wage" but not a minimum wage set by the state per se. Looking at constitutions, labor laws, and minimum wage laws across the region, a typical formulation is along the lines of Brazil's constitution, which states that the objective of a minimum wage is "to allow the worker and his family to live a materially, morally, and culturally dignified life."

Setting the Minimum Wage: State-Specific, Sector-Specific, and Demographic Group–Specific Levels

Within Latin America, "national" minimum wages coexist with state-sanctioned wage bargaining through three different models:

- Some countries (for example, Brazil and Chile) have a single "national" minimum wage, and employers and employees negotiate wages, either individually or through their respective organizations, with little state involvement. In the past, the state was involved in collective bargaining—and some countries, like Peru, still have such provisions on the books—but today wages by sector are negotiated between employers and their employees. Lately, some states have legislated minimum wages that are higher than the national minimum wage.

- Argentina, Ecuador, and Uruguay follow a second model that includes both a national minimum wage and strong state involvement in collective bargaining through wage councils. The minimum wage, however, is kept separate from state-supervised or state-sanctioned collective bargaining.

- In most of Central America the two issues come together, making for a plethora of minimum wages within each country. For example, Panama's latest law (2016) has 109 categories and about 20 different minimum wages, Costa Rica has 13 different sectoral minimum wages, Honduras has about 42, and El Salvador has 2 agricultural and 3 nonagricultural minimum wages. The Dominican Republic has wages not by sector (except for agriculture and security guards) but by firm size. Nonetheless, there is a trend toward convergence. Panama, for example, still sets wages for over 100 sectors, but successive laws have assigned the same minimum wage to different sectors. In El Salvador and Guatemala, only a few sectors currently have special minimum wages, mostly pertaining to agriculture and manufacturing.

(continued on next page)

Despite the many within-country variations, including some that persist in South America, the overall trend is clear—toward a single, unified minimum wage for all. However, this unifying trend is evolving faster in some dimensions and country aggregates than in others.

Wage-Setting Mechanisms

The usual mechanism for setting the minimum wage is through a tripartite wage council (comprising workers, employees, and government) that suggests the new minimum wage to the labor ministry, which then makes the final decision. There are variations on this theme. In Colombia and Panama, for example, if the wage council cannot reach a decision by consensus, the executive branch, through the labor ministry, may set the new wage by decree. Consensus rarely occurs, so the minimum wage is de facto set by decree.

In other countries (for example, El Salvador and Jamaica), the wage council exists only to advise the labor minister, who shoulders the full responsibility for setting the minimum wage. Finally, in many countries (such as Costa Rica, Paraguay, and Peru), the commission sends a majority proposal to the labor minister, who can either accept it or disregard it and set the wage himself or herself.

Two exceptions to all of the above are Argentina and Brazil, which are polar opposites in this regard. In Argentina, the National Council of Employment, Productivity, and the Minimum Wage is a bipartite commission of employers and employees with legal power to set the minimum wage The executive does not get involved except to convene the council. In contrast, Brazil has no such commission, and the minimum wage is currently set by a law approved by Congress. The current law states that the minimum wage will increase each year according to either the previous year's inflation or nominal GDP growth lagged two years, whichever is greater. Congress updates the law every four years.

In Colombia, the rate of increase was much more modest, and in Paraguay it has not increased in real terms since about 2003. Although workers in countries that already had high minimum wages in 1995 saw modest increases at best, the workers in economies where the floors were low saw high minimum wage increases (figure 5.1, panel a).

In Central America and Mexico, the pattern is less clear. Costa Rica, El Salvador, Guatemala, and Panama had minimum wages that were on the higher side in purchasing power parity (PPP) U.S. dollars. Honduras, Nicaragua, and particularly Mexico had minimum wages on the lower side. Workers in Guatemala, Nicaragua, Panama, and particularly Honduras saw the minimum wage increase rapidly.

Workers in Mexico, however, continue to languish under a low minimum wage, and workers in the Dominican Republic and El Salvador have seen the minimum wage rise and then fall such that its value in real terms has changed little since 1995 (figure 5.1, panel b).

Minimum wage growth during the 2000s in Bolivia, Brazil, Chile, Ecuador, and Uruguay has been higher than in most other Latin American countries and Organisation for Economic Co-operation and Development (OECD) countries (figure 5.1, panel c).

Looking at the minimum wage as a percentage of the median wage, we can divide Latin America into two groups of countries: one where this indicator has clearly increased, and one where this indicator has trended downward since 2002–03. In Bolivia, Paraguay, and Peru, the minimum wage has merely kept up with median wage growth, and in Colombia it has been falling since 2001 (figure 5.2, panel a). In Argentina, Brazil, Chile, Ecuador, and Uruguay, the minimum wage has risen faster than median wages (figure 5.2, panel b).

FIGURE 5.2: **Ratios of Minimum Wage to Median Wage in Latin America and Comparisons with Selected Organisation for Economic Co-operation and Development Countries**

a. Countries where ratio did not increase, 1995–2014

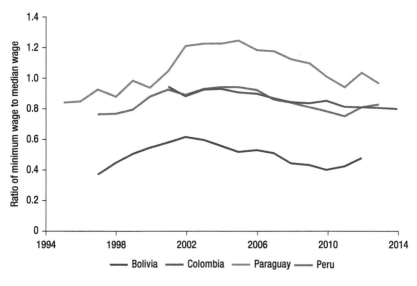

(continued on next page)

Ratios of Minimum Wage to Median Wage in Latin America and Comparisons with Selected Organisation for Economic Co-operation and Development Countries *(continued)*

b. Countries where ratio increased, 1995–2014

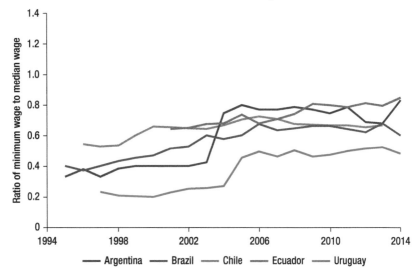

— Argentina — Brazil — Chile — Ecuador — Uruguay

c. Comparison with selected OECD countries, 2001 vs. 2012

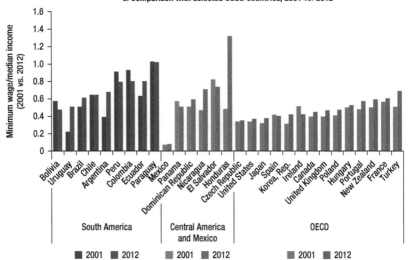

South America | Central America and Mexico | OECD

■ 2001 ■ 2012   ■ 2001 ■ 2012   ■ 2001 ■ 2012

Sources: Calculations based on official country data for minimum wages in Latin America. Median wages from Socio-Economic Database for Latin America and the Caribbean (SEDLAC), Universidad Nacional de la Plata (CEDLAS) and the World Bank (http://sedlac.econo.unlp.edu.ar/eng/). OECD.Stat (http://stats.oecd.org/) for OECD minimum and median wages.
Note: OECD = Organisation for Economic Co-operation and Development. Because a unified minimum wage does not exist in Central American countries, the lowest urban minimum in each country is selected as the de facto minimum wage. Mean wages are for full-time employers, employees, and self-employed workers who are ages 15–65. 0 and 99th percentile income not included.

Notice that, at the end of our period, the ratio of the minimum wage to the median wage has shown some convergence toward values between 0.6 and 0.8, with considerably less variation than in 1995. These values are high compared with high-income countries, where the minimum wage fluctuates between 0.37 and 0.6 of the median wage. Around the world, countries outside Latin America cluster around 0.4 (figure 5.2, panel c).

Extent and Evolution of Minimum Wage Compliance

To analyze compliance, we plot the percentage of workers who make less than one minimum wage against the ratio of the minimum wage to the median wage.[8] Among South American countries, Paraguay and, to a lesser extent, Colombia and Peru, have minimum wages that are quite high (figure 5.3, panel a). Perhaps needless to say, non-compliance is also high in all three countries, and 40 percent or more of the population makes less than the floor. Among Central American countries, Guatemala and Honduras are also in this situation (figure 5.3, panel b). Mexico is the country with the most room to increase its low minimum wage without significantly affecting compliance.

FIGURE 5.3: **Ratio of Minimum Wage to Median Wage and Noncompliance with the Minimum Wage, South America, and Central America and Mexico, 1995–2014**

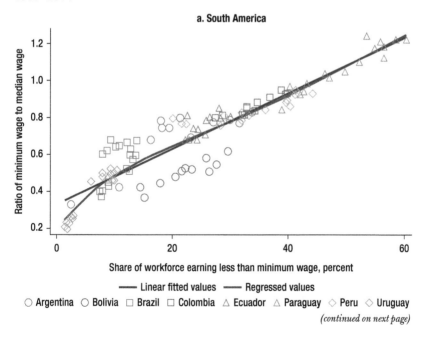

(continued on next page)

FIGURE 5.3: **Ratio of Minimum Wage to Median Wage and Noncompliance with the Minimum Wage, South America, and Central America and Mexico, 1995–2014** *(continued)*

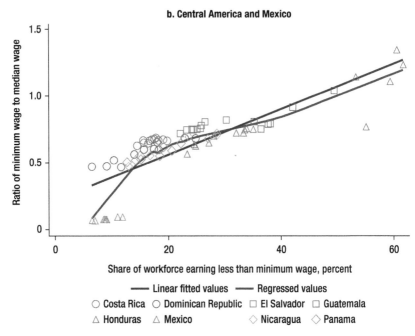

b. Central America and Mexico

Sources: Calculations based on official country data for minimum wages in Latin America; median wages from Socio-Economic Database for Latin America and the Caribbean (SEDLAC), Universidad Nacional de la Plata (CEDLAS) and the World Bank (http://sedlac.econo.unlp.edu.ar/eng/).

Note: Mean wages are for full-time employers, employees, and self-employed workers who are ages 15–65. 0 and 99th percentile income are not included. Each symbol represents a country in a given year. Minimum wages chosen are the lowest urban minimum wage in each country within often-complicated minimum wage schedules. Analyses along the lines of Gindling and Terrell (2007) for Costa Rica or Gindling and Trejos (2010) for El Salvador—which explicitly take into account the many values of the minimum wage—may be more adequate than the approach taken here, which defines the minimum wage as the lowest of these multiple minima.

Overall, the regional data show a negative correlation between the minimum wage level and compliance. Surprisingly, the compliance trade-off is almost linear: a 10 percent increase in the minimum-wage-to-median-wage ratio increases noncompliance by about 1 percentage point. This relationship is confirmed in regression analysis controlling for gross domestic product (GDP) growth and country fixed effects.

The negative relationship between the minimum wage level and compliance means that the advantages and drawbacks of increasing the wage floor in

Latin America must be analyzed differently than in developed countries. To determine whether increasing minimum wages is a desirable policy, the literature concerning OECD countries pits the unemployment effects of increasing the minimum wage against the compression of the earnings distribution of those who remain employed after a minimum wage increase.[9] However, in the developing world—and Latin America is no exception—this is a flawed approach because of imperfect compliance (Lotti, Messina, and Nunziata 2016). When analyzing the impact of raising wage floors in Latin America, one must analyze those whose incomes increase with the minimum wage, those who become unemployed, and those (many) who simply see the minimum wage pass them by with few effects upon their earnings.[10]

Variation across Countries in the Legal Force of Minimum Wage Laws

Given the heterogeneity of the minimum wage relative to the median wage, minimum wage legislation is binding in only a few countries. Figure 5.4 shows kernel estimates of the wage density for all salaried workers in various Latin American countries.[11] In Brazil and Chile, the spikes in density are high around the minimum wage (figure 5.4, panels a and b). They also increase in height, showing that more and more workers are making the minimum wage as it increases. Finally, there is a large drop-off to the left of the spike, showing reasonable compliance and suggesting that many of these workers are now in the spike, although, as everywhere in Latin America, some workers are to the left of the spike (indicating noncompliance).

In contrast, in Honduras and Peru, the minimum wage appears to be largely ignored (figure 5.4, panels c and d). There is no spike in the wage density, the area to the left of the minimum wage being as dense as the area to its right. In these high minimum wage countries, the effects of the wage floor are limited both by noncompliance and by the fact that any workers whose wages are being pushed up by the minimum are close to or above the median wage. A policy that increases the wages of the upper half can hardly be considered a policy for wage equality.

The final subgroup of countries comprises Mexico and Uruguay, which are countries with a low minimum-wage-to-median-wage ratio (figure 5.4, panels e and f). In Mexico, the blue and red vertical lines are far to the left of almost all the wage density, and the minimum wage there does not seem to affect the wage distribution. In Uruguay—where the minimum wage was so low as to catch almost no one in 2002 but where, 10 years later, the minimum wage had increased much faster than the median wage—there is no spike (although some of this may represent small sample sizes) and apparently no truncation just below it. The minimum wage there may have limited effects, neither pushing a great many workers forward nor leading them into unemployment.

Kernel Estimates of Wage Density for All Salaried Workers, Selected Latin American Countries

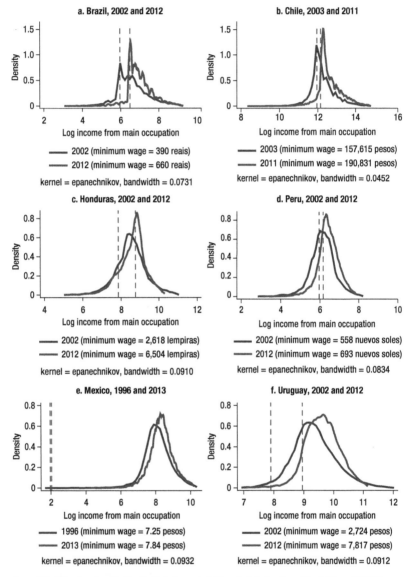

a. Brazil, 2002 and 2012

Log income from main occupation

—— 2002 (minimum wage = 390 reais)
—— 2012 (minimum wage = 660 reais)

kernel = epanechnikov, bandwidth = 0.0731

b. Chile, 2003 and 2011

Log income from main occupation

—— 2003 (minimum wage = 157,615 pesos)
—— 2011 (minimum wage = 190,831 pesos)

kernel = epanechnikov, bandwidth = 0.0452

c. Honduras, 2002 and 2012

Log income from main occupation

—— 2002 (minimum wage = 2,618 lempiras)
—— 2012 (minimum wage = 6,504 lempiras)

kernel = epanechnikov, bandwidth = 0.0910

d. Peru, 2002 and 2012

Log income from main occupation

—— 2002 (minimum wage = 558 nuevos soles)
—— 2012 (minimum wage = 693 nuevos soles)

kernel = epanechnikov, bandwidth = 0.0834

e. Mexico, 1996 and 2013

Log income from main occupation

—— 1996 (minimum wage = 7.25 pesos)
—— 2013 (minimum wage = 7.84 pesos)

kernel = epanechnikov, bandwidth = 0.0932

f. Uruguay, 2002 and 2012

Log income from main occupation

—— 2002 (minimum wage = 2,724 pesos)
—— 2012 (minimum wage = 7,817 pesos)

kernel = epanechnikov, bandwidth = 0.0912

Source: Calculations based on data from the Socio-Economic Database for Latin America and the Caribbean (SEDLAC), Universidad Nacional de la Plata (CEDLAS) and the World Bank (http://sedlac.econo.unlp.edu.ar/eng/).
Note: Vertical lines represent the log of the minimum wage in initial (red dashed) and final (blue dashed) year. Because a unified minimum wage does not exist in Central American countries, the lowest urban minimum wage is selected as the de facto minimum wage. Minimum wages are defined per month in Brazil, Chile, Honduras, Peru, and Uruguay, and per hour in Mexico, as per minimum wage policy in each country.

The Differentiated Effect of the Minimum Wage on Wage Inequality in Good and Bad Times

A common approach used to identify the effects of the minimum wage is to find a comparison group of people who resemble minimum wage workers but do not make the minimum wage. Following Corseuil and Carneiro (2001) and using panel data for Brazil (from the Monthly Employment Survey) and Paraguay (from the Continuous Employment Survey), we quantify worker flows from formal employment to unemployment and to informality just before and just after the legislation changes and the minimum wage increases. The treatment group in this analysis is composed of those whose earnings fall between the new and old minimum wages, including those who make exactly the old (but not the new) minimum wage. These individuals constitute the group whose wages will be set by the new minimum wage legislation. The comparison group includes (1) those whose wages fall just beneath the initial minimum wage, who are illegal or informal during both periods, and who are thus, in principle, not affected by the minimum wage; and (2) those whose wages fall just above the final minimum wage, and whose earnings thus are also not affected by the change.[12]

In Paraguay, the results on unemployment and formality depend on GDP growth. When GDP was growing fast (in 2010), the minimum wage increase sent no one into unemployment, showing actually positive effects (all significant at least at 10 percent). However, when GDP growth fell to a still-healthy 4–5 percent (in 2012), the elasticity turned negative, meaning that increases in the minimum wage would lead to small increases in unemployment. Regarding formality, no pattern in relation to GDP growth could be discerned.

Results for Brazil cover a larger period (2003–15), as presented in figure 5.5. They show that employment elasticity of the minimum wage depends on how well the economy is doing, albeit with a lag. The lag is not surprising, because the labor market in general lags the performance of the economy. GDP growth was high from 2008 to 2012, and during 2008–15 there are no unemployment effects of increasing the minimum wage. The trend is downward, and it would not have been a surprise if elasticity had turned negative again in 2016, as it was during the low-growth years before 2006. Regarding formality, the relationship appears less clear, but the high-growth years are also positive formality elasticity years. These results suggest that when the economy is doing well, Brazil has space to raise the minimum wage with small or no adverse effects on the labor market in terms of unemployment and informality.

The relationship between minimum wages and compliance also responds to GDP growth. Table 5.1 shows coefficients of cross-country regressions in which the percentage of the labor force making less than one minimum wage is the dependent variable, and the minimum-wage-to-median-wage ratio as well as GDP and GDP growth are the explanatory variables.

FIGURE 5.5: **Effects of the Minimum Wage on Unemployment and Formality in Brazil, 2003–15**

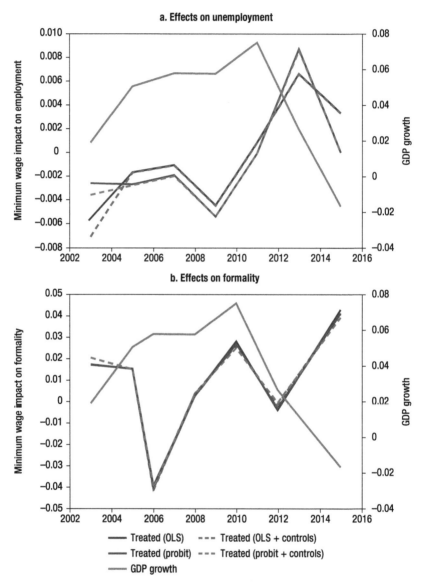

a. Effects on unemployment

b. Effects on formality

—— Treated (OLS)   === Treated (OLS + controls)
—— Treated (probit)   === Treated (probit + controls)
—— GDP growth

Sources: Calculations based on official country data for minimum wages in Latin America; Labor Database for Latin America and the Caribbean (LABLAC) (http://lablac.econo.unlp.edu.ar/eng/index.php).
Note: GDP = gross domestic product; OLS = ordinary least squares.

TABLE 5.1: **Cross-Country Regression of Minimum Wage Noncompliance as a Function of GDP, GDP Growth, and the Ratio of the Minimum Wage to the Median Wage**

Variables	Dependent variable: minimum wage noncompliance				
	(1)	(2)	(3)	(4)	(5)
a. South America					
Minimum wage/median income	0.37 (0.00)	0.32 (0.00)	0.35 (0.00)	0.36 (0.00)	0.34 (0.00)
Log GDP per capita	−0.03 (0.20)				−0.03 (0.26)
GDP per capita growth		−0.24 (0.15)			−0.20
Country dummies	Yes	Yes	Yes	No	Yes
N	128	121	128	128	121
R-squared	0.96	0.96	0.96	0.90	0.96
b. Central America					
Minimum wage/median income	0.38 (0.00)	0.41 (0.00)	0.41 (0.00)	0.27 (0.00)	0.37 (0.00)
Log GDP per capita	0.04 (0.41)				0.05 (0.31)
GDP per capita growth		−0.02 (0.95)			−0.08 (0.83)
Country dummies	Yes	Yes	Yes	No	Yes
N	114	112	114	114	112
R-squared	0.77	0.77	0.77	0.67	0.71

Source: Calculations using Labor Database for Latin America and the Caribbean (LABLAC) (http://lablac.econo.unlp.edu.ar/eng /index.php).

Regardless of the model specification, the effect of the minimum-wage-to-median-wage ratio on noncompliance is almost constant: an increase of 10 percent in this ratio leads to an increase of about 4 percentage points in noncompliance. Interesting, too, is that the equation clearly shows that GDP growth allows for lower effects of noncompliance from similar increases in the minimum wage. Column (2) shows that a 1 percentage point increase in GDP growth decreases noncompliance by 0.24 percentage points for South America, although the coefficient is only significant at the 15 percent level. The implication is that if GDP is growing at a 5 percent annual rate, for example, the minimum-wage-to-median-wage ratio could increase by up to 3 percent with no adverse effects on the percentage of individuals making less than the minimum wage.

Table 5.1 also shows the same coefficients for Central America. In this case, perhaps because of the fundamentally different nature of minimum wages in Central America, neither GDP level nor GDP growth seem to affect noncompliance with the minimum wage.

What were the consequences of minimum wage changes on the recent changes in wage inequality in the region? In line with the earlier discussion, the work of Ferreira, Firpo, and Messina (2017) suggests that, in Brazil, the consequences largely depended on macroeconomic conditions.[13] The authors use the framework recently proposed by Firpo, Fortin, and Lemieux (2009), which generalizes the traditional Oaxaca-Blinder decomposition to other statistics beyond the mean to analyze how changes in the wage structure can be traced back to changes in worker characteristics (the endowment effect) or changes in the returns associated with those characteristics (the structure effect).

Ferreira, Firpo, and Messina (2017) analyze the determinants of inequality (measured by the Gini coefficient) during the 1995-2012 period and two subperiods, 1995-2003 and 2003-12. The main difference between the two subperiods is that the first is a period of very low GDP growth, with declines of average and median earnings. The second subperiod is instead a period of rapid growth of GDP, median earnings, and average earnings. As discussed earlier, the minimum wage increased throughout the period, although much more rapidly during 2003-12 than during the first years of analysis.

Figure 5.6 summarizes the findings of Ferreira, Firpo, and Messina (2017) regarding the main drivers of inequality in Brazil. Interestingly, the study finds that, throughout the period, the contribution of the minimum wage was mildly regressive: the minimum wage increase was associated with a small increase in inequality of 1.2 Gini points for the period as a whole. This effect is driven primarily by noncompliance (the endowment effect). However, this overall impact hides very different behavior across subperiods. Low earnings growth during 1995-2003 implied that increases in the minimum wage were strongly associated with rising noncompliance. This endowment effect outweighed the positive impact on earnings for those workers earning the minimum. As a result, inequality increased.

On the other hand, the rapid increase of the minimum wage after 2003 is associated with a reduction in inequality. This is driven by two effects rowing in the same direction. Noncompliance declined (endowment effect), and those workers at the minimum (an increasing share) saw their earnings grow faster than average earnings.[14] Overall, Ferreira, Firpo, and Messina (2017) find that the contribution of the minimum wage to reducing inequality during the boom years was some 20 percent. Other factors, including the decline of the schooling and experience premiums discussed in chapter 3, appear to have played more important roles.

FIGURE 5.6: Decomposition of Factors Contributing to Wage Inequality Changes in Brazil, 1995–2003 vs. 2003–12

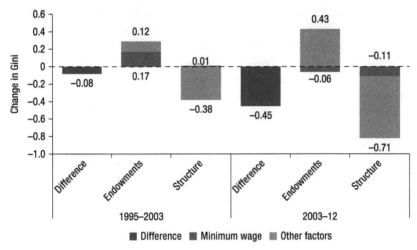

■ Difference ■ Minimum wage ▨ Other factors

Source: Ferreira, Firpo, and Messina (2017).
Note: Wage inequality changes measured by the changes in the (log) interquartile range between the 90th percentile and the 10th percentile. "Difference" refers to the difference in the endowment and structure change. "Endowments," or the composition effect, refers to changes in the distribution of workers' observable characteristics, keeping returns fixed. "Structure" refers to changes in returns, keeping the composition of employment fixed. "Other factors" includes differences based on changes in human capital, gender, race, urban and rural regions, and in the case of structure effects, unobservable characteristics.

The Role of Unionization in Wage Inequality

In developed countries, unions are usually associated with both higher pay and lower wage inequality. In addition to showing that the union wage premium is almost always positive and significant, the considerable literature on unions and wage inequality has shown that unions reduce both (1) the importance of standard wage-determining factors (schooling, occupation, gender, and race) on earnings; and (2) wage inequality as a whole among union members (Card 1992; DiNardo, Hallock, and Pischke 1997; Freeman 1980; Hirsch 1982). Some authors have argued that the fall in union membership has been one of the factors leading to higher inequality in the United Kingdom and the United States (DiNardo, Fortin, and Lemieux 1995; Gosling and Machin 1995).

As with minimum wages, things are not so simple in Latin America. First, unions are a heterogeneous factor throughout the region, ranging from Argentina's strong unions to Chile's low-coverage unions (Drake 2003). Furthermore, union membership in Latin America is often, but not always, higher among those in the upper half of the wage distribution, with public sector unions playing an important role. In light of this, the economic impact of unionization on inequality is likely to vary by country.

For example, Fairris (2003), using counterfactuals, finds that falling union density and falling union effectiveness caused the wage distribution in Mexico to be 11 percent more unequal than it would have been if unions had not lost their power in Mexico. On the other hand, the Mexican unions apparently have very small effects on wages but manage to preserve unskilled jobs (Maloney and Ribeiro 1999). In general, unionization in Latin America tends to be associated with public sector employment and state-owned enterprises.

Analyses of unionization trends and wage inequality in selected countries of the region included the following findings:

- *In Argentina,* little work has been done on the effect of unions on wage inequality. Gasparini, Marchionni, and Escudero (2001) discuss the possibility that increased union activity (of which there is no doubt) has led to greater wage equality, but they present little empirical evidence.

- *In Brazil,* where union members are mostly in the upper half of the income distribution, the fall in union density was an equalizing force (Abrache 1999; Menezes-Filho et al. 2005).

- *In Uruguay,* unions went from being banned during the 1973–84 military dictatorship to being participants in tripartite bargaining from 1984–91 and being completely free from 1992 onward. The results appear to have been positive, with collective bargaining between employers and unions leading to greater equality in the wage distribution and increasingly cooperative relations between labor and management (Cassoni, Labadie, and Fachola 2001).

The one fact that is present everywhere in Latin America is the fall in union density since the early 1990s. The studies mentioned above show that union density fell in Brazil from over 22 percent to under 17 percent; in Mexico, from over 30 percent to under 20 percent; in Peru, from close to 60 percent to close to 30 percent; and even in Uruguay, where, after an initial increase from zero to about 60 percent of workers, union density is about 15 percent (Saavedra and Torero 2005). However, we have surprisingly little information regarding the coverage of union contracts in the region. Automatic extension clauses are likely to be important in the formal sector of many countries, with the implication that wages negotiated by union representatives cover workers who are not unionized. Similarly, union-negotiated wages may affect workers who are not unionized through various spillover effects.

The available evidence on the role of unions in the structure of wages in Latin America poses numerous challenges, and is limited to a handful of countries.

However, some conclusions emerge. Overall, the effect of unions is more nuanced in Latin America than in OECD countries. It appears to depend on (1) where in the wage distribution unionized workers are to be found; (2) which institutions govern the unions (pertaining to whether nonunion workers get to benefit from union bargaining, whether there is firm-level or industry-level bargaining, and how involved government is in wage bargaining); and (3) the evolution of union density and in which industries it occurs. Most studies find that the effects are pro-equality (except in Brazil) and small (except in Uruguay) and that their magnitude is dwarfed by supply-and-demand factors, transfers, or even the minimum wage.

Conclusions

Institutional and regulatory factors are not equally binding in all Latin American countries. Brazilian minimum wage legislation appears to be the most binding in the region, followed by such legislation in Peru and Colombia.[15] Formality has been on the rise, but the levels of informality in the region are still high and vary substantially across countries. The share of the workforce that is unionized is largest in Peru and Argentina (around 30 percent), followed by Mexico, Brazil, and Uruguay (around 20 percent), but it is even lower in the other countries.

This chapter has identified, based on new and existing evidence, three country-specific factors that determine the extent to which labor market institutions—specifically, minimum wages and the level of unionization—equalize (or not) the distribution of wages:

- *The extent to which minimum wages are binding.* This largely depends on the placement of the minimum wage in the distribution of wages. However, the higher the minimum wage, the higher the noncompliance with the law. Thus, countries in Latin America face a trade-off between the level of minimum wages and compliance with the law. In countries where the minimum wage is close to or higher than the median, the minimum wage is associated with noncompliance levels of 40 percent or more (two in five workers make less than the wage floor). In these cases, further increases in the minimum wage are unlikely to be equalizing. Kernel analysis suggests that in Brazil and Chile, where the minimum wage is 60–70 percent of the median wage, the spike is big, and the wage distribution to the left and to the right of the minimum wage is markedly different. Consequently, minimum wages are highly binding. In countries such as Colombia and Paraguay, there are fewer signs of binding minimum wages: the minimum wage is close to the median wage, the spike is small, and the wage distribution to the left and right of the minimum wage appears more or less the same. In various Latin American countries, this ratio of the minimum wage to the median wage has risen to around 0.6, a level at which the minimum wage apparently still has an equalizing effect on the wage distribution.

- *Overall economic growth and minimum wages.* A country's economic environment is important. Both cross-country regressions and panel analysis suggest that it is possible to increase the minimum-wage-to-median-wage ratio if the economy is growing strongly and less possible if it is not. The evidence is reinforced by detailed microdata analysis for Brazil (Ferreira, Firpo, and Messina 2017). During a period of slow growth and falling average wages (1995–2003), increases in the minimum wage were inequality-enhancing, as an increasing fraction of workers were not covered by the law (that is, their wages fell below the minimum wage). During the high-growth period that followed (2003–12), which was characterized by rising average earnings, the rapidly growing minimum wage substantially helped reduce earnings inequality as noncompliance with the law declined. A growing economy also makes increasing formalization possible and may help lead to formalization among lower-earning workers, a feature that chapter 2 identified as important for the recent inequality reduction trends.

- *Effects of falling union density.* The trend in falling union density has coexisted with falling wage inequality, which is at odds with developed-country literature, but a crucial distinction regards *who* is ceasing to be unionized. If union workers are concentrated in the upper tail of the earnings distribution, then falling union density may lead to higher equality. However, when nonunionized workers benefit from higher, union-negotiated wages, as in much of the region, unions will have equalizing effects even when union density is low (as in Uruguay).

What do we actually know about the effect of regulations and institutions on wage inequality? Reviewing the existing and newly collected evidence, it is clear that the effect of institutional and regulatory variables on wage inequality is context-specific. It is possible, however, to assert that active minimum wage policies may reduce wage inequality, potentially at the cost of higher unemployment and informality. Moreover, the relationship of the minimum wage level and noncompliance with the law is almost constant: an increase of 10 percent in the minimum-wage-to-median-wage ratio leads to an increase of about 4 percentage points in noncompliance.

We know much less about the effect of unions on the distribution of earnings. Given the fragmented nature of unionization in the region, the effect of unions depends on where the unionized workers lie along the income distribution and on what the unions' preferences are concerning inequality among their members. The few results in the literature are mixed and country-specific, with falling unionization being either equalizing or unequalizing depending on the country context.

Annex 5A. Supplementary Minimum Wage Information

TABLE 5A.1: Changes in Minimum Wage Indicators, Selected Latin American Countries, 1995–2003, 2003–13, and 1995–2013

(annualized change, percentage points)

Country	Change in ratio of minimum wage to median wage	Change in minimum wage noncompliance rate
	a. 1995–2003	
South America		
Argentina	1.2	1.0
Bolivia	1.5	1.7
Brazil	0.8	2.5
Chile	0.5	2.3
Ecuador	n.a.	n.a.
Peru	2.7	2.1
Uruguay	0.1	0.3
Central America and Mexico		
Costa Rica	n.a.	n.a.
Dominican Republic	0.7	1.9
El Salvador	−0.5	−0.2
Honduras	1.1	2.0
Mexico	−0.3	−4.6
Nicaragua	n.a.	n.a.
Panama	1.0	1.1
	b. 2003–13	
South America		
Argentina	−2.6	5.7
Bolivia	−0.7	−1.2
Brazil	−0.4	0.8
Chile	−0.6	0.3
Ecuador	0.5	1.2
Peru	−1.2	−1.0
Uruguay	0.7	2.6

(continued on next page)

TABLE 5A.1: **Changes in Minimum Wage Indicators, Selected Latin American Countries, 1995–2003, 2003–13, and 1995–2013** *(continued)*
(annualized change, percentage points)

Country	Change in ratio of minimum wage to median wage	Change in minimum wage noncompliance rate
b. 2003–13 *(continued)*		
Central America and Mexico		
Costa Rica	0.3	0.2
Dominican Republic	0.5	0.9
El Salvador	−0.2	−0.6
Honduras	2.8	5.4
Mexico	0.0	6.3
Nicaragua	1.4	1.4
Panama	−0.6	−0.6
c. 1995–2013		
South America		
Argentina	−0.9	3.6
Bolivia	0.3	0.1
Brazil	0.1	1.5
Chile	−0.1	1.2
Ecuador	n.a.	n.a.
Peru	0.5	0.4
Uruguay	0.4	1.6
Central America and Mexico		
Costa Rica	n.a.	n.a.
Dominican Republic	0.6	1.3
El Salvador	−0.3	−0.4
Honduras	2.1	3.9
Mexico	−0.1	1.4
Nicaragua	n.a.	n.a.
Panama	0.1	0.1

Sources: Calculations based on the Socio-Economic Database for Latin America and the Caribbean (SEDLAC), Universidad Nacional de la Plata (CEDLAS) and the World Bank (http://sedlac.econo.unlp.edu.ar/eng/). Real exchange data from the Internal Revenue Service, U.S. Treasury. Minimum wages from official country data.
Note: Mean wages for full-time employers, employees, and self-employed workers ages 15–65. Income for the 0 and 99th percentile is trimmed. n.a. = not applicable.

TABLE 5A.2: **Correlations of Changes in the Minimum Wage with Changes in Inequality-Related Indicators, Selected Latin American Countries, 1995–2003, 2003–13, and 1995–2013**

Indicator	Change in ratio of minimum wage to median wage	Change in minimum wage noncompliance rate
	a. 1995–2003	
Change in Gini total income	−0.1956* (0.0861)	−0.1956* (0.0861)
Change in Gini labor income	0.1261 (0.2714)	0.1261 (0.2714)
Change in returns to skill (completed tertiary vs. primary or less)	0.0314 (0.7851)	0.0314 (0.7851)
Change in returns to skill (completed tertiary vs. high school)	−0.0266 (0.8173)	−0.0266 (0.8173)
Change in the labor supply (completed tertiary vs. primary or less)	−0.1345 (0.2404)	−0.1345 (0.2404)
Change in the labor supply (completed tertiary vs. high school)	−0.1322 (0.2487)	−0.1322 (0.2487)
Change in aggregate domestic demand	−0.0321 (0.7804)	−0.0321 (0.7804)
Change in real exchange rate	−0.0260 (0.8216)	−0.1645 (0.1324)
Change in Gini not due to observables	0.1733 (0.1292)	0.2303* (0.0399)
Change in the ratio of minimum wage over median wage	1	
Change in the minimum wage noncompliance rate	0.6098* (0.0000)	1
	b. 2003–13	
Change in Gini total income	−0.0130 (0.8758)	0.0145 (0.8593)
Change in Gini labor income	−0.0053 (0.9487)	0.0580 (0.4776)
Change in returns to skill (completed tertiary vs. primary or less)	−0.0489 (0.5548)	0.0372 (0.6495)

(continued on next page)

Indicator	Change in ratio of minimum wage to median wage	Change in minimum wage noncompliance rate
b. 2003–13 *(continued)*		
Change in returns to skill (completed tertiary vs. high school)	0.0021 (0.9808)	−0.0210 (0.8045)
Change in the labor supply (completed tertiary vs. primary or less)	−0.0958 (0.2469)	−0.0667 (0.4141)
Change in the labor supply (completed tertiary vs. high school)	0.0557 (0.5011)	−0.0335 (0.6824)
Change in aggregate domestic demand	0.0126 (0.8792)	−0.1965* (0.0153)
Change in real exchange rate	−0.0479 (0.5633)	0.1070 (0.1896)
Change in Gini not due to observables	0.0347 (0.6852)	−0.0758 (0.3698)
Change in the ratio of minimum wage over median wage	1	
Change in the minimum wage noncompliance rate	−0.2981* (0.0002)	1
c. 1995–2013		
Change in Gini total income	−0.0527 (0.4431)	0.0090 (0.8937)
Change in Gini labor income	0.0323 (0.6388)	0.0454 (0.4991)
Change in returns to skill (completed tertiary vs. primary or less)	−0.0166 (0.8093)	0.0731 (0.2762)
Change in returns to skill (completed tertiary vs. high school)	−0.0002 (0.9980)	−0.0012 (0.9861)
Change in the labor supply (completed tertiary vs. primary or less)	−0.1150 (0.0935)	−0.0665 (0.3219)
Change in the labor supply (completed tertiary vs. high school)	0.0182 (0.7912)	−0.0582 (0.3857)
Change in aggregate domestic demand	−0.0179 (0.7943)	−0.1643* (0.0138)
Change in real exchange rate	−0.0395 (0.5652)	0.0036 (0.9567)

(continued on next page)

TABLE 5A.2: Correlations of Changes in the Minimum Wage with Changes in Inequality-Related Indicators, Selected Latin American Countries, 1995–2003, 2003–13, and 1995–2013 *(continued)*

Indicator	Change in ratio of minimum wage to median wage	Change in minimum wage noncompliance rate
c. 1995–2013 *(continued)*		
Change in Gini not due to observables	0.0734 (0.2957)	0.0274 (0.6940)
Change in the ratio of minimum wage over median wage	1	
Change in the minimum wage noncompliance rate	0.1507* (0.0278)	1

Sources: Gini coefficients adapted from Rodríguez-Castelán et al. (2016). Other data: authors' calculations based on the Socio-Economic Database for Latin America and the Caribbean (SEDLAC), Universidad Nacional de la Plata (CEDLAS) and the World Bank (http://sedlac.econo.unlp.edu.ar/eng/). Aggregate domestic demand data from the World Bank's World Development Indicators (http://data.worldbank.org/data-catalog/world-development-indicators). Real exchange data from the Internal Revenue Service, U.S. Treasury. Minimum wages from official country data.

Note: "Domestic demand" includes private consumption, public consumption, and gross capital formation. For all information regarding wages, the 1st and 99th percentiles for every country, year, gender, and education levels are trimmed. Gini not attributable to observables controls log of hourly wage with a set of 16 education dummies and 39 potential experience dummies. Mean wages for full-time employers, employees, and self-employed workers 15–65 years old. 0 and 99th percentile income trimmed.

Significance level: * = 1 percent.

Annex 5B. Who Makes the Minimum Wage in Latin America?

The impact of the minimum wage on household income inequality depends not only on its impact on the wage distribution, but also crucially on who makes the wage floor and where those earners fall in the household income distribution. If minimum wage earners are mostly in the lower tail of the household income distribution, even an imperfectly binding minimum wage is more likely to have a large impact on the income distribution. This is usually the case when those who make the wage floor are the primary breadwinners in the household. On the other hand, if most minimum wage earners are spouses or children of primary earners who make much more than the minimum wage, the effect will be diluted because of their higher position in the household income distribution.

In any case, the increase in primary workers making the minimum wage should show up as a shift in the distribution of minimum wage workers toward the lower end of the household income distribution. In other words, the minimum wage should become more progressive if more primary workers are earning it. One way to see this is through a concentration curve, which shows, on the horizontal axis, the accumulated per capita household income and, on the vertical axis, the concentration of the benefit or unit being measured—in this case, minimum wage workers.

A concentration curve that is arched toward the northwest (upper-left) corner of the graph is pro-poor, because most of the benefits being measured accrue to the lower tail of the household income distribution. Conversely, a concentration curve arched toward the southeast (lower-right) corner is pro-rich, because most of the benefits being measured lie in the upper tail of the income distribution. A concentration curve that is a straight line from (0,0) to (1,1) corresponds to equal benefits for rich and poor, because every 1 percent increase in income corresponds to a 1 percent increase in the distribution of the benefits being measured (in this case, minimum wages). Figure 5B.1, panels a and b, show the concentration curves of minimum wage workers by per capita household income percentile in Brazil and Uruguay in 2002 (in red) and 2014 (in blue).

The concentration curve for Brazil shows that minimum wage workers are more or less equally spread throughout the household income distribution. About 60 percent of the minimum wage workers come from households at or below the median household income, which indicates the effect is slightly progressive but not overwhelmingly so. Hence, Brazil—which in the 2000s was

FIGURE 5B.1: **Effect of the Minimum Wage on Different Household Income Levels, Selected Latin American Countries**

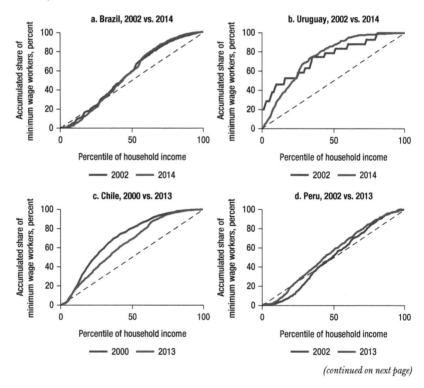

(continued on next page)

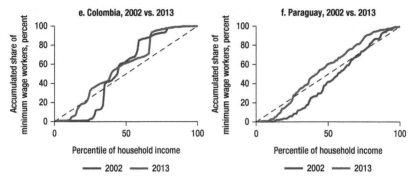

e. Colombia, 2002 vs. 2013

f. Paraguay, 2002 vs. 2013

Percentile of household income

——— 2002 ——— 2013

Source: Calculations based on data from the Socio-Economic Database for Latin America and the Caribbean (SEDLAC), Universidad Nacional de la Plata (CEDLAS) and the World Bank (http://sedlac.econo.unlp.edu.ar/eng/).
Note: Relative to the concentration curves shown, by year, the straight diagonal lines represent a perfect-equality scenario—that is, if rich and poor were to benefit equally from the minimum wage.

the poster child for the minimum wage in the labor market—ceases to be so when we consider the effect of the minimum wage on welfare.

The concentration curve for Uruguay, on the other hand, shows a much more pro-poor minimum wage. The fact that the minimum wage was so low in 2002 is responsible for the stepwise curve for that year, and thus it is perhaps best not to pay it too much attention. But in 2014 the distribution of minimum wage workers in Uruguay, almost 80 percent of whom reside in the poorest 40 percent of households, is definitely pro-poor. By this criterion, the minimum wage in Uruguay is much more redistributive (in terms of household income distribution) than that of Brazil.

What do the concentration curves look like for Chile and Peru? Remember that Chile is a medium-minimum-wage country while Peru is a high-minimum-wage country (relative to each country's median labor earnings). In Chile, the concentration curves of minimum wage workers arch upward, benefiting lower-income families and pulling the household income distribution toward equality (figure 5B.1, panel c). Although the curves are less pro-poor than those of Uruguay, remember that Chile has a higher minimum wage than Uruguay does. However, from 2000 to 2013 the minimum wage became less pro-poor in Chile. Peru's concentration curve, on the other hand, resembles Brazil's, with the minimum wage distributed almost equally throughout all the percentiles (figure 5B.1, panel d), making it less pro-poor. However, a note is in order here: an equally distributed benefit, such as Peru's minimum wage, is still a strongly redistributive force. In an unequal society, giving the same thing to everyone is a progressive policy.

Finally, let us look at Colombia and Paraguay, the two South American countries with traditionally high minimum wages. Both, as expected, show a minimum wage that is less pro-poor than those of the other countries seen here. In Colombia, the stepwise pattern shows that few people make the minimum wage and that they are almost all concentrated in the middle of the income distribution (figure 5B.1, panel e). The panel also shows that virtually no one in the poorest decile of the household distribution makes the minimum wage. More or less the same occurs in Paraguay: in 2002, there were more minimum wage workers in the upper half of the household income distribution than in the lower half (figure 5B.1, panel f). In 2013, there were only slightly more in the lower half.

Notes

1. Other institutions such as employment protection and unemployment insurance may also affect inequality, but are likely to have had second-order effects during this period. Severance payments are the most important form of income protection for workers in Latin America. Employment protection may affect workers' wages, and depending on their bargaining power may affect low- and high-skilled workers differently (Leonardi and Pica 2013). Employment protection laws have changed very little in Latin America during the last two decades, making them unlikely candidates to explain the observed changes in earnings inequality. Similarly, unemployment insurance may affect wages after reemployment through their effects on reservation wages and unemployment duration (Schmieder, von Wachter, and Bender 2016). The coverage of unemployment benefits in the region is tremendously low. During the 2000s, Brazil had the highest coverage, reaching out to less than 13 percent of the unemployed. Argentina and Chile do not even cover 5 percent of the unemployed (Alaimo et al. 2015). Even if changes in unemployment benefits took place during the period, they are unlikely to have significantly affected earnings inequality. Changes in payroll taxation may have had a more important role on changes in the wage structure during the last decade. Payroll taxes may be fully or partially shifted to wages (Gruber 1997; Kugler and Kugler 2009) and affect relative pay by altering the informal/formal trade-offs (Kugler, Kugler, and Herrera-Prada 2017). Understanding the importance of recent changes in payroll taxation on the evolution of wage inequality constitutes an important avenue for further research.

2. Downward wage rigidity refers to a decreasing ability to reduce wages.

3. As discussed later in this chapter, the extent to which the minimum wage is "binding" can be defined in terms of the relation between minimum and median wages in the specific distribution.

4. After falling almost 40 percent in real terms from 1968 to 1990, the federal minimum wage in the United States stayed more or less constant up to 2007. Despite eventual increases to keep up with inflation, it was broadly constant and quite low in real terms. State laws sprang up in reaction to the erosion of the federal minimum wage and have provided a source of variation that has been frequently used as an identification strategy. The debate on the effects of the minimum wage in the United States started in the early 1990s and centered on unemployment effects. Although Card and Krueger (1993) found no unemployment effects, Abowd, Kramarz, and Margolis (1999) and Neumark, Schweitzer, and Wascher (2000) found employment elasticities of 0.4 or higher. The fact remains that the absolute number of people who may have lost their jobs because of minimum wage increases was modest because the variations in the minimum wage were modest. More recent reviews of the literature conclude that unemployment effects tend to be small but positive (Belman and Wolfson 2014; Doucouliagos and Stanley 2009). However, the U.S. debate over modest effects may soon change. The federal minimum wage has already had a

relevant increase since 2007 (40 percent over three years), and if Congress were to pass a $12 per hour minimum wage, the U.S. debate would enter a new phase. As recently as July 2009, only 6.5 percent of hours worked in the United States were paid at the minimum wage of $7.25 per hour. At $12 per hour, the U.S. federal minimum wage would be in line with those of other developed countries, and its effect would likely increase (Autor, Manning, and Smith 2010).

5. This increase directly affects not only earnings of minimum wage workers but also many social benefits that are indexed to changes in the minimum wage. Recent analysis suggests that although Brazil's current minimum wage level is in line with international comparators (as measured either as a share of gross national income per worker or as a share of median or mean wages), it has grown faster than in most Latin American countries in recent years and, in 2012–13, faster than productivity growth in a third of Brazilian manufacturing firms (Silva, Almeida, and Strokova 2015).

6. Most studies on the United States find that the minimum wage has modest effects on inequality (Autor, Katz, and Kearney 2008; Goldin and Katz 2007; Lemieux 2008). They show that the minimum wage was not the main reason why the wages of lower-paid workers lost purchasing power over the past few decades. Other, more-structural causes, such as changes in the demand for skill, are more important than the minimum wage in determining the wage distribution in the United States. Important exceptions to this view are DiNardo, Fortin, and Lemieux (1995) and Lee (1999), who find that the erosion of the minimum wage had been one of the most important factors in increasing lower-tail inequality (as measured by the 10th–50th percentile ratio).

7. Throughout the region, it is common to use the minimum wage as a more general unit of account or numeraire, for instance, in quoting wages or monetary contracts in general. The numeraire effect refers to the bunching of wages at round multiples of the minimum wage, because the statutory minimum wage is often used as the numeraire, or base measure of value, for wage negotiations. See also Messina and Sanz-de-Galdeano (2014).

8. "Less than one minimum wage" is defined as less than 0.95 of the minimum wage to allow for some reporting error.

9. See Meer and West (2015) for a recent survey of the literature on OECD countries.

10. Note, however, that employees who make wages below the minimum wage may still see their earnings influenced by minimum wage legislation in the presence of lighthouse effects (signals conveyed by statutory minima to wage-setting in the informal sector).

11. The panels cover only those countries with a single minimum wage, avoiding the complexities of multiple minimum wages in Central American countries.

12. A limitation of this approach is that the minimum wage may affect those who are just below or above the minimum wage through various spillover effects (Autor, Manning, and Smith 2010; Maloney and Nuñez-Mendez 2004). This chapter combines this approach with other distributional identification strategies and contrasts the results to circumvent this limitation.

13. The minimum wage automatic adjustment rule introduced in 2006 in Brazil establishes that each year's increase is to be equal to the GDP growth rate of two years prior. The minimum wage policy should be looked at in light of the economic cycle. This rule might mean significant increases in the minimum in the beginning of downturns. If not accompanied by raising labor productivity, they can unduly undermine unskilled-job generation and formalization during downturns, with negative effects on inequality.

14. Similarly, and considering data for all countries in Latin America, the correlation coefficient between changes in the ratio of the minimum wage to median wage was 0.61 in the 1995–2003 period and −0.3 in the 2003–12 period.

15. As discussed earlier in this chapter, the extent to which the minimum wage is "binding" can be defined in terms of the relation between minimum and median wages in the specific distribution.

References

Abowd, J. M., F. Kramarz, and D. N. Margolis. 1999. "Minimum Wages and Employment in France and the United States." NBER Working Paper 6996, National Bureau of Economic Research, Cambridge, MA.

Abrache, J. S. 1999. "Do Unions Always Decrease Wage Dispersion? The Case of Brazilian Manufacturing." *Journal of Labor Research* 20 (3): 425–36.

Alaimo, Veronica, Mariano Bosch, David S. Kaplan, Carmen Pagés, and Laura Ripani. 2015. "Empleos para crecer." Banco Interamericano de Desarrollo, Washington, DC.

Alves, G., V. Amarante, G. Salas, and A. Vigorito. 2012. "La desigualdad del ingreso en Uruguay entre 1986 y 2009." Working Paper 12-03, Instituto de Economía (IECON), Montevideo, Uruguay.

Arango, C. A., and A. Pachón. 2004. "The Minimum Wage in Colombia: Holding the Middle with a Bite on the Poor." Bank of the Republic, Bogota, Colombia.

Autor, D. H., L. F. Katz, and M. S. Kearny. 2008. "Trends in U.S. Wage Inequality: Revising the Revisionists." *Review of Economics and Statistics* 90 (2): 300–23.

Autor, D. H., A. Manning, and C. L. Smith. 2010. "The Contribution of the Minimum Wage to U.S. Wage Inequality over Three Decades: A Reassessment." Finance and Economics Discussion Series. Divisions of Research & Statistics and Monetary Affairs, Federal Reserve Board, Washington, DC.

Bell, L. A. 1997. "The Impact of Minimum Wages in Mexico and Colombia." *Journal of Labor Economics* 15 (3): S102– S135.

Belman, D., and P. Wolfson. 2014. *What Does the Minimum Wage Do?* Kalamazoo, MI: Upjohn Institute Press.

Bravo, D., and D. Contreras. 1998. "Is There Any Relationship between Minimum Wage and Employment? Empirical Evidence Using Natural Experiments in a Developing Economy." Discussion Paper 157, Universidad de Chile, Santiago.

Card, D. 1992. "The Effect of Unions on the Distribution of Wages: Redistribution or Relabelling?" NBER Working Paper 4195, National Bureau of Economic Research, Cambridge, MA.

Card, D., and A. B. Krueger. 1993. "Minimum Wages and Employment: A Case Study of the Fast Food Industry in New Jersey and Pennsylvania." NBER Working Paper 4509, National Bureau of Economic Research, Cambridge, MA.

Cassoni, A., G. Labadie, and G. Fachola. 2001. "The Impact of Unions on the Economic Performance of Firms." Working Paper 15/01, Department of Economics, Universidad de la República, Montevideo, Uruguay.

Corseuil, C. H., and F. G. Carneiro. 2001. "Os Impactos do Salário Mínimo sobre Emprego e Salários no Brasil: Evidências a Partir de Dados Longitudinais e Séries Temporais." Research report for the Department of Social Studies, Institute for Applied Economic Research (IPEA), Brasilia.

Corseuil, C. H., M. Foguel, and M. Hecksher. 2015. "Efeitos dos Pisos Salariais Estaduais sobre o Mercado de Trabalho: Uma Nova Abordagem Empírica." Discussion Paper 1887, Institute for Applied Economic Research (IPEA), Brasilia.

DiNardo, J., N. M. Fortin, and T. Lemieux. 1995. "Labor Market Institutions and the Distribution of Wages, 1973–1992: A Semiparametric Approach." NBER Working Paper 5093, National Bureau of Economic Research, Cambridge, MA.

DiNardo, J., K. Hallock, and J. S. Pischke. 1997. "Unions and Managerial Pay." NBER Working Paper 6318, National Bureau of Economic Research, Cambridge, MA.

Doucouliagos, H., and T. D. Stanley. 2009. "Publication Selection Bias in Minimum Wage Research? A Meta-Regression Analysis." *British Journal of Industrial Relations* 47 (2): 406–28.

Drake, P. 2003. "El movimiento obrero en Chile: De la Unidad Popular a la Concertación." *Revista Ciencia Política* 23 (2): 148–58.

Fairris, D. 2003. "Unions and Wage Inequality in Mexico." *Industrial and Labor Relations Review* 56 (3): 481–97.

Ferreira, F. H. G., S. P. Firpo, and J. Messina. 2017. "Ageing Poorly? Accounting for the Decline in Earnings Inequality in Brazil, 1995–2012." Policy Research Working Paper 8018, World Bank, Washington, DC.

Firpo, S., N. Fortin, and T. Lemieux. 2009. "Unconditional Quantile Regressions." *Econometrica* 77 (3): 953–73.

Freeman, R. B. 1980. "Unionism and the Dispersion of Wages." *Industrial and Labor Relations Review* 34 (1): 3–23.

Gasparini, L., M. Marchionni, and W. Sosa Escudero. 2001. "La distribución del ingreso en la Argentina." Center for Distributive, Labor and Social Studies (CEDLAS), Universidad Nacional de La Plata, Argentina.

Gindling, T. H., and K. Terrell. 2004. "Legal Minimum Wages and the Wages of Formal and Informal Sector Workers in Costa Rica." IZA Discussion Paper 1018, Institute for the Study of Labor (IZA), Bonn.

———. 2006. "Minimum Wages, Globalization and Poverty in Honduras." IZA Discussion Paper 2497, Institute for the Study of Labor (IZA), Bonn.

———. 2007. "The Effects of Multiple Minimum Wages throughout the Labor Market: The Case of Costa Rica." *Labour Economics* 14 (3): 485–511.

Gindling, T. H., and J. D. Trejos. 2010. "Reforzar el cumplimiento de los salarios mínimos en Costa Rica." Salvadoran Foundation for Economic and Social Development (FUSADES), San Salvador.

Goldin, C., and L. F. Katz. 2007. "The Race between Education and Technology: The Evolution of U.S. Educational Wage Differentials, 1890 to 2005." Working Paper 12984, National Bureau of Economic Research, Cambridge, MA.

Gosling, A., and S. Machin. 1995. "Trade Unions and the Dispersion of Earnings in British Establishments, 1980–90." *Oxford Bulletin of Economics and Statistics* 57 (2): 167–84.

Grau, N., and O. Landerretche. 2011. "The Labor Impact of Minimum Wages: A Method for Estimating the Effect in Emerging Economies Using Chilean Panel Data." Working Paper 329, Department of Economics, University of Chile, Santiago.

Gruber, J. 1997. "The Incidence of Payroll Taxation: Evidence from Chile." *Journal of Labor Economics* 15 (S3): 72–101.

Hernández, G., and E. Pinzon. 2006. "El efecto del salario mínimo sobre el empleo y los ingresos." *Archivos de Economía* 316. Departamento Nacional de Planeación (DNP), Colombia.

Hirsch, B. T. 1982. "The Interindustry Structure of Unionism, Earnings, and Earnings Dispersion." *Industrial and Labor Relations Review* 36 (1): 22–39.

Kugler, A., and M. Kugler. 2009. "Labor Market Effects of Payroll Taxes in Developing Countries: Evidence from Colombia." *Economic Development and Cultural Change* 57 (2): 335–58.

Kugler, A., M. Kugler, and L. O. Herrera-Prada. 2017. "Do Payroll Tax Breaks Stimulate Formality? Evidence from Colombia's Reform." NBER Working Paper 23308, National Bureau of Economic Research, Cambridge, MA.

Lee, D. 1999. "Wage Inequality in the United States during the 1980s: Rising Dispersion or Falling Minimum Wage?" *Quarterly Journal of Economics* 114 (3): 977–1023.

Lemieux, T. 2008. "The Changing Nature of Wage Inequality." *Journal of Population Economics* 21 (1): 21–48.

Lemos, S. 2004. "The Effects of the Minimum Wage on Wages, Employment and Prices." IZA Discussion Paper 1135, Institute for the Study of Labor (IZA), Bonn.

Leonardi, M., and G. Pica. 2013. "Who Pays for It? The Heterogeneous Wage Effects of Employment Protection Legislation." *Economic Journal* 123: 1236–278.

Lotti, G., J. Messina, and L. Nunziata. 2016. "Minimum Wages and Informal Employment in Developing Countries." World Bank, Washington, DC. Unpublished.

Maloney, W. F., and J. Nuñez-Mendez. 2004. "Measuring the Impact of Minimum Wages: Evidence from Latin America." In *Law and Employment: Lessons from Latin America and the Caribbean*, edited by J. J. Heckman and C. Pagés. Chicago: University of Chicago Press.

Maloney, W. F., and E. P. Ribeiro. 1999. "Efficiency Wage and Union Effects in Labor Demand and Wage Structure in Mexico: An Application of Quantile Analysis." Policy Research Working Paper 2131, World Bank, Washington, DC.

Maurizio, R. 2014. *Labour Formalization and Declining Inequality in Argentina and Brazil in 2000s: A Dynamic Approach*. ILO: Geneva.

Meer, J., and J. West. 2015. "Effects of the Minimum Wage on Employment Dynamics." *Journal of Human Resources* 51 (2): 500–22.

Menezes-Filho, N., H. Zylberstajn, J. Chahd, and E. Pazello. 2005. "Unions and the Economic Performance of Brazilian Establishments." In *What Difference Do Unions Make? Their Impact on Productivity and Wages in Latin America*, edited by P. Kuhn and G. Márquez. Washington, DC: Inter-American Development Bank.

Messina, J., and A. Sanz-de-Galdeano. 2014. "Wage Rigidity and Disinflation in Emerging Countries." *American Economic Journal: Macroeconomics* 6 (1): 102–33.

Neri, M., G. Gonzaga, and J. M. Camargo. 2000. "Efeitos informais do salário mínimo e pobreza." IPEA Discussion Text 724, Institute for Applied Economic Research, Brasilia.

Neumark, D., M. Schweitzer, and W. Wascher. 2000. "The Effects of Minimum Wages Throughout the Wage Distribution." NBER Working Paper 7519, National Bureau of Economic Research, Cambridge, MA.

Rodríguez-Castelán, C., L. F. López-Calva, N. Lustig, and D. Valderrama. 2016. "Understanding the Dynamics of Labor Income Inequality in Latin America." Policy Research Working Paper 7795, World Bank, Washington, DC.

Saavedra, J., and M. Torero. 2000. "Labor Market Reforms and Their Impact on Formal Labor Demand and Job Market Turnover: The Case of Peru." IDB Working Paper 121, Inter-American Development Bank, Washington, DC.

———. 2005. "Union Density Changes and Union Effects on Firm Performance in Peru." In *What Difference Do Unions Make? Their Impact on Productivity and Wages in Latin America*, edited by P. Kuhn and G. Márquez. Washington, DC: Inter-American Development Bank.

Schmieder, J. F., T. von Wachter, and S. N. Bender. 2016. "The Effect of Unemployment Benefits and Nonemployment Durations on Wages." *American Economic Review* 106 (3): 739–77.

Silva, J., R. Almeida, and V. Strokova. 2015. *Sustaining Wage and Employment Gains in Brazil: A Skills and Jobs Agenda*. Directions in Development: Human Development Series. Washington, DC: World Bank.

Ulyssea, G., and M. Foguel. 2006. "Efeitos do Salário Mínimo Sobre o Mercado de Trabalho Brasileiro." IPEA Discussion Text 1168, Institute for Applied Economic Research, Brasilia.

6
Conclusions and Policy Reflections

Introduction

What caused the changes in wage inequality in the past two decades in Latin America? Looking to the future, will the current economic slowdown be regressive? This volume has taken up these two questions by reviewing relevant literature and providing new evidence on what we know from conceptual, empirical, and policy viewpoints.

The answer to the first question can be broken down into several parts, although the bottom line is that the changes in wage inequality resulted from a combination of three big forces: (1) education expansion and falling returns to skill (the supply-side story); (2) shifts in aggregate domestic demand (in South America in the 2000s) that favored unskilled workers; and (3) exchange rate appreciations from the commodity boom and the associated shift to the nontradable sector that changed interfirm wage differences. Other forces had a non-negligible but secondary role in some countries, while they were not present in others. These include the rapid increase of the minimum wage and a rapid trend toward formalization of employment, which played a supporting role but only during the boom.

Understanding the forces behind recent trends also helps to shed light on the second question. The analysis in this volume suggests that the economic slowdown is putting the brakes on the reduction of inequality in Latin America—and will likely continue to do so.

Review of the Trends

The reduction of wage inequality in Latin America in the 2000s was a regionwide phenomenon (in 16 of the 17 countries studied) that occurred after a decade of either stagnation or moderate increases.[1] This reduction was the main driver of the decline in household income inequality—even more important than the emergence of conditional cash transfer programs, the expansion of pension coverage, or changes in household demographics.[2] Behind this reduction in wage inequality was faster wage growth for workers at the bottom of the wage distribution. Such commonalities are surprising given the differences across countries in employment and production structure, terms of trade, institutions, and regulations.

While overall wage inequality trends were common across countries, the magnitude of the reduction and the year in which it started varied. Overall, although wage inequality in some countries started to fall slowly in the mid-to-late 1990s, the decline became sharp in 2003. The biggest difference across the region was the magnitude of the reduction in the 2000s across subgroups of countries in different geographical areas. Specifically, wage inequality fell more in countries in South America relative to Central America and Mexico. In both groups of countries, the wages of low-earning workers grew. Although wages for the top 10 percent also rose in South America (albeit less than for the bottom 10 percent), they fell in Central America and Mexico.[3]

Causes of the Declines in Wage Inequality

This volume has organized the possible causes for the declines in wage inequality around three explanations:

- *Labor supply factors*, such as education expansion and its effect on falling returns to skill

- *Labor demand conditions,* including (1) shifts in domestic demand, (2) falling interfirm wage differences among similar workers driven by exchange rate appreciation from the commodity boom and the associated shift in demand to the nontradable sector, and (3) technological change and traditional trade channels

- *Institutional factors* such as minimum wage policies and a rapid trend toward formalization of employment.

The following sections review the evidence on each of these explanations.

Labor Supply Factors: Education Expansion and Falling Returns to Skill

The relative supply of skills (as proxied by educational attainment) has expanded steadily across Latin American countries since the 1980s. This expansion contributed to the decline of wage inequality by reducing the education premium (Card and Lemieux 2001; Katz and Murphy 1992). Moreover, in the 2000s, there was a combination of sharply rising unskilled wages with falling employment in unskilled occupations, as shown in the cases of Brazil and Peru. Without labor supply changes (in terms of both quantity and quality), these patterns at the bottom of the wage distribution are hard to reconcile; that is, these patterns are inconsistent with solely an outward demand shift for unskilled workers.

However, the evolution of the relative supply of skilled workers alone does not suffice to explain the observed trends in wage inequality. First, it cannot explain the downward change in the trajectory of the education premium in the early 2000s.[4] That is, the wage premium for college-educated workers versus workers with a primary education or less fell in the 2000s but not during the 1990s. The education expansion started earlier (in the 1980s), and since then the relative supply of skills has followed a steady upward trend without any notable acceleration in the 2000s. If supply-side trends were the sole driver of wage inequality, we would have seen a fall in returns to skills and a decline in inequality in the 1990s, but that did not occur. Second, relative labor supply trends in South America are not much different from those in Central America and Mexico. Hence, they cannot explain the much stronger reduction of inequality in South America. Third, the education premium fell during the 2000s for both old and young workers. If old and young workers are imperfect substitutes, the education premium should have fallen more for young workers, whose relative supply of skills changes more rapidly. This was not observed in the data.

Labor Demand Conditions

Since the 1990s, the region has had many important changes in labor demand conditions that have reduced wage inequality. The following section discusses these changes and how they have translated into demand for different types of labor.

Shifts in Domestic Demand and Rising Wages for Unskilled Workers

This book emphasizes the role of the tightness or softness of market conditions in wage inequality in the region. In the 2000s, aggregate domestic demand trends were radically different in South America than in Central America and Mexico. In South America, the period was marked by a strong increase in domestic demand that reflected the spending effect of positive terms-of-trade improvements, which responded to the commodity price boom but also to large capital flows to the region. In turn, South America witnessed the region's largest fall in returns to skill and thus the largest fall in wage inequality. The observed surge in demand was associated with a larger employment expansion in the nontradable sector than in the tradable sector. This could have reduced the skill premium for two distinct reasons: (1) differences in skill intensities across sectors, or (2) differences in the supply elasticities of skilled versus unskilled workers.

- *Differences in skill intensities across sectors*

The conventional wisdom, particularly in South America, posits that the expansion of demand brought about by real exchange rate appreciation in the 2000s led to a larger expansion in labor demand in the nontradable sector than in the tradable sector, favoring the relatively less-skill-intensive sectors.[5] The underlying assumption was that the nontradable sector in Latin America is more intensive in unskilled labor than the tradable sector. Hence, increases in the demand for nontradable goods and services would benefit less-educated workers the most. This could be the case, for example, if growth in nontradables were accounted for by growth in the construction sector, which is less skill-intensive than most sectors.

Evidence for the region, however, contradicts this assumption. In South America, on average, the nontradable sector is more skill-intensive than the tradable sector. Some relatively less-skill-intensive nontradable sectors expanded considerably—particularly construction, whose workers' level of education is below average. Yet, the construction industry has a relatively small employment share (around 7 percent in most countries), and other nontradable sectors that are high-skill-intensive expanded as well—business services, for example. Moreover, the extent of sectoral reallocation to nontradable sectors was relatively small (De la Torre et al. 2015).

- *Differences in the supply elasticities of skilled versus unskilled workers*

De la Torre and Ize (2016) (formalized in De la Torre et al. 2015) develop a different explanation for the impact of domestic aggregate demand on the tradable versus nontradable sector. If the unskilled labor supply is less responsive than the skilled labor supply to increases in demand, the surge in domestic aggregate demand, even if symmetric in skill intensity, could have reduced the skill premium (given that skilled labor supply rose). This asymmetry in supply elasticities across skilled and unskilled workers is plausible in a context of rapidly growing aggregate labor demand and employment and a falling relative supply of unskilled workers. When aggregate demand increases, the diminishing reservoir of unskilled workers results in a less-elastic supply of workers and, hence, in higher wage increases. The observed wage and employment changes by skill level in South America are consistent with this hypothesis. In fact, estimates of supply elasticities show small differences across worker groups but are in line with lower supply elasticity for unskilled labor (Bargain and Silva, forthcoming).

In sum, the combination of a falling supply of unskilled workers and changes in demand resulted in a notable reduction of the skill premium that contributed to the decline of inequality in the region. The importance of the demand channel, and the mechanism through which it operated, differed across countries. In Central America and Mexico the terms-of-trade shock was not there, and the mild reduction of inequality is more likely to have been supply-driven. In South America, the sharp rise in the terms of trade raised domestic demand and the demand for nontradables. In some South American countries, this triggered the demand for certain services that are unskilled-labor-intensive. In others, it created unskilled-labor shortages, which may have resulted in rapidly rising wages if the unskilled labor supply was relatively inelastic. This book claims that all three ingredients—rising terms of trade, increased demand for nontradables, and shortages of unskilled labor—were present in most cases.

More in-depth country studies will be needed to quantify the importance of each channel in each particular context.[6]

Falling Interfirm Wage Differences among Similar Workers

Importantly, the causes of falling wage inequality in the 2000s highlighted so far cannot explain falling wage differentials among workers with similar education, labor market experience, and occupation, which accounts for more than half of the decrease in earnings inequality. During 2001–13, the changes in pay differences between skill groups contributed 48 percent of the total change in wage variance. The remaining 52 percent was associated with changes in pay differences within groups. Over 1997–2001, the change in the "between" variance had accounted for 34 percent of the change in overall variance of wages, and the rest was explained by differences within skill groups.

Hence, this book has explored factors that could explain wage differences among observationally similar workers. These factors might include differences in skills across workers that are not observable in employment surveys—for example, in cognitive abilities such as reading and math as well as socioemotional skills. A complementary explanation is the importance of differences in wages paid across sectors or even across firms (for workers in the same sector and with the same occupation or skill level) and changes in those differences.

Research for this book has found that most of the initial wage inequality and its subsequent decline took place within sector-occupations. Naturally, pay differentials for workers who are employed in the same sector and occupation could occur because of differences in pay either between firms (with more-productive firms presumably paying more to attract and retain better workers) or within firms (with firms having pay policies that allow for large pay gaps between workers with the same skills employed in the same occupation but in different departments or areas). Our results show that most of the initial wage inequality within sector-occupations, as well as its subsequent decline, is associated with interfirm (as opposed to intrafirm) wage differentials and their dynamics.

Changes in wage inequality resulting from changes in interfirm pay differentials for observationally similar workers can arise from three sources: (1) changes in pay heterogeneity across firms, (2) changes in heterogeneity among workers, or (3) changes in the degree to which the most desirable workers and the most productive firms find each other (Card, Heining, and Kline 2013). Separating these three sources of variation requires data whereby workers and firms can be identified and followed over time. This analysis was possible only for Brazil and Costa Rica, and more research is needed to understand whether the conclusions for these two countries can be generalized. But the findings are interesting: In Costa Rica, the only country in our sample where wage inequality *increased*, the main component behind this trend was increasing heterogeneity in pay across firms. In Brazil, where wage inequality *decreased* significantly in the 2000s, the heterogeneity in pay across firms declined the most.[7]

What could explain the observed changes in interfirm wage dispersion and the change in overall wage inequality that occurs through this channel? Firm heterogeneity provides another lens through which demand forces may affect wage inequality. The reported contributions of increased international trade, the commodity boom, and the emergence of China as a major consumer of commodities discussed so far did not account for the role of heterogeneity across firms. To the extent that these global forces affect interfirm wage differentials, their overall effects on wage inequality may be different.

In this more complex setting, we argue below that the fall in interfirm wage dispersion in South America could be the result of exchange rate appreciation from the commodity boom and the associated rise in the employment share of the non-tradable sector. It is important to note that, in this context, the combined effect of these factors on wage inequality operates through their effect on interfirm wage dispersion rather than through their effect on the skill premium. We argue that the interplay of exchange rate appreciations and firm heterogeneity is important to understand the evolution of wage inequality.

• *Exchange rate appreciation*

The observed exchange rate appreciation in South America relative to several important export destinations negatively affected firms' export participation. This, in turn, decreased wages among the more-productive exporting firms relative to the less-productive firms in the same industry. Because more-productive firms also tend to pay higher wages, this process decreases within-sector wage inequality. The converse is true for countries where the exchange rate has depreciated or where trade costs fell. Moreover, in commodity-boom countries that witnessed a significant exchange rate appreciation, the observed Dutch disease effects were associated with a shift to the nontradable sector (from the tradable sector). Because interfirm wage differentials are lower in the nontradable sector, this process may have reduced interfirm wage dispersion and therefore overall wage inequality.

Although the role of exchange rate appreciation seems more prominent, there are at least two other factors that could have played a role in the fall in interfirm wage dispersion in some countries: (1) narrowing dispersion in firm productivity (or, alternatively, the value added per worker becoming increasingly delinked from worker pay); and (2) changes in minimum wage policies.[8]

• *Narrowing dispersion in firm productivity*

Many developed countries have experienced widening dispersion in labor productivity, leading to an increase in earnings inequality. The available data from Costa Rica do not allow for an analysis of this indicator, but if the global trend occurred there, it could have been a source of the country's rising wage inequality. The sources of this widening dispersion could include transitory shocks or a more volatile environment for firms, greater sorting, or entry-exit dynamics. Preliminary evidence for Brazil does not suggest that firms' labor productivity distribution became less disperse (Alvarez et al., forthcoming).[9] Instead, value added per worker appears to have become increasingly delinked from worker pay during this period (Alvarez et al., forthcoming; Silva, Almeida, and Strokova 2015). This process could result in lower wage inequality even if workers' and firms' fundamentals are not altered. Hence, more research is needed, but the available evidence does not confirm that the fall in inequality resulted from narrowing dispersion in firm productivity.

- *Changes in minimum wage policies*

Latin American countries differed markedly in their institutional wage policies such as the minimum wage. How economic rents are split between capital and labor can be affected by the dynamics of the minimum wage. More specifically, a larger share of a firm's profits is likely to fall into workers' hands when the minimum wage becomes more binding. If remuneration policies across firms become less heterogeneous—because, for example, a higher but more similar share of the benefits from the employment relationship is distributed to workers—wage inequality falls. This channel is a plausible cause of falling interfirm wage dispersion and may have operated to varying degrees across countries. However, its importance depends on how high the minimum wage is and by how much it increased. The country-specific role that changes in minimum wage policies played in the observed changes in interfirm wage differentials and their impact on overall wage inequality is an important topic for further research. Note that the minimum wage policies are expected to have a *broader* effect on wage inequality beyond the *specific* effect on interfirm wage dispersion, as discussed below.

Technological Change and Traditional Trade Channels

The literature usually focuses on two forces that can raise the relative demand for skilled labor: (1) skill-biased technological change and (2) trade liberalization. In countries such as the United States, research and opinion surveys suggest that these forces—particularly technological change—are the primary drivers of changes in wage inequality (Autor, Katz, and Krueger 1998; Berman, Bound, and Griliches 1994; Feenstra and Hanson 1999; Goldin and Katz 2007; Krueger 2012). Polarization of occupations in the labor market—a more recent version of the technological change hypothesis—had an important impact on the compensation of U.S. workers and, through this channel, on wage inequality (Autor et al. 2014; Autor and Dorn 2013). This phenomenon consisted of an expansion in the demand for skilled and unskilled occupations to the detriment of middle-skilled jobs, which tend to entail tasks that are easily codifiable and, hence, can be performed by machines (Autor et al. 2014; Autor and Dorn 2013).

The evidence for Latin America, however, suggests that technological change was not the main driver of inequality in the region. Wages expanded rapidly in low-paying occupations relative to high-paying occupations. Skill-biased technological change would have caused the opposite effect. Also, there is little evidence of labor market polarization. In fact, the evidence of occupation polarization is weak for most countries of the region and for other developing countries (Maloney and Molina 2016; Messina, Pica, and Oviedo 2016).

Regarding the traditional role of trade, the Stolper-Samuelson theorem suggests that trade liberalization in countries where unskilled labor is relatively abundant will lead to an increase in both the relative price of unskilled-labor-intensive sectors and the relative return to unskilled labor, and therefore to a reduction in wage inequality.[10] Although most trade liberalization occurred in the 1990s, wage inequality was stagnant or rising in Latin America during that period (Goldberg and Pavcnik 2007), while inequality fell only in the 2000s (Halliday, Lederman, and Robertson 2015). Hence, Stolper-Samuelson trade effects cannot explain the timing of the downward trend in wage inequality.[11]

Other trade shocks could have been at play, such as the commodity boom triggered by the emergence of China as a major consumer of commodities. Recent studies indicate that the *direct* effects of the commodity boom on wage inequality in the region can account for only a small share of the fall in wage inequality in the 2000s (Adão 2015). However, the commodity boom also had *indirect* (spending) effects, as discussed below.[12]

Institutional Factors: Minimum Wage Policy and Employment Formalization

Country-specific factors such as minimum wage policy played a more prominent role in some countries than in others.[13] With few exceptions (Bolivia, Colombia, Paraguay, and Peru), the real minimum wage rose during the 2000s. In Brazil, in particular, increases in the minimum wage significantly helped reduce inequality during the boom years. However, the Brazilian case also shows that although a rising minimum wage decreased inequality during the boom, it had also increased inequality during the slow growth period of the 1990s as noncompliance increased (Ferreira, Firpo, and Messina 2017). In fact, noncompliance with the minimum wage is high in most countries of the region, limiting its potential role to compress the distribution of wages.[14]

Reduced informality of employment is another factor that helped reduce inequality in some countries. With some exceptions, the growth and policy changes of the 2000s translated into a sizable reduction of informal employment. Results also indicate that, in the 1990s, only high-wage workers exited from informality, while in the 2000s most of those who became formal were low-wage workers. Evidence in this book shows the changes in formalization by percentile in Argentina, Brazil, and Bolivia (high-, medium-to-high-, and low-formality countries, respectively). In all three countries, the changes from the mid-1990s to the early 2000s coincided with increased inequality, with workers below the median wage becoming more informal and workers above the median wage increasing their formalization. In contrast, from 2002 onward, the formalization process appeared to be strongly equalizing in all three countries, particularly in Brazil.

Reductions in informality, especially when concentrated among the unskilled, help to reduce inequality through two channels: (1) they reduce within-group inequality, because workers with equivalent skills are paid less in the informal sector; and (2) they reduce between-group inequality, because the wage penalty of being informal is not evenly distributed across skill groups and is concentrated among unskilled workers. The decompositions in this book suggest that declining informality played an important role in inequality reductions during the 2000s in Argentina, Brazil, Mexico, and Peru. In Bolivia, Chile, and Uruguay, the impact was smaller.

Shifting Wage Inequality Trends: The Remaining Challenges

What have we learned? First, the expansion of education was the great equalizer in Latin America, but it is not a sufficient explanation for the trends observed since the 1990s. Second, the tightness of market conditions in South America led to falling wage inequality when combined with increasing skill supply.

Still, neither explanation sheds light on important wage differentials across workers with similar skills, education, and occupation. Hence, a third factor emerges as a key demand-side factor: the exchange rate appreciation from the commodity boom and the associated shift in demand to the nontradable sector, which narrowed inter-firm wage differences.

Finally, other forces played a non-negligible but secondary role in some countries, although they were not present in others. These include the rapid increase of the minimum wage and a rapid trend toward formalization of employment, which played a supporting role but only during the boom.

The increase in access to education in the region (including higher education, where enrollment doubled in the past decade) was accompanied by an increase in equality of opportunities (Ferreyra et al. 2017). This was an important positive development. However, for the trend to be sustainable, the quality of education also needs to improve. The evidence on "garage universities" suggests that new programs did accept students from lower socioeconomic backgrounds without lowering standards, suggesting an efficient expansion of the higher education system (Camacho, Messina, and Uribe 2016; Ferreyra et al. 2017). However, governments need to remain vigilant to the pressures that increasing demand for education may impose on the system, because that demand will likely continue to increase.

Growth was a fundamental driver of improvements in labor market outcomes (Araujo et al. 2016), which in turn were the main drivers of reductions in inequality in the 2000s. These improvements were particularly pro-poor. As noted earlier, the reduction in wage inequality was fundamentally driven by strong wage increases at the bottom of the distribution, with important effects on poverty. Labor earnings at the top of the wage distribution also increased (except in Mexico) but at much lower rates than at the bottom. Over the same period, the relative supply of skilled labor increased among young workers of all socioeconomic backgrounds, but the rise was much more pronounced among the poor than among the non-poor, contributing to their increase in average earnings.

Minimum wage changes played a supporting role in reducing the region's wage inequality during the 2000s, with limited displacement effects. Likewise, fast economic growth in South America supported reductions of informality in most countries of that region. During the period, formal labor market insertion increased more among low-wage workers than among high-wage workers, making this phenomenon an additional factor in the decline of wage inequality.

Despite these positive developments, important challenges remain. The region remains highly unequal. The average years of education among the working-age population has increased significantly, but the current level remains below that of comparable countries, which leaves room for improvement. The poor lag behind the non-poor in many aspects, including educational endowments. These educational disadvantages take a long time to reverse, and they make poor workers' job mobility and access to and retention of high-productivity jobs harder, particularly when labor demand is weak and there is slack in the labor market.

Looking to the Future: How Will the Drivers of Wage Inequality Evolve?

One important conclusion of this book is that the increase in domestic demand (hence the economic cycle) driven by the rising terms of trade in South America mattered for wage inequality. These trends are not permanent. The gross domestic product (GDP) growth slowdown that started in mid-2011 has already slowed or halted the reduction of wage inequality in the region. Countries such as Brazil, where the slowdown has been pronounced, are diverging from the rest of South America (Calvo-González et al. 2017). Between 2011 and 2015, the region's average Gini coefficient fell from 48.8 to 47.0 points, a much smaller annual reduction than the decrease from 54.7 to 48.8 points between 2002 and 2011. Similarly, the labor Gini coefficient fell from 42.0 to 40.2 between 2011 and 2015, a much smaller annual reduction than the decrease from 47.3 to 42.0 between 2002 and 2011.

Will the slowdown completely reverse the gains? On the one hand, the skilled labor supply is likely to continue to increase, thus pushing down wage inequality. On the other hand, growth in aggregate domestic demand has slowed, and spending booms of similar magnitude and origin are unlikely to continue. The extent of interfirm wage differences is likely to remain large and provide an important channel through which demand forces affect wage inequality, but perhaps moving now in the opposite direction (toward greater wage dispersion among similar workers), as real exchange rates of South American economies and elsewhere have depreciated. This will be the case if production shifts from nontradable to tradable sectors. Finally, this slower expansion of domestic demand is also likely to crowd out space for the minimum wage to rise without significant adjustments in employment. To sum up, lower growth could continue to slow the reduction of wage inequality and increase household income inequality if unemployment effects are large.

However, the effects of the slowdown do not necessarily have to be symmetrical to the effects of the boom years—that is, wages of unskilled workers that rose significantly do not necessarily have to fall in the same proportion. This is the case for at least two reasons. First, the region is unlikely to enter a contraction of similar and opposite magnitude to that of the boom; rather, it is entering an era of slow growth. Second, to the extent that labor markets remain relatively tight, the wages of unskilled workers are to some extent protected by the existing minimum wage policy and downward wage rigidities.

Conclusions: How to Row against the Tide?

Wage inequality fell in Latin America in the 2000s. This remarkable achievement was a result of the expansion of education, but only because it was combined with economic growth. Because of the economic slowdown, further progress will require extra work. This book has not addressed the welfare implications of inequality reduction, and not all reduction in wage inequality is welfare-maximizing. However, there are policies that might both reduce inequality and enhance welfare. Two examples are expanding the coverage and quality of education for children from disadvantaged households, and improving competition policies.

Regarding trends in wage inequality due to observable characteristics of workers, this book has found that the expansion of education and, the associated fall in the skill premium, were the key drivers of wage inequality reduction. Given the current levels of education in Latin America, there is still scope for reducing wage inequality through investment in early learning, schooling and college education, and apprenticeships. Enhancing educational quality is essential for building skills that translate into higher wages and sustainable livelihoods. Moving forward, continuing expansion of education to cover the most vulnerable households and improving the quality of education, particularly for children from low-income households, will help reduce wage inequality and enhance welfare.

Regarding the reduction in wage inequality due to unobservable characteristics of workers, this book has highlighted the role of exchange rate appreciation, particularly in South America. The mechanism in this case is unrelated to education. Rather, it is related to changes in the distribution of productivity across firms. Eliminating policies that try to protect inefficient firms (such as corporate subsidies that allow low-productivity firms to remain in the market), improving antitrust and competition policies, and promoting trade liberalization could reduce within-group inequality based on unobservable characteristics and enhance welfare.

The increase in the minimum wage was also important in some countries. A note of caution is needed regarding minimum wage policies, however. Despite pressures to keep raising the minimum wage, this policy should be viewed in light of the economic cycle. Lower domestic demand crowds out space for the minimum wage to rise with limited employment adjustments. Regulatory approaches such as the minimum wage, which reflect society's search for fairness, may be effective in raising the welfare of unskilled, low-income workers during upturns. However, if not accompanied by rising labor productivity, they can also unduly undermine unskilled-job generation and formalization during downturns, with negative effects on inequality.

Latin America has historically been a region vulnerable to external shocks, whether caused by changes in world demand, international interest rates, or terms of trade. The importance of commodities in its trade makes South America particularly sensitive to fluctuations in commodity prices. Latin America as a whole seeks to expand the importance of less-vulnerable sources of economic growth that rely on increasing productivity through technology and trade, not just through increases in aggregate domestic demand. In this new setting, the durable social gains from lower wage inequality—protected in both the short run and long run—are critical.

In times of slower growth and more stable terms of trade, firms need to find new ways to stay competitive. Market reforms to promote competition and increase international economic integration may enable global forces such as technology and trade to emerge as even more important sources of productivity growth. Because the size of the tradable sector is likely to expand, however, greater firm heterogeneity in that sector could potentially spur further inequality. If coupled with more progressive tax systems, the positive effects of trade and technological change on overall employment and growth could open space for further investment in human capital and redistribution, ultimately contributing to both sustained and vigorous economic growth and further decreases in inequality in Latin America.

Notes

1. Wage inequality declined vigorously in Latin America in the 2000s, by about 6 Gini points between 2002 and 2013. In contrast, wage inequality increased by an average of about 1.3 Gini points in countries outside Latin America during this same period.

2. Factors that led to changes in household demographics included increasing female labor force participation and declining fertility rates.

3. For a detailed analysis of declining wages for skilled workers in Mexico and the drivers of this decline, see Campos-Vázquez, López-Calva, and Lustig (2016).

4. This point is presented formally by Fernández and Messina (2017), who show the evolution of the skill premium in Argentina and Chile using two different models. The first model builds a

counterfactual evolution of the skill premium as predicted by changes in the relative supply of skilled and unskilled workers. The second shows the model's predictions once changes in labor demand are allowed for. The model that limits the variation of the skill premium to changes in labor supply overpredicts the reduction of the skill premium, missing fundamental dynamics because it fails to predict the increase in the wage premium during the first half of the period (approximately up to 2002). It then subsequently understates the decline in the skill premium in the two countries after 2002. By contrast, the model in which demand changes are introduced produces a much better fit of the data.

5. This would happen because demand for tradables can be satisfied via imports, while demand for nontradables cannot. As the nominal exchange rate appreciates, the domestic price of tradable goods falls.

6. Although estimating the relative importance of labor supply trends (education expansion) versus labor demand trends is complex, available estimates in Fernández and Messina (2017) and Gasparini et al. (2011) suggest that these forces played complementary roles.

7. This book follows Card, Heining, and Kline (2013) and estimates a model with additive fixed effects for workers and firms. This model disentangles the contribution to interfirm pay differentials of three factors: (1) the dispersion in quality across employers (firm fixed effects), (2) the dispersion in ability across workers (worker fixed effects), and (3) the degree to which the most desirable workers are paired with the most productive firms (covariance of worker and firm effects). The book presents results for Costa Rica and Brazil. In Costa Rica, the rise in variance of firm effects accounts for 33 percent of the total increase in wage inequality, and the rise in variance of worker effects accounts for 21 percent, with a rise in their covariance and the residual explaining the remainder. In Brazil, the fall in variance of firm effects accounts for 41 percent of the total decline in wage inequality, and the fall in variance of worker effects accounts for 20 percent, with a fall in their covariance and the residual explaining the remainder.

8. Interfirm wage differentials could also be driven by differences in the method of organization used by different firms, which could well be also the result of learning-by-exporting.

9. Note that more research is needed to draw definitive conclusions, because this analysis uses data covering formal employment only.

10. Since the emergence of China, trade has received renewed attention as a driver of wage inequality (Autor, Dorn, and Hanson 2013).

11. Note, however, that Stolper-Samuelson trade effects might occur with a lag if labor markets adjust slowly. Moreover, they depend on the relative skill-intensity of the liberalized sectors. Evidence on relative goods prices for Mexico indicates that when the country joined the GATT (General Agreement on Tariffs and Trade), it protected less-skill-intensive industries. When Mexico joined NAFTA (the North American Free Trade Agreement), however, the relative price of skill-intensive goods reversed its rise (Robertson 2004).

12. Direct effects result from the sectoral responses of employment and wages to an observable sector-level demand shift, while indirect effects result from spending effects of positive terms-of-trade improvements.

13. The minimum wage policy does not have the same effects on wages in all Latin American countries. To some extent, this is because their structure varies by country. For example, the minimum wage in some countries, such as Mexico and Uruguay, is very low, affecting a small number of workers. Minimum wages in this context are unlikely to have large effects on inequality. In contrast, the Brazilian minimum wage increased rapidly during the 2000s, and by 2014 it was getting closer to the median wage. Colombia and Peru are close followers.

14. Interestingly, Ferreira, Firpo, and Messina (2017) find that, throughout the 1995–2012 period, the contribution of the minimum wage in Brazil was mildly regressive: the minimum wage

increase was associated with a small increase in inequality of 1.2 Gini points for the period as a whole. This effect was driven primarily by noncompliance (the endowment effect). However, this overall impact hides very different behavior across subperiods. Low earnings growth during 1995–2003 implied that increases in the minimum wage were strongly associated with rising noncompliance. This endowment effect outweighed the positive impact on earnings for those workers earning the minimum. As a result, inequality increased. On the other hand, the rapid increase of the minimum wage after 2003 was associated with a reduction in inequality. This was driven by two effects rowing in the same direction: noncompliance declined (endowment effect), and those workers at the minimum (an increasing share) saw their earnings grow faster than average earnings. Overall, Ferreira, Firpo, and Messina (2017) find that the contribution of the minimum wage to the reduction of inequality during the boom years was some 20 percent.

References

Adão, R. 2015. "Worker Heterogeneity, Wage Inequality, and International Trade: Theory and Evidence from Brazil." Job Market Paper, Massachusetts Institute of Technology, Cambridge, MA.

Alvarez, J., F. Benguria, N. Engbom, and C. Moser. Forthcoming. "Firms and the Decline of Earnings Inequality in Brazil." *American Economic Journal: Macroeconomics.*

Araujo, J.T., E. Vostroknutova, M. Brueckner, M. Clavijo, and K. M. Wacker. 2016. "Beyond Commodities: The Growth Challenge of Latin America and the Caribbean." Paper presented at the Latin American Development Forum, World Bank, Washington, DC.

Autor, D., and D. Dorn. 2013. "The Growth of Low-Skill Service Jobs and the Polarization of the U.S. Labor Market." *American Economic Review* 103 (5): 1533–597.

Autor, D., D. Dorn, and G. Hanson. 2013. "The China Syndrome: Local Labor Market Effects of Import Competition in the United States." *American Economic Review* 103 (6): 2121–168.

Autor, D., D. Dorn, G. Hanson, and J. Song. 2014. "Trade Adjustment: Worker-Level Evidence." *Quarterly Journal of Economics* 129 (4): 1799–860.

Autor, D., L. Katz, and A. Krueger. 1998. "Computing Inequality: Have Computers Changed the Labor Market?" *Quarterly Journal of Economics* 113 (4): 1169–214.

Bargain, O., and J. Silva. Forthcoming. "Labor Supply Elasticities: Evidence for Latin America." Policy Research Working Paper, World Bank, Washington, DC. Available at: https://sites.google .com/site/joanasilvaweb/.

Berman, E., J. Bound, and Z. Griliches. 1994. "Changes in the Demand for Skilled Labor within U.S. Manufacturing: Evidence from the Annual Survey of Manufacturers." *Quarterly Journal of Economics* 109 (2): 367–97.

Calvo-González, O., R. A. Castañeda, M. G. Farfán, G. Reyes, and L. D. Sousa. 2017. "How Is the Slowdown Affecting Households in Latin America and the Caribbean?" Policy Research Working Paper 7948, World Bank, Washington, DC.

Camacho, A., J. Messina, and J. P. Uribe. 2016. "The Expansion of Higher Education in Colombia: Bad Students or Bad Programs?" IDB Discussion Paper 452, Inter-American Development Bank, Washington, DC.

Campos-Vázquez, R. M., L. F. López-Calva, and N. Lustig. 2016. "Declining Wages for College-Educated Workers in Mexico: Are Younger or Older Cohorts Hurt the Most?" Policy Research Working Paper 7546, World Bank, Washington, DC.

Card, D., J. Heining, and P. Kline. 2013. "Workplace Heterogeneity and the Rise of West German Wage Inequality." *Quarterly Journal of Economics* 128 (3): 967–1105.

Card, D., and T. Lemieux. 2001. "Can Falling Supply Explain the Rising Return to College for Younger Men? A Cohort-Based Analysis." *Quarterly Journal of Economics* 116 (2): 705–46.

De la Torre, A., G. Beylis, A. Ize, and D. Lederman. 2015. *Jobs, Wages and the Latin American Slowdown*. Latin America and the Caribbean Semiannual Report (October). Washington, DC: World Bank.

De la Torre, A., and A. Ize. 2016. "Employment, Wages, Distribution, and the Latin American Deceleration." Background paper, World Bank, Washington, DC.

Feenstra, R. C., and G. H. Hanson. 1999. "Productivity Measurement and the Impact of Trade and Technology on Wages: Estimates for the U.S., 1972–1990." *Quarterly Journal of Economics* 114 (3): 907–40.

Fernández, M., and J. Messina. 2017. "Skill Premium, Labor Supply and Changes in the Structure of Wages in Latin America." IDB Working Paper 786, Inter-American Development Bank, Washington, DC.

Ferreira, F. H. G., S. P. Firpo, and J. Messina. 2017. "Ageing Poorly? Accounting for the Decline in Earnings Inequality in Brazil, 1995–2012." Policy Research Working Paper 8018, World Bank, Washington, DC.

Ferreyra, M. M., C. Avitabile, J. Botero Alvarez, and S. Urzua. 2017. *At a Crossroads: Higher Education in Latin America and the Caribbean*. Directions in Development: Human Development Series. Washington, DC: World Bank.

Gasparini, L., S. Galiani, G. Cruces, and P. Acosta. 2011. "Educational Upgrading and Returns to Skills in Latin America: Evidence from a Supply-Demand Framework, 1990–2010." Policy Research Working Paper 5921, World Bank, Washington, DC.

Goldberg, P., and N. Pavcnik. 2007. "Distributional Effects of Globalization in Developing Countries." *Journal of Economic Literature* 45 (1): 39–82.

Goldin, C., and L. F. Katz. 2007. "Long-Run Changes in the U.S. Wage Structure: Narrowing, Widening, Polarizing." NBER Working Paper 13568, National Bureau of Economic Research, Cambridge, MA.

Halliday, T., D. Lederman, and R. Robertson. 2015. "Tracking Wage Inequality Trends with Prices and Different Trade Models: Evidence from Mexico." Policy Research Working Paper 7471, World Bank, Washington, DC.

Katz, L. F., and K. M. Murphy. 1992. "Changes in Relative Wages, 1963–1987: Supply and Demand Factors." *Quarterly Journal of Economics* 107 (1): 35–78.

Krueger, A. 2012. *Struggling with Success: Challenges Facing the International Economy*. Singapore: World Scientific.

Maloney, W. F., and C. Molina. 2016. "A Note on Labor Market Polarization in the Developing World." World Bank, Washington, DC. Unpublished.

Messina, J., G. Pica, and A. M. Oviedo. 2016. "Job Polarization in Latin America." World Bank, Washington, DC. Unpublished. Available at: http://www.jsmessina.com.

Robertson, R. 2004. "Relative Prices and Wage Inequality: Evidence from Mexico." *Journal of International Economics* 64 (2): 387–409.

Rodríguez-Castelán, C., L. F. López-Calva, N. Lustig, and D. Valderrama. 2016. "Understanding the Dynamics of Labor Income Inequality in Latin America." Policy Research Working Paper 7795, World Bank, Washington, DC.

Silva, J., R. Almeida, and V. Strokova. 2015. *Sustaining Employment and Wage Gains in Brazil: A Skills and Jobs Agenda*. Directions in Development: Human Development Series. Washington, DC: World Bank.